INTRODUCTION TO THE WORLD'S MAJOR RELIGIONS

Introduction to the World's Major Religions

CHRISTIANITY

Volume 4

Lee W. Bailey

Lee W. Bailey, General Editor

GREENWOOD PRESS
Westport, Connecticut • London

Library of Congress Cataloging-in-Publication Data
available on request from the Library of Congress.

British Library Cataloguing in Publication Data is available.

Copyright © 2006 by Lee W. Bailey

ISBN: 0–313–33634–2 (set)
     0–313–33327–0 (vol. 1)
     0–313–32724–6 (vol. 2)
     0–313–33251–7 (vol. 3)
     0–313–32683–5 (vol. 4)
     0–313–32846–3 (vol. 5)
     0–313–33590–7 (vol. 6)

First published in 2006

Greenwood Press, 88 Post Road West, Westport, CT 06881
An imprint of Greenwood Publishing Group, Inc.
www.greenwood.com

Printed in the United States of America

The paper used in this book complies with the
Permanent Paper Standard issued by the National
Information Standards Organization (Z39.48–1984).

10 9 8 7 6 5 4 3 2 1

Introduction to the World's Major Religions
Lee W. Bailey, General Editor

Judaism, Volume 1
Emily Taitz

Confucianism and Taoism, Volume 2
Randall L. Nadeau

Buddhism, Volume 3
John M. Thompson

Christianity, Volume 4
Lee W. Bailey

Islam, Volume 5
Zayn R. Kassam

Hinduism, Volume 6
Steven J. Rosen

CONTENTS

SET FOREWORD

This set, *Introduction to the World's Major Religions,* was developed to fill a niche between sophisticated texts for adults and the less in-depth references for middle schoolers. It includes six volumes on religions from both Eastern and Western traditions: Judaism, Christianity, Islam, Hinduism, Confucianism and Taoism, and Buddhism. Each volume gives a balanced, accessible introduction to the religion.

Each volume follows a set format so readers can easily find parallel information in each religion. After a Timeline and Introduction, narrative chapters are as follows: the "History of Foundation" chapter describes the founding people, the major events, and the most important decisions made in the faith's early history. The "Texts and Major Tenets" chapter explains the central canon, or sacred texts, and the core beliefs, doctrines, or tenets, such as the nature of deities, the meaning of life, and the theories of the afterlife. The chapter on "Branches" outlines the major divisions of the religion, their reasons for being, their distinctive doctrines, their historical background, and structures today. The chapter on "Practice Worldwide" describes the weekly worship practices, the demographic statistics indicating the sizes of various branches of religions, the global locations, and historical turning points. The chapter on "Rituals and Holidays" describes the ritual practices of the religions in all their varieties and the holidays worldwide, such as the Birth of the Buddha, as they have developed historically. The chapter on "Major Figures" covers selected notable people in the history of each religion and their important influence. A glossary provides

definitions for major special terms, and the index gives an alphabetic lo-
cator for major themes. A set index is included in volume 6 (to facilitate
comparison).

In a world of about 6 billion people, today the religion with the greatest
number of adherents is Christianity, with about 2 billion members, com-
prising 33 percent of the globe's population. Next largest is Islam, with about
1.3 billion members, (about 22 percent). Hindus number about 900 million
(about 15 percent). Those who follow traditional Chinese religions number
about 225 million (4 percent). Although China has the world's largest population, it is officially Communist, and Buddhism has been blended with
traditional Confucianism and Taoism, so numbers in China are difficult
to verify. Buddhism claims about 360 million members (about 6 percent
of the world's population). Judaism, although historically influential, has
a small number of adherents—about 14 million (0.2 percent of the world's
population). These numbers are constantly shifting, because religions are
always changing and various surveys define groups differently.[1]

Religions are important elements of the worldview of a culture. They
express, for example, the cultural beliefs about cosmology, or picture of the
universe (e.g., created by God or spontaneous), and the origin of humanity (e.g., purposeful or random), its social norms (e.g., monogamy or polygamy), its ways of relating to ultimate reality (e.g., sacrifice or obedience
to law), the historical destiny (e.g., linear or cyclical), life after death (e.g.,
none or judgment), and ethics (e.g., tribal or universal).

As the world gets smaller with modern communications and global
travel, people come in contact with those of other religions far more frequently than in the past. This can cause conflicts or lead to cooperation, but
the potential for hostile misunderstanding is so great that it is important
to foster knowledge and understanding. Noting parallels in world religions
can help readers understand each religion better. Religions can provide
ethical guidance that can help solve serious cultural problems. During war
the political question "why do they hate us?" may have serious religious
aspects in the answer. New answers to the question of how science and
religion in one culture can be reconciled may come from another religion's
approach. Scientists are increasingly analyzing the ecological crisis, but the
solutions will require more than new technologies. They will also require
ethical restraint, the motivation to change the destructive ecological habits
of industrial societies, and some radical revisioning of worldviews. Other
contemporary issues, such as women's rights, will also require patriarchal
religions to undertake self-examination. Personal faith is regularly called

into consideration with daily news of human destructiveness or in times of crisis, when the very meaning of life comes into question. Is life basically good? Will goodness in the big picture overcome immediate evil? Should horrendous behavior be forgiven? Are people alone in a huge, indifferent universe, or is the ultimate reality a caring, just power behind the scenes of human and cosmic history? Religions offer various approaches, ethics, and motivations to deal with such issues. Readers can use the books in this set to rethink their own beliefs and practices.

NOTE

1. United Nations, "Worldwide Adherents of All Religions by Six Continental Areas, Mid-2002," *World Population Prospects: The 1998 Revision* (New York: United Nations, 1999).

PREFACE

Christianity is now the world's largest religion, with its adherents numbering about a third of the world's population. It has three major branches: Eastern Orthodoxy (about 12 percent of Christians), Roman Catholicism (59 percent), and Protestantism (29 percent). Along with Judaism and Islam, it is a major monotheistic religion that professes belief in one god. Its founder was Jesus, born a Jew in Israel about 2,000 years ago, who taught a radical, reformist ethic and was crucified. His followers believe that he was resurrected, and they took his teachings beyond reform to start a new religion. The Eastern Orthodox Church was the foundational portion of the church. The Roman Catholics separated from the Orthodox in 1054 CE, and then the Protestants began new traditions in 1517. Protestantism is diverse but can be divided into four major branches: Lutheran, Anglican, Calvinist, and Free Churches.

Christianity has formed part of the basic structure of Western culture's worldview and morality. Drawing on Jewish tradition, the Orthodox Church defined the basic principles of monotheism against the fading polytheist classical world. This gave a cosmic, universal sense to morality that helped overcome tribal revenge struggles and a unified picture of the cosmos behind the scientific assumption of a logically consistent universe. The early Orthodox defined the relation of Jesus's humanity to his divinity (that clarified his being powerfully divine and not just another human hero), the meaning of the Trinity (that incorporated the cosmic, historical, and constantly present elements of the divine), began the monastic tradition, and spread the faith to new kingdoms such as in Russia. The medieval Roman Catholic Church helped rebuild Europe during and after the fading Roman Empire gave way to marauding tribes sweeping across Europe. Its monasteries, hospitals, and schools helped rebuild a stable society, its soaring cathedrals helped lead the heart from lower to higher concerns, and the role of the Pope was strengthened in an effort to improve the religion. Beginning in the sixteenth century, Protestantism supported the rise of a direct, private relationship to God, more individual freedom, mass literacy that increased the importance of all believers reading the Bible, more democracy as opposed to hierarchical church institutions, increasing faith in human capabilities, optimism about improving the world, the rise of the middle class, and its culture of commerce and technological innovation.

Today the church faces some equally serious challenges. The mechanical worldview of industrial society is gaining ground with every new technology. How will the church respond, with its ancient biblical worldview? How will the church respond to the argument for random, meaningless evolution versus the argument for purposeful design of the universe? How will Christians react to new social developments brought by secularization, mass education, and new technologies, such as birth control? Will the monotheistic effort to overcome ethnic, racial, and national conflicts and instead seek global ethics succeed in the face of wars and ecological crises? Will the church be able to draw believers toward the changes and the higher purposes needed? Such are the momentous and urgent issues for Christians to wrestle with. Understanding the faith's history, beliefs, and practices will help everyone move into the future more wisely.

Care has been taken to try to fairly represent previously under-represented groups in Christianity. Some major thinkers are integrated into the text, and others are mentioned briefly, then profiled in more depth in Chapter Six, "Major Figures". The mainstream Christian churches are represented here, but it is impossible to name and examine all the thousands of Protestant, independent Free Churches around the world, so we describe representative denominations. The major theological and organizational themes of various denominations will be stressed, so one can identify them when combined in any particular church. Some religions that seem to be Christian but that emphasize fringe beliefs or add additional sacred texts to the orthodox canon cannot be included here.

The terms "pagan," "heathen," and "barbarian," are heavily weighted Christian terms describing people of other religions whom Christians opposed. They are put here in quotation marks, indicating that they may at times be called "non-Christian." The study of world religions now uses the dating system BCE and CE, to be more neutral and apply to all religions. The numbers are the same as the Christian calendar. The new BCE means "Before the Common Era," using the same numbers as the old BC (Before Christ). The new CE means "Common Era," also using the same numbers as the old AD (*Anno Domini* or Year of Our Lord). Biblical texts in the discussion can be located by using a concordance, which is an index to the Bible.

ACKNOWLEDGMENTS

Many thanks go to consultants for this book, including Dr. Mary Skinner, Rev. Dr. Allison Stokes, Fr. Scott Kubinski, Chaplain Mary Humenay, Rev. Stephen Lilly, Fr. Leo Reinhardt, Rev. Bud Dolch, Rev. Rebecca Dolch, Rev. Charles Thompson, and the numerous other ministers and priests I spoke to and churches that I visited.

Statue of Jesus with Sacred Heart. © Getty Images/32285.

INTRODUCTION

JESUS

Christianity began as a small reform movement within Jewish culture in Israel, led by Jesus of Nazareth (4 BCE–29 CE). Israel was under the rule of the Roman Emperor Caesar Augustus (63 BCE–14 CE) when Jesus was born. The Jews were a small nation with an unusual religion for the time, which insisted that there was only one God (monotheism).

Christian tradition records that Jesus was born of a virgin mother, Mary. Jesus began teaching at the age of 30. He gathered a group of 12 close followers called "disciples" or "apostles." Some hoped he would lead a political revolt against Rome, but he did not. Instead he called for several spiritual reforms, some of which had been taught before by Jewish prophets, such as Isaiah, who called his people back to God's purpose.

Jesus spoke with such wisdom and courage that he eventually convinced his followers that he could not be an ordinary human, but must be God in human form. But his call to a challenging spiritual life angered many, and so the Romans crucified him. This would have been another tragedy of a brave reformer in the Jewish prophetic tradition, killed for his boldness, except that his followers proclaimed that their master was resurrected from the dead. This stirred his 12 disciples powerfully, for it meant that eternal life beyond the grave overcomes life's sufferings and injustices. Jesus's 12 disciples (apostles in Catholicism) grew into a larger number of apostles who spread the Gospel (good news) and founded new groups called churches (*ekklesia*) along the eastern Mediterranean coast, west to Rome. Their inspiring teacher (*rabbi*) came to be seen as the Messiah (*Christos*), a divine figure. For about 300 years, Christians were persecuted. Early missionaries such as Paul, traveled around the Mediterranean, teaching and converting. By 100 CE there were an estimated 300,000 new Christians.

Christianity later became the state religion in 380 under the Byzantine Emperor Theodosius the Great. The Roman Empire was crumbling, burdened by a vast empire, a large army, and invading tribes. In the midst of medieval invasions, plagues, wars, knights, and castles, Christians built monasteries, hospitals, orphanages, libraries, schools, and cathedrals. Christian leaders struggled against widespread, ancient, crude customs such as blood revenge and endless tribal feuds. Medieval scholars later began a new Christian calendar declaring Jesus's birth to be the year zero. Modern scholars uncovered evidence that his birth was more likely about four years before the year zero in today's calendar.

THREE DIVISIONS OF THE CHURCH

The early medieval Christian Church was based in Constantinople (now Istanbul, Turkey), center of the Byzantine Empire. In Italy, the Bishop of Rome gained increasing authority as he worked to protect Rome from invasions and to Christianize the crumbled Roman Empire in the West. The original Greek-speaking Byzantine Church split away from the Latin-speaking Roman Church in 1054 CE, and became the Eastern Orthodox Church. This church spread west to Greece, up to the Balkan states, and north to Russia. The Roman Church called itself the Roman Catholic Church, spread west to Spain and north into Western Europe, and organized under the Pope. In 1517 CE in Germany, Martin Luther started the third division of Christendom, called the Protestant Reformation, that expanded across northern Europe and to North America. Protestants branched into four overlapping divisions: the Lutheran Church, the Anglican Church, the Calvinist Churches, and the Free (or Anabaptist) Churches.

CONTEMPORARY DIVISIONS

While the three major divisions of the church continue, contemporary issues have drawn new groups together that often cross old organizational lines.

Conservative

Today Conservative Christians tend to accept the Roman Catholic Pope's or an Orthodox Patriarch's authority. Conservative Protestants include fundamentalists, evangelicals, and pentecostals, in numerous denominations. These groups interpret the Bible rather literally. They also tend to support male leadership and oppose abortion and same-sex marriages. They tend to maintain the exclusivist idea that their branch of Christianity is the only true religion, and others are false. Conservative Christians are growing in numbers, mainly due to church and population increases in Asia, Latin America, and Africa.

Mainstream

Both conservatives and liberals can be found in mainstream (or mainline) denominations, such as the Methodist, Presbyterian, or Anglican churches. The large middle-ground population of most churches may or may not accept church rulings from above, may or may not interpret the Bible more symbolically, and may or may not welcome scientific and technological advances, such as the theory of evolution. Some welcome the ordination of women, use gender-neutral language in liturgy, and work against racial prejudice, while others do not. They may respect other world religions but have minimal relations with them. They may hold to ancient liturgies or blend them with new forms.

Liberal

Liberal, left-wing, and radical Christians, such as some American Baptist, Lutheran, and United Church of Christ churches, strive to rethink many basic principles of the faith, such as theism, the masculine image of God. They seek to reform the church, interpret the Bible more symbolically, and may break with their church hierarchy on issues such as ordination of women or ordination and marriage of gays and lesbians. They may use both male and female images of God or explore the ancient goddess traditions. They respect most scientific knowledge and seek to reconcile it with religious views. They welcome many technological advances but increasingly reject those that are becoming ecological problems. They welcome relations with other world religions.

INTERPRETATION

The question of interpretation (or hermeneutics) is central to understanding current church debates. How should Christians interpret the Bible? Was Jesus the Son of God, the messiah sent from heaven to save a sinful world, a wise human, a prophet, a political revolutionary, or a monastic reformer? Traditional, Orthodox, evangelical and fundamentalist Christians interpret the Bible largely as a historical document, factually inerrant, and a literal, authoritative guide to beliefs and ethical behavior. Conflicts with science, as with the creation account in Genesis, may be answered with theories such as Creation Science. Liberal Christians see the Bible as partly historical, as in the existence of Jesus, and partly symbolic, as in the creation account. This is an old debate. Long ago the early Christian theologian Origen (c. 185–254 CE) pointed out the various layers of biblical truth: literal, moral, and allegorical. Symbolic language for them points to truths.

Nineteenth-century German scholars began a careful linguistic, archaeological, and textual historical-critical study of the Bible called "historical-critical" analysis. This method provided the scholarly tools for a radically new way of seeing the Bible as a collection of numerous texts, written and edited over a thousand-year period. Scholars seek evidence outside the Bible to verify to some degree the historical veracity of biblical events, such as the Babylonian kings' records of their battles with Israel, or the Roman Josephus's record of Jesus's existence.[1] Some texts long taken by some to be literally true now reveal contradictions, such as the two versions of creation (Genesis 1:1 to 2:4, and 2:4 to 3:24), in which the sequences of plants and human creation are opposite. To liberals, the Bible blends historical with mythic, symbolic literature meant to convey the theological reality of God. But conservative believers generally reject this interpretive method as too skeptical and undermining faith.

Christianity has spread the word of Jesus's teachings about faith, hope, love, and eternal life for two millennia, has inspired millions, has given many peace, and has been an important part of the foundations of Western civilization. Christianity has also been shaped by its culture. It is a highly complex cultural phenomenon that now faces new challenges and will continue to change.

NOTE

1. Ian Wilson, *Jesus: The Evidence* (San Francisco: HarperSanFrancisco, 1996).

TIMELINE

4 BCE	Birth of Jesus, founder of Christianity in Bethlehem, Israel.
29 CE	Crucifixion and Resurrection of Jesus in Jerusalem.
34	Conversion of Saul to St. Paul, the first major Christian theologian.
c. 40–64	Paul travels, writes letters (epistles) to new churches.
70	Destruction of Jerusalem by Romans; Jews scatter in Diaspora.
c. 70–95	"New Testament" Gospels of Mark, then Matthew and Luke written.
c. 95	Book of Revelations written.
c. 90–100	Gospel of John written.
238	"Barbarian" Goth army crosses Danube River into Roman Empire.
306	Emperor Constantine begins Byzantine Empire in Constantinople.
313	Constantine orders full toleration of Christianity.
325	Council of Nicaea, called by Constantine, clarifies early beliefs.

380	Christianity officially becomes imperial religion of Roman Empire.
c. 382–405	Canon (official texts) of Old (Hebrew) and New (Greek) Testaments set.
400s	Use of Eastern Orthodox Liturgy of St. John Chrysostom begins.
404	Jerome (342–420, a biblical scholar in Bethlehem) finishes Latin translation of Bible called "Vulgate."
410	Rome sacked by Visigoth invaders.
426	Theologian St. Augustine writes book *City of God*, to refute charge that Christianity caused the downfall of Rome.
431	St. Patrick, a missionary in Ireland, brings Christianity to Celts.
c.450	Attila the Hun's army sweeps across Eastern Europe into Italy.
455	Vandals sack Rome.
476	Visigoths conquer Spain and most of Gaul (France).
497	Ostrogoth King Theodoric declared King of Italy.
525	St. Benedict organizes Western monasticism in Italy.
532–37	St. Sophia Church built in Constantinople by Emperor Justinian.
572	Lombards conquer northern Italy.
590–604	Pope Gregory I ("The Great") claims wide papal authority.
622	Beginning of spread of Islam from Mecca, Arabia.
638	Jerusalem and Egypt taken by Arabs.
680–754	Life of Boniface, missionary to Germany.
711	Muslims enter Spain, begin rule.
732	Muslims defeated in Tours, France.
800	Charlemagne crowned Holy Roman Emperor by Pope Leo III.

988	Russian Prince Vladimir in Kiev chooses Eastern Orthodox Church.
1054	Split between Roman Catholic and Eastern Orthodox churches.
1095	Pope Urban II launches first Crusade to take Jerusalem from Muslims.
1099	Jerusalem sacked, Christian Crusaders rule.
1163–1200	Gothic-style Notre Dame Cathedral built in Paris.
1187	Muslim military leader Saladin takes Jerusalem from Christians.
1194–1220	Gothic-style Notre Dame Cathedral built in Chartres, France.
1209	St. Francis of Assisi, Italy, founds Order of Mendicant Friars.
1232	Inquisition begins in Germany and Spain to find heretics.
1274	A definitive Catholic theology, *Summa Theologica*, published by Theologian Thomas Aquinas.
1321	Italian poet Dante's *Divine Comedy*, with the culminating medieval Christian view of the afterlife, published.
1388	English scholar John Wycliffe translates Bible into English, against church law.
1412–31	French mystic Joan of Arc leads an army against the invading English.
1440–1505	Ivan III ("The Great"), first Russian Czar, claims Moscow to be Third Rome, new center of Eastern Orthodox Church.
1453	Fall of Constantinople to Muslim Ottoman Turks, renamed Istanbul.
1492	Muslims and Jews expelled from Spain by Catholics after long battle.
	Italian explorer Christopher Columbus reaches Americas.

1499	Italian artist Michelangelo completes sculpture *Pietà* (Jesus lying in mother Mary's arms) in Rome.
1506–1590	St. Peter's Basilica, center of Catholic Church, designed by Bramante, Michelangelo, and others, built in Rome.
1508–12	Michelangelo paints fresco ceiling of Sistine Chapel, Rome.
1517	Theologian Martin Luther's "95 Theses" begins Protestant Reformation. "Anabaptist" (Free) Churches emerge in Switzerland and Germany.
1523	Priest Ulrich Zwingli leads Reformation in Zürich. Balthasar Hubmaier begins Anabaptist church near Zürich.
1526	William Tyndale translates New Testament into English.
1527	Anabaptist Schleitheim Confession defines Anabaptist theology.
c. 1528	Martin Luther composes hymn "A Mighty Fortress Is Our God."
1532	King Henry VIII gains supremacy over English Church.
1545	Roman Catholic Reformation begins with Council of Trent.
1533–1603	Queen Elizabeth I reigns over England and Ireland.
1554–60	Russian Orthodox St. Basil's Cathedral built in Moscow.
1559	John Calvin's *Institutes* leads Reformed Church theology.
1562	St. Teresa of Avila, Spain, reforms Catholic Carmelite convents.
1588	English Navy defeats Catholic Spanish Armada's attack on England.
1598	Edict of Nantes orders toleration of French Protestants; revoked 1685.

1609	First Baptist Church formed in Amsterdam.
1611	Protestant King James Bible translated into English.
1618–48	Bloody Thirty Years War between Catholics and Protestants stains Europe.
1620	English Congregationalist Pilgrims (Puritans) sail to Massachusetts.
1661	Scotland becomes Presbyterian, led by Calvinist minister John Knox.
1667	English poet John Milton completes *Paradise Lost*.
1668	English mystic George Fox founds Friends (Quakers).
1675–1710	Anglican St. Paul's Cathedral built in London, designed by Christopher Wren.
1682	William Penn founds Pennsylvania colony, welcomes Quakers.
1689	English Parliament's "Toleration Act" allows religious liberty.
1693	Free Church Amish denomination begins in Switzerland.
1706	First Presbyterian Church in American colonies founded.
1725–60	First Great Awakening in American colonies spreads emotional piety.
c. 1734	Anglican Charles Wesley writes "Hark, the Herald Angels Sing."
1738	Wesley brothers and Whitefield begin Methodism in England.
1740	Composer George Handel writes *Messiah* oratorio in England.
c. 1770	Anglican priest John Newton writes "Amazing Grace."
1787	Free Church African Methodist Episcopal Church begins in United States.
1794	William Blake prints "Ancient of Days" engraving of God in England.

1852	Russian Orthodox monastic leader Margarita Tuchkova dies.
1853	U.S. Protestant Antoinette Brown (later Blackwell) ordained first woman minister.
1858	Catholic girl St. Bernadette sees visions of Virgin Mary in Lourdes, France.
1860's	Holiness/Pentecostal church begins in United States.
1869–70	First Vatican Council declares Papal infallibility.
1878	Composer Peter Tchaikovsky composes "Liturgy of St. John Chrysostom."
1893	First Parliament of World Religions in Chicago.
1900	Composer James Weldon Johnson writes "Lift Every Voice and Sing."
1900–1910	First Fundamentalist dogmas published in United States.
1901	American Standard Version of Bible translated into English.
1917	Russian Communists begin to persecute Russian Orthodox Church.
1929	Vatican City formed in Rome as 108-acre sovereign state for Pope.
1933	German Protestant theologian Paul Tillich flees Nazis.
1934	German ministers' Barmen Declaration opposes Nazis.
1939–45	German Nazi Holocaust destroys 6 million Jews and other "undesirables."
1945	German Lutheran pastor Dietrich Bonhoeffer executed by Nazis.
	Ancient *Nag Hammadi Library* scrolls discovered in Egypt.
1947	Ancient *Dead Sea Scrolls* discovered in Israel.
1948	World Council of Churches founded in Amsterdam.

1946–52	Protestant Revised Standard Version of Bible published.
1958	Pope John XXIII elected.
1962–65	Second Vatican Council allows many Catholic reforms.
1963	Rev. Martin Luther King, Jr. gives "I Have a Dream" speech, highlighting U.S. civil rights movement for racial equality.
1973	Peruvian Scholar Gustavo Gutierrez supports Catholic Liberation Theology.
1978	John Paul II elected Pope.
	Mother Teresa awarded Nobel Peace Prize for helping dying destitutes in Calcutta, India.
1980	Archbishop Oscar Romero assassinated in El Salvador for supporting poor peasants.
1980s	Protestant televangelists active in United States.
1984	South African Archbishop Desmond Tutu awarded Nobel Peace Prize for his work to end apartheid.
1989	Soviet Communism collapses and Russian Orthodox Church rebuilds.
	Barbara C. Harris is the first Anglican woman to be ordained Bishop.
1993	Papal encyclicals reinforce opposition to artificial birth control.
1997	Second Parliament of World Religions in Capetown, South Africa.
1999	Orthodox Patriarch Bartholomew I calls eco-damage a sin.
2000	Protestant mainstream membership declines, Evangelicals increase.
	Catholic and Protestant clergy numbers decrease Christian population in Asia, Africa, and Latin America begins to outnumber that in northern hemisphere.

2002	Seven women illegally ordained as Catholic priests on Danube River.
2003	Disputes increase over Catholic priest child abuse and Protestant gay marriages and ordinations.
	U.S. Episcopalians in New Hampshire ordain gay bishop Gene Robinson.
2004	Third Parliament of World Religions in Barcelona, Spain.
2005	Roman Catholic dioceses continue financial struggles in priest child abuse losses due to lawsuit cash settlements. Many close parishes (Boston), some go bankrupt (Tucson, Arizona; Portland, Oregon; Spokane, Washington; St. George, Canada).
	Pope John XXIII dies.
	German Cardinal Joseph Ratzinger elected Pope Benedict XVI.
	Four women illegally ordained as Catholic priests on St. Lawrence River.
	Large Protestant interdenominational megachurch, Lakewood Church (in Houston, Texas) moves into stadium to accommodate 16,000.

1

HISTORY OF FOUNDATION

Christianity grew out of Judaism, adopting its monotheism (belief in one god), its ethical focus on humanity instead of nature, and its history. From a human perspective, Jesus, its founder, was a Jewish reformer or prophet who was crucified for his beliefs. From the Christian perspective, Jesus was the Son of God, the Messiah or Christ sent to save believers from their sin and suffering and to begin the new religion by showing God's power to heal suffering, guide social justice, and overcome the fear of death with the promise of eternal life. Christians were first persecuted by Romans, then, beginning with Emperor Constantine's conversion, Christianity became the official religion of the Roman Empire under Emperor Theodosius in 380 CE. This move from persecuted to ruling religion was a great change, but the church still had many political and theological problems to solve. The old polytheistic pagan religions did not just fade away, and among Christians many debates raged over issues such as the divinity of Christ.

JUDAISM

Initially a reform movement within Judaism, Christianity adopted the Jewish sacred books written in Hebrew, the *Tanakh,* and called it the "Old Testament." In Judaism, the first five books are called the *Torah,* or the "Books of Moses": Genesis, Exodus, Leviticus, Numbers, and Deuteronomy.

Moses

About 1200 BCE, the Hebrew people had been enslaved in Egypt under Pharaoh Ramses II, when their leader, Moses, led a rebellion to freedom in Israel (see biblical book of Exodus). This is the earliest historical biblical event with any external evidence (the Egyptian "Merneptah Stele"). In Egypt the Hebrews obviously knew the polytheistic religion of Egypt. In tradition, Moses led the Hebrew Exodus from slavery to Mount Sinai northeast of Egypt and was said to have received the Ten Commandments from God. Like other ancient legal codes such as Hammurabi's laws in Babylon, the Hebrews' Ten Commandments carved in stone 10 basic theological and ethical laws. Over the years more laws were appended, adding up to 613 laws establishing the moral foundation for the new people. According to biblical scholarship, they gathered together 12 tribes who slowly invaded and conquered the lands of Canaan, Samaria, and Philistia, which later became Israel. The importance of Law was that it helped to reduce the abuses of power of a local chieftain who could rule by personal power and whim and to combat the ancient problem of retribution, or unregulated revenge movements that continue old cycles of violence, like fruitless gang warfare.

Historically, Moses may have introduced the theological doctrine of monotheism to the Hebrews, briefly attempted before in Egypt by Pharaoh Akenaton, during the Hebrews' time there. Monotheism is important for its elevation of God to cosmic significance above nature and for unifying and universalizing the moral and logical principles of the cosmos. This is distinct from most polytheistic religions, which divinized nature spirits, ancestor spirits, as well as cosmic creator divinities. Monotheism claimed to be superior to all these divinities, to incorporate all their powers into one God, and to externalize evil from divinity. Most importantly, monotheism affirms that the one God who created the universe is ultimate reality. It is more powerful than any other powers, is the force of goodness, and thus ultimately overcomes any evil and suffering in the world. Monotheism's slow suppression of polytheism did not eliminate the powers that they symbolized in the world, such as war and love, it just said that these forces were not divine and not as powerful as the one God. Monotheism unified the universe into a single, high moral and rational unity, which eventually made possible theories of a universal morality and science, beyond local tribal loyalties and conflicts. Monotheism began with the portrayal of God as a masculine deity and led to the image of His being remote from earth. Both views are now debated.

God creating the universe in William Blake's "The Ancient of Days." Courtesy of the Art Archive/British Museum/Eileen Tweedy.

Theism was an ancient aspect of religion that pictured the mysterious forces responsible for the world to be like humans. This sense of God as personal conveyed the qualities of the creator as life-giving, caring, loving, and giving guidance. Ancient religions saw their gods in animals as well, as can be seen by the animal-headed deities of Egypt, such as Horos (son of winged Isis and Osiris), who was pictured as having a falcon head. This meant that Horos appeared in the sky as a falcon. But the Hebrews eventually rejected all animal images of God, such as the Golden Calf. Instead they wanted to humanize religion and move it away from polytheism and nature religions that believed that they had to ritually satisfy the overarching needs of gods of the ocean, the winds, hunting, agriculture, and ancestors. Humanizing religion meant focusing on the moral behavior of humans rather than satisfying nature and ancestor spirits. It also affirmed the value and dignity of the individual person. This newly revealed God of the Hebrews liberated them from Egyptian slavery, with Moses's leadership, according to the book of Exodus, and gave them laws based on divinely inspired ethics.

Abraham

Ancient religions often required sacrifices of valuable animals, even humans, in the belief that they must please the ancient gods so that the gods would provide them with goods like food and military victory. The Hebrews rejected human sacrifice, as is expressed in the story of Abraham who did not sacrifice his son, Isaac (Genesis 22). There is no external verification that Abraham was a historical person, so he may be legendary, but in tradition he lived about 1700 BCE. He was, it is recorded, told by God (as a test of his faith) to sacrifice his only son, Isaac. But at the last minute God sent a ram instead and saved the boy's life, thus symbolizing the end of human sacrifice for early Hebrews. Animal and grain sacrifice continued, however, in the temple of Jerusalem, until just after Jesus's time, when the Romans destroyed the Jewish temple in Jerusalem in 70 CE. For most Christians, Jesus is seen as the last sacrifice to God, who died to save believers from their sins and satisfy God's judgment on sinful humanity. This further elevated the value of each person. In biblical tradition, Abraham is the founding father of Israel, as given in the covenant with God, who also told Abraham to have all his male descendents circumcised as a sign of the covenant.

David

King David, who lived about 1010–970 BCE, is said to have fought Canaanites as a youth, unified Hebrew tribes, then led Israel to Jerusalem as the new capital city. He married Bathsheba, and their son Solomon built the first Temple. But later the army of the large Assyrian Empire came from the East (now Iraq) and conquered much of Israel in 722 BCE. Then Babylonia, replacing Assyria's rule, attacked Israel and finally conquered Jerusalem in 586 BCE, taking most all of the Hebrews (except the Samaritans) into slavery in Babylon.

The Prophets

During this time a number of prophets, such as Isaiah, Jeremiah, and Ezekiel, spoke. In the ancient world a thoughtful, spiritual prophet was often consulted to gain an understanding of the will of God. When Babylon was conquering Israel, several prophets wrote about what the people were asking: "Why does our nation suffer again so miserably at the hand of foreign imperial armies?" The biblical prophets' answers were not always welcome, for the prophets said that the nation was not being true to its God and was being punished. Criticizing insincere temple worship, Isaiah said God did not like temple rituals that ignored social justice. His vision was that God scorned the traditional temple celebrations, especially the blood sacrifices, and cared more for the needs of orphans and widows. God was calling not for routine temple rituals, Isaiah proclaimed, but for sincere faith and social justice. This is why the nation suffered military defeat, the prophets said. This aspect of God shows God's judgment.

Isaiah's second message was more hopeful, for it expressed the theology of God's merciful forgiveness and power of salvation from suffering. God promised a Messiah to his people, Isaiah announced, a new leader who would bring peace and justice. This side of God is called his mercy. This hope for a Messiah has been a theme in Jewish thought since, but Jews have been wary of false messiahs who promise a lot but are easily defeated.

From Babylon to Rome

After about 50 years captivity in Babylon, the Jews were released by the conquering Persians and they returned to Israel to build a new temple beginning about 515 BCE, as recorded in the biblical books of Ezra and Nehemiah. Subsequent imperial conquests of Israel's valued trade routes came from the Greek Alexander the Great in 332 BCE, followed by Hellenistic rule and cultural influence, such as the Greek language and philosophy. A successful revolt, led by the Jewish clan called the Maccabees in 167 BCE, returned rule to Jews for about 100 years. Then the Romans, who appointed Herod to rule Israel, dominated the Jews beginning in 63 BCE. The first of four kings named Herod, he was a Palestinian who married a Jewish princess and converted to Judaism. He was a cruel tyrant hated by the Jews.

Jews at that time generally divided into two major groups. The Sadducees, comprised mostly of the wealthy aristocratic classes and temple priests, denied resurrection and reward or punishment in the afterlife. The Pharisees were the more middle-class Jews, devoted to the Law (Torah), including ritual observances and belief in resurrection and reward and punishment in the afterlife. Two smaller groups were the Zealots, who advocated violent rebellion against Rome, and the monastic Essenes, known mostly from the 1947 discovery of the Dead Sea Scrolls. These leather scrolls with revered writings were hidden, when Rome attacked, in caves by the Dead Sea and were discovered 2,000 years later. They reveal that the Essenes, both men and women who withdrew from mainstream Jewish life, practiced simple ascetic spirituality and shared a sacred meal of bread and wine. Their texts stressed the eternal soul, the early coming of the end of the world, and the coming of a religious "Teacher of Righteousness," who opposed a "Wicked Priest."[1]

The Jews repeatedly revolted against Roman oppression, and the Roman army finally sacked and burned Jerusalem and its temple in 70 CE. The bruised Jewish nation then began its Diaspora, or dispersion throughout the Mediterranean world and into Babylon, North Africa, Spain, Germany, and Russia. Without a central temple, Judaism shifted its theology away from temple priests and sacrifice toward local synagogue teachers—rabbis, drawn mostly from the Pharisees.

JESUS

Jesus's Birth

According to the New Testament Gospels, during the reign of Caesar Augustus in Rome, a Jewish child was born in Israel who would found the Christian religion. Jesus's birth is described as quite humble. His earthly father was Joseph, a carpenter. His mother was Mary, and they lived in Nazareth, north of Jerusalem in the region of Galilee. This humble birth indicates his alignment with the poor and outcasts with whom he associated as a man. By tradition, Mary was a virgin betrothed to Joseph, but she was pregnant before their wedding. It is written that an angel appeared to Joseph and told him not to leave her, because the virgin birth was to fulfill a divine prophecy. Mary was also visited by an angel, Gabriel, who told her that she was to bear the son of God. She responded gracefully, accepting her role and emphasizing God's intent to "exalt those of low degree," so she expected that her son would bring justice to the poor.

Required by a Roman census to return to his home town, Joseph took pregnant Mary to Bethlehem, south of Jerusalem. The crowds filled the inns because of the census, so the couple had to stay in a stable, which may have been a cave. According to the New Testament, Mary gave birth to Jesus there and laid him in a manger, which is a feeding bin for animals, in place of a cradle. Shepherds came, saying that a bright-shining angel sent them to find the newborn Savior. According to tradition, kings and priests from the East (such as the Persian Zoroastrian Magi) also came, for they

The adoration of the Magi and circumcision of Jesus, from the 1200s, Monastery of St. Agnes, Perugia, Italy. © Getty Images/FA01002.

also believed in the birth of a savior and had been following a star to Jesus's birthplace, bringing gifts of gold and incense.

As Jesus grew up, it is recorded that John the Baptist, a man of the wilderness dressed in camel's hair and leather, appeared fiercely preaching repentance and baptized people with water, saying he was preparing the way for another. When Jesus was about 30 years old, John began Jesus's ministry by baptizing him in Israel's Jordan River.

Jesus's Ministry and Teachings

After his baptism, Jesus went to the wilderness for a 40-day retreat. The Bible story tells that Jesus was unsuccessfully tempted there with worldly power by the devil. When he returned he learned of John's arrest, apparently for his fiery preaching, by Roman-dominated King Herod. Sensing danger, Jesus went north to rural Galilee and began preaching repentance of sinfulness in the synagogues. He said he was sent to liberate the oppressed.

Jesus began gathering apostles in the Jewish fishing villages along the western shore of the Sea of Galilee: Simon Peter, Andrew, James, and John. By tradition he went to nearby Capernaum and cast out a demon from an unclean man and healed many others of illnesses. It was said that he healed the blind, lame, and lepers. He gathered 12 main disciples and other apostles, including Mary from the village of Magdala.

It is told that once Jesus was walking and a woman touched the edge of his robe seeking healing. She had suffered from a hemorrhage for 12 years. It was forbidden for men and women to touch each other in public, according to Jewish Law, but Jesus responded compassionately, telling the woman to take heart, for her faith had made her well. His healing extended intentionally to the poor and the meek. He said that they would be comforted and blessed.

As recorded in the New Testament, Jesus often spoke in metaphors and stories called parables. He called his listeners "the light of the world" and urged people to seek true treasures, not earthly treasures that decay and are stolen, but authentic spiritual treasures, such as peace and love.

From a human perspective, Jesus may have seen himself as a reformer in the prophetic tradition of Judaism, rather than the founder of a new religion. But the Gospels describe a stronger picture of him as divine Messiah, a spiritual power existing for all time. Much as Jewish Prophets had emphasized the importance of avoiding empty adherence to religious law, Jesus stressed sincere motivation. But he saw this reform as fulfilling the true spirit of the Law, not abolishing it. He taught that the purpose of religious rules is not to believe and obey blindly, but to remember God and live in harmony with God's will.

Similarly it is said that Jesus challenged the ancient law of retaliation, an eye for an eye and a tooth for a tooth. The ancient Jewish law was intended to limit punishment to an equal and fair response, instead of allowing an escalation of retaliation in conflict. But Jesus went further and preached a radical, highly challenging ethic that stresses not just behavior, but sincere inner spiritual motivation. Loving your neighbors and hating your enemies only breeds ethnic hatred. Better to love your enemies and pray for your persecutors, he taught.

Jesus's Crucifixion and Resurrection

According to tradition, Jesus led his disciples to Jerusalem during the third year of his ministry for the Jewish Passover celebration of the Exodus from Egyptian slavery. Jerusalem, an ancient walled city densely populated with a maze of narrow streets and steps and filled with pilgrims for the holiday, was overshadowed by the Roman rulers. Jesus rode a donkey into Jerusalem into the "Golden Gate" before the great Temple. Many of the admiring crowd saw him, spread garments and palm tree branches on the ground before him, and rejoiced. Today this is celebrated as Palm Sunday. According to tradition, Jesus now intensified his criticism of insincere religion and social injustice. In the only account of his anger and violence, Jesus entered the temple area and overturned the tables of the moneychangers and sellers of sacrificial animals, accusing them of being a den of robbers in a house of prayer. Echoing the Prophets, he again condemned hypocrisy in religion, angering many in the archaic temple, filled with the smell of incense, with blood running down from the sacrificial animals on the altar.

On the night of the Passover celebration, it is recorded that Jesus led his disciples in the traditional Jewish Passover meal, which was later called his Last Supper. He used the traditional Jewish bread and wine, but he transformed their meaning, saying that the bread was his body and the wine was his blood. This reference to eating and drinking Jesus's body and blood alludes to the very ancient practices of sacrifice, such as the Passover sacrificial Lamb. Jesus's words now show an increased sense of being a divine Messiah sent from heaven.

Jesus's death, inevitable in an ancient culture that routinely executed protesters, was hastened by the betrayal of one of his disciples, Judas Iscariot. The Gospel texts portray Jesus as fully aware of his destiny and of his coming betrayal by Judas. Jesus led the disciples to the Garden of Gethsemane, just outside Jerusalem, where he prayed. He asked the disciples to stay awake and guard him, but they fell asleep, symbolic of failure to honor and protect the divine. Judas led a crowd with weapons to seize Jesus in the garden that night and kissed Jesus as a sign for the crowd to take him—now a classic image of betrayal by a trusted friend.

Jesus was taken to the temple high priests, it is told, who asked whether he was the Messiah, the Son of God. Three answers are given in the Gospels. In Matthew, Mark, Luke, and John: "Jesus said to him "you have said so" (Matthew 26:64), or "And Jesus said, 'I am'" (Mark 14:62), or "If I tell you, you will not believe" (Luke 22:67). Each of these, whether an evasive or direct answer, concludes with the saying: "But from now on the Son of man shall be seated at the right hand of the Power of God" (Luke 22:69), indicating Jesus's anticipated return to his heavenly position seated next to God's throne. Christians could thus say that Jesus knew he was Messiah from before his birth. These texts suggest a cautious disclosure of Jesus's self-understanding as Messiah (see also Ch. 2, Texts and Tenets).

It is written that the chief priests, who found Jesus guilty of claiming to be a king of the Jews, sent him to Pilate, the Roman governor of Judea. Pilate asked Jesus, "Are you king of the Jews?" and Jesus again replied evasively, "You have said so," according to the gospels of Matthew, Mark, and Luke, but "My kingship is not of this world," in John. Pilate did not find Jesus guilty, but the mob demanded his crucifixion, even after Pilate offered to release a prisoner for the Passover holiday. The crowd instead cried out to release another prisoner, Barabbas, who had been imprisoned for an insurrection and murder, and to crucify Jesus.

The tradition says that Jesus was whipped, then taken with his cross to the execution grounds called Calvary, or Golgotha ("place of a skull"), just outside the city walls. He was hung on a cross between two criminals. Through his pain, Jesus is said to have cried out: "Father, forgive them, for they know not what they do" (Luke 23:33). He was mocked and offered sour drinks such as vinegar. Jesus breathed his last as his grieving followers and family looked on.

Joseph of Arimathea, a member of the city council, offered to take Jesus's body. He wrapped it in a linen shroud and laid him in a rock-hewn tomb.

Christ crucified, in Stations of the Cross series, at Immaculate Conception Roman Catholic Church, Ithaca, New York. Courtesy of the author.

This was the day Christians now call Good Friday. A heavy rock was rolled before the tomb door, and Roman soldiers were posted to guard the place. Two days later, now called Easter or Pascha Sunday, two women apostles went to the graveyard to see the tomb. In four different Gospel accounts, there was a great earthquake, and an angel, a young man, or two men dressed in dazzling apparel. The heavy stone door to the tomb was rolled back, and Jesus's body was gone. The angel or man is said to have told them not to be amazed because Jesus had risen and was not there.

It is told that his mother, Mary, saw Jesus standing outside the tomb, not recognizing him at first. One of Jesus's close followers, Mary Magdalene, ran to find Peter and another apostle, and they all hurried back to the tomb, finding only the linen shroud. Jesus told Mary Magdalene that he was ascending to heaven. Jesus then revealed himself to the disciples elsewhere after this. To assure them that he was truly embodied, resurrected, and not just a spirit, Jesus ate a piece of fish and invited the most skeptical one, "doubting" Thomas, to place his hand on his wounds.

If Jesus's story had ended at the cross, without the resurrection account, there would be no Christianity. He would have been just another prophet who tried to reform his culture's religion, who was tragically rejected and killed. But the resurrection affirmed to later believers that Jesus was not just another human hero. He came to be seen as a divine figure visiting earth from a transcendent, heavenly realm, come to teach awareness of the presence and true nature of ultimate reality, and to save believers from suffering, evil, and death. This theology is first apparent in the Gospel of John. Jesus's resurrection elevates his entire life and teaching, placing them in a new realm of faith beyond earthly existence. It re-visions Jesus to be divine, as the Messiah or Christ. As Christianity spread, it welcomed people of all social classes and all nationalities. Christians later concluded that Jesus is paradoxically fully human and fully divine, both a human prophet and a divine savior who brought the promise of eternal life to all Christians.

PAUL

Paul, originally named Saul, was a Jew who, after Jesus's death, was one of a number of persecutors who hated the new Christians and put many in jail (Acts 8:3). But he was converted by a dazzling vision of Jesus resurrected to the new "way" and changed his name to Paul. His most important accomplishment was to universalize Christianity. Paul spread beyond Jewish communities the gospel of Jesus as a savior who challenges social injustices, gives strength in suffering, overcomes death, promises eternal life, and calls for love. He reached out to Greek-speaking gentile believers, saying that they did not have to be circumcised or keep the entire Jewish Law. He taught the importance of faith in God's justice (and not obedience to the law) as the proper motive for ethical behavior. God's love and grace, he said, were freely given and not to be earned by sacrifices or good behavior. He was somewhat patriarchal toward women but also said that there is no male or female, slave or free, in Christ, and he had many women followers. His letters became New Testament books. He was executed in Rome in 65 CE.

THE EARLY CHURCH

As it developed, early Christianity had a wide appeal for several reasons. It drew upon a wide range of traditions—Hebrew monotheism, the Jewish prophetic ethical tradition, possibly the Persian Zoroastrianism's concept of a cosmic conflict between good and evil, and the idea of a god-man coming to Earth to bring salvation, also known in several other religions, such as in Egypt and Greece. Christian theology developed in the atmosphere of ancient "mystery religions" that taught a cosmic savior, baptism, and a sacred meal. Christianity also welcomed greater rights of participation in worship for women than some other religions and gained respect from the courage of persecuted martyrs such as Stephen, who was stoned to death for preaching the new faith. Another martyr, Perpetua, a North African woman, refused to renounce Christianity in 203 CE. She was 22 years old, nursing her child while in prison, and had remarkable visions assuring her of her coming entry into the next world. She was thrown to wild animals, then stabbed with a sword. The courage and faith of such martyrdom, showing strong belief in life after death, inspired many to become Christians. Christianity had a stronger appeal to the poor and oppressed than many religions, because Jesus taught the equality of all in the sight of God and exalted the poor and humble over the rich and mighty. This was a seed of Western democracy.

The early Church had many issues, both theological and organizational, to solve. The early devout believers saw the Church as a community of mystics, guided by the divine Light. They met in homes, with little formal leadership aside from the hostesses. Later, others envisioned an organized society with uniform rules, a set ritual, and a formal, hierarchical, male priesthood.

The early church produced several apologists, or theologians, who explored important emerging questions of the faith. For example, Justin Martyr (100–165), who taught in Ephesus (in Asia minor, now Turkey) and Rome, emphasized truth and reason. He argued that Jesus was the divine Logos ("reason," or "meaning") shared by all peoples, and that those who lived before Jesus, like the Greek philosopher Socrates, were Christians if they lived according to reason.

Irenaeus (130–200) studied in Rome and became bishop of Lyons (France). He attacked forms of Gnosticism (which, envisioning the world as evil, saw the biblical God as a lesser, imperfect deity, and taught a "secret knowledge" enabling escape from this world). He clearly stated major themes of the emerging faith: the goodness and universal intellect of God, his plan for saving believers from evil, its perfection in Jesus, and the offer of salvation from suffering. Humans can find beauty in God's glory, he taught, and participate in God's Holy Spirit. When loving those who wrong them, they participate in God's goodness.

Tertullian (160–220), born in Carthage, North Africa, was the first theologian to write in Latin and to develop the theology of the Trinity. For him God, Jesus, and the Holy Spirit were one in quality, substance, and power, but distinct in sequence, aspect, and manifestation. He was one of the church fathers who saw martyrdom as a baptism, leading the church to believe that the blood of those who die for the faith without baptism are baptized by their blood.[2]

The Egyptian theologian Origen (185–254) led an ascetic life and taught the logical coherence of the world and God's love and providence. Influenced by Greek philosophy, he taught that creation is eternal and that souls pre-exist this life. He taught that scripture has three levels of meaning: the literal, the inner, and the deeper, more cosmic, allegorical, and spiritual. He rejected the literal meaning of the biblical creation account. He made a lasting distinction between moral development, rational perception of divine wisdom in the world, and direct, mystical contact with God's mysterious presence.[3]

As the Roman Empire slowly faded from both internal weakness and external attack, between 300 and 600 CE, the church stepped in to fill the need for order in Europe. One way of strengthening moral order was the medieval church's affirmation of the last judgment. This is the belief that after death the soul will be judged for its earthly ethical behavior and rewarded in Heaven or punished in Hell. This belief was also known in other cultures, such as in Egypt and Persia. In chaotic times when law enforcement was

Christ ascending to heaven in the post-resur-
rection appearance to the apostles, stained-glass
window at St. Paul's United Methodist Church,
Ithaca, New York. Courtesy of the author.

weak, fear of Hell offered a motive for internalized ethical self-control, even
if it was based on fright, rather than sincere motivation. Christians did not
see this world as evil, but reacted against the harshness around them by
aiming toward heaven.

The Byzantine Emperors Constantine and Theodosius

Christianity's path to becoming the official religion of the Empire began
when in 312 the Roman general Constantine saw a vision of a cross and
interpreted this as a sign from the Christian God that helped him win a
battle. The Roman Empire was fading by then, burdened by a vast Empire, a
large, expensive army, continuing poverty, injustice, oppression, and invading (or immigrating) barbarian tribes, such as the Visigoths. After he became Emperor, Constantine in 313 moved the Imperial capital from Rome
east to more secure Byzantium, which was renamed Constantinople after
him. Constantine granted unlimited freedom of religion across the Roman

Empire in the Edict of Milan in 313, which allowed the Church to expand
without persecution. In 321 he endowed church buildings and made Sunday a public holiday, apparently because he saw Christianity as a faith that
could unite the Empire.

Constantine summoned the important Council of Nicaea in 325, where he
assembled bishops and theologians to discuss how to handle issues such as
Arianism. This theology (named after its teacher, Arius), widespread among
the newly Christianized tribes that invaded Rome, believed that Jesus was
not divine but was a human hero. The council rejected Arianism. The first
short Nicene Creed was formulated to express their decision and was later
expanded by the Council of Chalcedon in 451, which also proclaimed Jesus
to be paradoxically fully divine and fully human. Christianity officially became the state religion in 380 under the Emperor Theodosius (379–395),
who also prohibited all non-Christian religions and sacrificial rituals.

THE EARLY EUROPEAN MIDDLE AGES

As Roman authority declined, invading tribes gradually plundered Europe. Visigoths sacked Rome in 410 and moved on to settle in Spain and
southern Gaul around 476. Around 450, Attila the Hun's army swept down
and conquered Italy. The Germanic Vandals left a trail of devastation across
Europe and pillaged Rome in 455. In 497 the Ostrogoths conquered Italy.
In 570 the Lombards gained control of northern Italy. In 711 North African
Muslims ("Moors") invaded Spain. After the collapse of Rome, agriculture
declined, roads, bridges, and aqueducts fell into disrepair, education and
thus literacy declined, and vulnerability to crime increased. Europe shifted
away from urban Roman rule to rule by local, land-owning nobility. Slowly
the Christian Church, between the fourth century and the fourteenth century, suppressed, converted, or conquered the many ancient tribal religions
of Europe's invading tribes, such as the Germans, Franks, Goths, Vandals,
and Celts. Sometimes Christians blended their traditions, as when they
adopted ancient goddesses as saints, like the Celtic Bridget. Other times
Christians suppressed pagans with wars, if their beliefs were too contrary,
as with the Albigensians, who saw the world as evil.

In the midst of invasions, diseases, and wars, aristocrats became knights
and built castles to consolidate their power. Christians built monasteries,
hospitals, orphanages, libraries, schools, and cathedrals. Bishops emerged
as regional Christian leaders and struggled against widespread, ancient,
crude customs such as blood revenge and fruitless tribal feuds. Bishops

sought to tame the brutal robbers by decreeing the "peace of god" for holy days. The Church thus slowly helped civilize and unify Europe. It did not always live up to its high goals, but at their best, Christian bishops, monasteries, and theologians all played important civilizing roles.

Augustine

The Bishop of Hippo North Africa, Augustine (354–430 CE) became the most important of early Medieval Christian theologians. He wrote the first surviving autobiography, *Confessions,* describing his deepest feelings, including his pain about fathering a child with his mistress, which shaped his view of sex as sinful. He also wrote *The City of God,* arguing against those who blamed Christians for the fall of Rome. His ideas decided several major Christian theological issues, such as why there is evil in God's world, called the problem of theodicy.

Monasticism

During the turbulent wars and erosion of the Roman Empire and the slow development of medieval institutions, many men and women retreated to monasteries to live their faith more intensely, to evade violence, to protest a growing worldliness among church authorities, and to help rebuild Europe. Some have lived isolated, but most in communities. Early monasticism was informal and unregulated, and many monks wandered about. Nuns tended to live in small domestic communities. As monasteries and convents formed, organization was required and rules were written.

St. Basil (c. 329–79) founded Eastern Orthodox monasticism. An educated Greek, he wrote rules, originally for lay people, that guided the Basilian monks about 360 CE. Most Orthodox monks still follow the same rules of St. Basil. He crafted the phrase that the Trinity is "three persons in one substance" and wrote the Liturgy of St. Basil, still used in the Orthodox rite. The colorful domed church in Moscow's Kremlin Square is named after him.

St. Benedict of Nursia (c. 480–547) organized rules and a communal system in Italy that became the classic model for centuries of subsequent Western monasteries. The Benedictine Rule that he wrote ordered a monk's life into three parts: prayer, study, and work, including their own education and copying by hand of the Bible and other texts. Monks and nuns take vows of poverty, chastity, obedience, and stability. The Benedictine Order, known also as the Black Monks after their robes, is still widely spread. By the ninth century, monasteries were an important social institution, founding schools, hospitals, and cathedrals. Accumulating vast landholdings and farms, they became an integral part of the feudal system.

Other important monastic orders of the Catholic Church include the twelfth-century Carthusians, Cistercians, and the Orders of Chivalry, who were leaders in the Crusades. The Augustinians, Franciscans, and Dominicans committed themselves to voluntary poverty, preaching, and serving believers' pastoral needs, as distinct from the earliest monastic purpose of serving God by personal sanctification. By the early 1200s a monastic school developed into the first Western university in Paris, and others soon followed in Italy (Bologna, Naples), England (Oxford, Cambridge), and Spain (Salamanca, Valencia). The Spaniard Ignatius of Loyola founded the Society of Jesus, or Jesuits, in 1534. Orthodox monks to this day inspire many with their mystical literature and icon painting. They have been greatly revered and some become bishops. Catholic monks and nuns have historically produced beautiful music, copied valuable texts, and created social services such as hospitals, orphanages, schools, and cathedrals. Anglicans have monastic orders as well. But King Henry VIII firmly abolished his era's widespread but lax monasticism by acts such as beheading resistant Carthusian monks in 1535. Their large properties were confiscated, so now monasticism is a minor portion of Anglican tradition.

Celibacy

Celibacy is the practice of sexual abstinence. Some of Jesus's first apostles were married and took their wives with them as they traveled (I Corinthians 9:5). However, Paul's early biblical distinction between spirit and flesh led to Christian division over ascetic practices, such as fasting and celibacy, intended to elevate the spirit above flesh. These practices are common in most religions. In the early Middle Ages, some, but not all, priests adopted celibacy. Early Western church councils gave clergy the right to marry, but this allowed priests in the aristocratic tradition to focus on accumulating property in order to pass both property and priesthood down to their sons. This was seen as a distraction from the spiritual role of priests, so priestly celibacy was required in Catholic law, first about 306 CE at the Council of

Elvira, Spain. It gradually spread, but did not stop some medieval priests from marrying or taking concubines. Priestly celibacy was promoted more firmly by the Papacy beginning in the eleventh century. By the Second Vatican Council (1962–65), Catholic celibacy was debated again, some arguing that it should be optional for priests. But Pope John XXIII insisted on its continuation. Now it is seen as a way for the priests to focus on their vocation undistracted by family obligations.

Missionaries

The Church spread its message through many missionaries. Patrick of Ireland (about 389–461 CE), son of a British Christian, was kidnapped by Irish sailors and spent six years as a slave in Ireland. Then, in response to a dream, he escaped back to England. He was inspired to become a priest, then ordained as a bishop and sent back to Ireland as a missionary, where he was the first to convert many among royal families, after contests with ancient Celtic Druid priests. At the royal center, Tara, he astonished them with a "miraculous" way of lighting a fire. He established ascetic communities that became monasteries—important pastoral, educational, and artistic centers. In legend he was said to have killed all the snakes in Ireland, probably symbolic of the archaic religions and other poisonous conflicts.

Anglo-Saxon Christians, notably Boniface (680–754), became missionaries from England to kingdoms that became Germany. With Pope Gregory II's support, Boniface went to Hesse and Thuringia, where he was successful in converting many. He established monasteries and bishoprics and led reforming councils to correct abuses. Thus, the foundations of the Christian church were laid in the early Middle Ages, and it expanded and solidified with missionaries, churches, and monasteries. The Eastern Orthodox Church expanded into Russia by 988, where now almost half its members reside.

The Roman Catholic Church slowly converted the tribal invaders and indigenous inhabitants of Western Europe. Its Latin was blended with the ancient tribal languages as the church expanded into European regions that became Italy, Spain, France, Germany, England, Scotland, the Netherlands, Belgium, and Ireland. In 1517 Protestantism developed, splintered into numerous denominations, and spread from northern Europe to North America and beyond. From these beginnings, Christianity became the world's largest religion, with great influence in shaping European and American cultures.[4]

NOTES

1. Geza Vermes, ed. *The Complete Dead Sea Scrolls in English* (New York: Allen Lane/Penguin, 1997).

2. *Catechism of the Catholic Church* (New York: Doubleday, 1995), item 1258.

3. G. R. Evans, ed. *The First Christian Theologians* (Oxford: Blackwell, 2004).

4. Williston Walker, et al., *A History of Christian Church* (New York: Scribner's, 1985).

2

TEXTS AND MAJOR TENETS

Since many men were literate in Jewish and Greek cultures in Jesus's time, the records of emerging Christianity were written down, saving it from extinction. These texts became the authoritative textual foundation for the development of Christian beliefs, or tenets—the Bible. Adopting the Jewish holy books as the "Old Testament," Christians added to it the "New Testament" that recorded Jesus's life and teachings, and the theological teachings of Paul and other early church leaders. As history unfolded, the three branches of the church each adopted slightly different versions of the Bible. Early issues that the church had to solve involved disputes over the nature of Jesus's divinity, the extent and nature of human sinfulness, and the growing structure of the church. Councils met to debate these issues and issued creeds, such as the Nicene Creed (an early statement of Christian faith stressing Jesus's divinity, 325 CE). Theologians such as Augustine (354–430 CE) wrote definitive texts.

SACRED TEXTS: THE OLD TESTAMENT AND THE NEW TESTAMENT

The Old Testament

Traditionalists believe that the Bible was inspired by God and, although written by human hands, is literally true and error-free. The great leader of the Hebrew Exodus out of Egypt named Moses, they believe, wrote the first five books of the Bible. But by looking closely at biblical language, history, and archaeology, critical analysis shows that the composition of the Bible was far more complex. Though one could still believe it to be inspired by God, it was written by many hands and edited centuries after the writing. Events that happened long after Moses's death, for example, are recorded in the fifth book, Deuteronomy, that he supposedly wrote. The Bible includes both history and poetry, both intended to teach the acts of Israel's God in history. The study of world religions has shown numerous parallels that Jews and Christians may have absorbed from other cultures. The account of Noah's Ark, for example, has a direct parallel in the Babylonian story of Uta-Napishtim, which was available to Hebrews during their exile in Babylon around 550 BCE.[1]

After the destruction of Jerusalem by the Romans in 70 CE, Jewish rabbis gathered to decide which of their many sacred scrolls were to become the canon, or the official holy text. By about 100 CE the rabbis had agreed to the contents of their canon, called the *Tanakh*, written in Hebrew. *Tanakh* is an acronym for *Torah* (the 5 books of Moses), *Navi'im* (the Prophets), and *Kethuvim* (Wisdom Literature or Writings). The Jewish *Tanakh* became the Christian Old Testament, because Christians saw Jesus as bringing a new testimony of God's will. Many major Jewish themes were absorbed into Christianity, most notably monotheism's cosmic scope, the Law's stress on ethical responsibility, the prophetic tradition on sincerity and social justice, the messianic tradition, and the value of each individual.[2]

The shortest Christian canon now is the Protestant, listed here. The additional Apocryphal and Deuterocanonical books included in the Catholic, Orthodox Greek, and Orthodox Slavonic Bibles are listed afterward.

1. The Pentateuch (five scrolls): The traditional five books of Moses include Genesis, Exodus, Leviticus, Numbers, and Deuteronomy. Genesis includes the creation account and the traditions of the Jewish Patriarchs Abraham, Isaac, Jacob, and Joseph. Exodus describes the history of the Exodus from Egypt and the beginning of the Torah, or Law of Israel in the Ten Commandments received by Moses. Leviticus, Numbers, and Deuteronomy assemble ritual traditions, laws, and the early historical traditions of Israel.

2. The historical books: Joshua, Judges, I & II Samuel, I & II Kings, I & II Chronicles, Ezra, and Nehemiah describe Israel's early historical traditions, including that of kings such as David and Solomon.

3. The books of the Prophets who criticized Israel's faults and promised God's forgiveness and a Messiah. They include the major prophets Isaiah, Jeremiah,

Ezekiel, and Daniel, and the 12 minor prophets: Hosea, Joel, Amos, Obadiah, Jonah, Micah, Nahum, Habakkuk, Zephaniah, Haggai, Zechariah, and Malachi.

4. The Wisdom Writings, including a drama of unjust suffering about Job, a good man who lost all his wealth and children, yet still believed in God's justice. It was borrowed and adapted from a Babylonian source. The many Psalms (songs of praise) sung in worship were recorded, as well as the Lamentations, texts grieving over Israel's defeat by Babylon and slavery there for about 50 years. In addition are included the books of Esther and Ruth, two heroic women; Proverbs, or short traditional wisdom sayings; Ecclesiastes, expressing doubt about God's goodness ultimately overcoming evil; and the Song of Solomon, a love poem.

The Apocryphal and Deuterocanonical Books include four groups:

1. Books and additions to the above books in the Roman Catholic, Orthodox Greek, and Slavonic Bibles: Tobit, Judith, additions to Esther, Wisdom of Solomon, Ecclesiasticus (or the Wisdom of Jesus Son of Sirach), Baruch, The Letter of Jeremiah (Baruch, Ch. 6), additions to Daniel (Prayer of Azariah, Song of the Three Jews, Susanna, Bel and the Dragon), 1 Maccabees, 2 Maccabees.
2. The books in the Orthodox Greek and Slavonic Bibles only: Esdras, Prayers of Manasseh, Psalm 151, 3 Maccabees.
3. Book in the Orthodox Slavonic Bible and the Latin Vulgate Appendix: 2 Esadras
4. Book in the Appendix to the Orthodox Greek Bible: 4 Maccabees.

Many of these books were included in early church Bibles, such as the 1611 English King James translation. But the English Puritan Protestant reformers disapproved of them and demanded that they be dropped. They were and now do not appear in Protestant Bibles.

What was the known origin of the biblical texts? Many *Tanakh* texts were oral tradition or written fragments of current books for centuries, then written down in Hebrew (a dialect of the ancient Canaanite language) and assembled beginning probably after King David's reign, perhaps around 900 BCE. The collection grew informally until the fall of Jerusalem to the Romans. About 30 years after the fall of Jerusalem in 70 CE, a group of Hebrew scholars (the "Masoretes") edited the Hebrew scrolls that originated from the sixth to the tenth centuries BCE and copied them into an authoritative canonical Hebrew text now called the Masoretic Text (MT). During the second century CE, a Greek translation of the Old Testament was undertaken by about 70 scholars (or completed in 72 days, in another tradition) in Alexandria and thereafter called the "Septuagint" (LXX), meaning "seventy." This is still the preferred Old Testament Greek text for the Eastern Orthodox Church. The Roman Catholic Bible was for centuries the Latin "Vulgate" translation from the Hebrew and Greek by Jerome, finished in 404 CE. Now different language groups use their translations, such as the New American Version.

People in Israel and neighboring regions in Jesus's time spoke Aramaic, an ancient Semitic language closely related to ancient Hebrew, spoken from the ninth century BCE until the present. It originated among the Arameans of northern Syria and was spread by the conquering Assyrians. It became a widespread Near Eastern language until the Greek invasion, then declined when the Arabs invaded Israel. Several Old Testament Aramaic passages are inserted into the Hebrew text, as in the account of Laban and Jacob making a covenant about marriage in Genesis 31:47.

The New Testament

The New Testament was written in Koiné Greek, a Hellenistic dialect of ancient Greek and the written language of educated people at the time. But certain passages, such as Jesus's cry on the cross: *"Eli, Eli, lama sabachthani?"* (My God, My God, why hast thou forsaken me?) (Matthew 27:46, Mark 15:34) are in Aramaic. Another New Testament Aramaic word is *Golgotha* ("place of the skull,") where Jesus was crucified. Whether Jesus spoke many passages in Greek, or Gospel authors translated his spoken Aramaic into written Greek is unknown, but Greek was the more literary language of the time. Ancient New Testament Greek texts number about 5,000 fragmentary scrolls of parchment or papyrus. The first New Testament Greek fragments known to be translated into Latin were found in some scrolls from North Africa from the second to fifth centuries. The Latin Vulgate, combining Jerome's Old Testament and Latin translations of various Greek manuscripts, was the standard Catholic Bible until 1943. Many Protestant Reformers returned to the ancient Hebrew Masoretic text for their Old Testament translations and added translations from various Greek manuscripts. Today the scholarly English *New Revised Standard Version: Holy Bible* includes all texts from all three branches: Orthodox, Catholic, and Protestant. It also strives to avoid use of male pronouns when both males and females are meant.[3]

The New Testament begins with the four Gospels: Matthew, Mark, Luke, and John. Each book tells of Jesus's birth, teaching, crucifixion, and resurrection. The first three are called the "synoptic" Gospels, because they are similar, repeating accounts of Jesus's life with variations. They were written down between about 70 to 95 CE. Matthew has the longest version of the Lord's Prayer, Mark's is the shortest and probably the oldest text, and Luke has the most extensive birth narrative.[4] The Gospel of John is similar to the synoptic Gospels but has a stronger mystical and Greek influence, such as the opening cosmic statement: "In the beginning was the Word (Greek: *logos*), and the Word was with God, and the Word was God." For John, Jesus is seen as a divine, eternal "Word" or cosmic principle of meaning, as well as the Hebrew Messiah (Greek: *Christos*), who speaks mystically of "living water," "living bread," and "living light."

Unlike the Synoptic gospels, John emphasizes the divinity of Jesus from the beginning of the universe, his role in creation, and his becoming flesh (incarnated) on earth as Son of God. His ministry takes three years, according to John, but only one year according to the Synoptic Gospels. This more cosmic portrayal has a stronger Greek flavor than the more earthly Hebrew image of Jesus as Prophet and saving Jewish Messiah sent from God. It was written about 90–100 CE, later than the Synoptics.

There is no account of Jesus's birth in John, and John includes several unique accounts not in the Synoptics, such as the marriage in Cana where Jesus turns water into wine, the Samaritan woman at the well, forgiveness of the woman caught in adultery who was about to be stoned, and Jesus washing the feet of his disciples. Whereas Jesus's reply to the Roman governor of Judea Pilate's question "Are you King of the Jews?" in Matthew, Mark, and Luke is "You have said so," in John, Jesus's reply is complex, including "My kingship is not of this world" (John 18). The risen Christ also shows himself to the disciples more often in John than in the Synoptic Gospels.

John's view of Jesus pre-existing his human life as the Word and clearly aware of himself as divine, bringing eternal life to believers, is a "high Christology," or a transcendent view of Jesus as divine. This is evident in several passages, such as: "For God so loved the world that he gave his only Son, that whoever believes in him should not perish but have eternal life" (John 3:16). In John, Jesus discussed his upcoming death and resurrection with more foresight than in the Synoptic Gospels: "now I am going to him who sent me… . A little while, and you will see me no more; again a little while, and you will see me" (John 16: 5,16). As opposed to the higher Christology that sees Jesus as divine, a lower Christology stresses Jesus's human side as a Jewish reformer, who was misunderstood and persecuted, but was merely human. Christians concluded, however (at the Council of Chalcedon in 451), that Christ was paradoxically both fully divine and fully human.

The Gospels are followed by the book of the Acts of the Apostles, describing the events after Jesus's death, such as the martyrdom of Stephen, who was stoned to death for preaching Christianity, and the conversion of Saul to Paul and his travels. Some of the first apostles were married and took their wives on their journeys(I Corinthians 9:5). Then follow several letters or "Epistles" from Paul (or attributed to Paul) written to various new churches: Romans, I & II Corinthians, Galatians, Ephesians, Philippians, Colossians, I & II Thessalonians, I & II Timothy, Titus, and Philemon. Other books are not usually attributed to Paul: Hebrews, James, I & II Peter, I, II, & III John, and Jude. Paul's epistles were written before the Gospels, between about 40 or 51 to 64 CE. Concluding the New Testament, the book of Revelation (The Apocalypse of John) is a dramatic visionary description of beliefs about the end of the world.

Many other texts about Jesus that circulated for some time after his life have varying versions of his teachings. Two were the ancient Gospel of the Ebionites, which includes Jesus saying: "I have come to destroy sacrifices." and the Gospel of Thomas, saying "The Kingdom is inside of you, and it is outside of you. When you come to know yourselves, then you will become known." Several such ancient texts were found in Egypt in 1945, in a collection of scrolls called the *Nag Hammadi Library*.[5]

The decisions as to which manuscripts were to be the official New Testament (canon) were made in the century leading up to 400 CE, when bishops in various Mediterranean cities were listing what they considered to be the canonical texts inspired by God's spirit. The heart of the New Testament is divine revelation—the *kerygma,* or the "preaching," in Greek, as distinct from the *didache,* or "teaching." Jesus preached about the "Kingdom of God" and the power of redemption in teaching, healing, and miracles, offering meanings for life, such as love and eternal life.

Nineteenth-century biblical scholars revealed numerous errors of translation from the Hebrew and Greek, due to centuries of poor copying and translations from the Greek, Aramaic, Syriac, and Latin. They updated Jerome's 404 Latin Catholic Vulgate edition and the 1611 English Protestant King James Version. Old English forms of "thou," thee," and "thine" now seemed archaic and were certainly not used in the early church. So the Church of England authorized a new translation in 1870. This was the

"English Revised Version" of 1885. The "American Standard Version" was published in 1901. Later scholars refined these into the "Revised Standard Version" (RSV) in 1952, authorized by the U.S. National Council of Churches. Further textual discoveries in the twentieth century, such as the Dead Sea Scrolls, led to more refinement of interpretations. Of course there are numerous editions of the Bible in many languages—in English, the *Orthodox Study Bible,* the *Catholic Study Bible,* the *Oxford Study Bible,* and others. The National Council of Churches sponsored the 1989 *New Revised Standard Version* (NSRV) that is ecumenical, including Orthodox, Catholic, and Protestant texts, and that uses more gender-neutral language.

TWENTIETH-CENTURY TEXT DISCOVERIES

The Dead Sea Scrolls are ancient scrolls found in jars in caves near Qumran, Israel, in 1947, that dated from the centuries around Jesus's life. Written in Hebrew and Aramaic, they are far older than any other existing Christian texts (which are copies of earlier texts). Their cave locations connect them with the nearby ancient Jewish Essene sect that apparently lived in a monastery at Qumran, on the steep desert hill above the Dead Sea, near Jerusalem. They are apparently part of a temple library, hidden during the wars with Rome. One passage says: "From the source of His righteousness is my justification, and from His marvelous mysteries is the light in my heart." They give important background to the life of Jesus and teaching of Christianity but are written in somewhat coded language, so are not specific. They refer, for example, to a "Teacher of Righteousness" who "knew all the mysteries of the Prophets" forecast the end of the world, and, when persecuted by a "Wicked Priest," had to flee into exile. Some thinkers identify this teacher with Jesus, but the vague references could fit other figures. Researchers assembling the fragments, translating, and interpreting the texts have aroused controversy.[6]

The Nag Hammadi scrolls are ancient papyrus scrolls discovered in Upper Egypt in 1945. Translations of Greek originals into the ancient indigenous language of Egypt called Coptic, they date from around the 4th century CE. They include mystical writings, such as "The Gospel of Thomas," "The Gospel of Mary," and "The Thunder Perfect Mind," which includes the words: "I was sent forth from the power ... I am the wife and the virgin, I am the silence that is incomprehensible." They give a fascinating picture of the various types of theology swirling around the developing Christian church. Ancient Gnosticism, for example, emphasized experiential *gnosis* (knowledge) of the divine, as opposed to faith, and saw Jesus as more human than orthodox Christians did.

A major effort to distinguish the actual historical events in the Bible from the possibly added teachings in poetry, mythology, or beliefs began in the nineteenth century. In 1985 the biblical scholar Robert Funk convened the "Jesus Seminar" to analyze the historical validity of all ancient texts about Jesus. More than 200 international biblical scholars have debated and voted on which texts about Jesus have the most historical validity and which may be secondary additions.[7] Debates about themes such as mysticism, story, women, resurrection, apocalypse, theism, and healing have persisted in the difficult task of attempting to distinguish the historical events of Jesus's life from the theological interpretations added later as the church developed. This effort to distinguish authentic words of Jesus from later additions is rejected by conservative traditionalists who accept the Bible in its entirety as God's revelation. Others stress the value of metaphors such as "living water" in revelation.

MAJOR TENETS

As Christianity developed, it clarified its basic beliefs, tenets, and doctrines. Some of those became central elements of the Western worldview.

Major Christian Doctrines

Theism

Christians believe that God is the ultimate reality of the universe, the transcendent creator and ruler of the world. God is seen as being personal, with human-like qualities. Adopting the God of the Jews, Christians continued the patriarchal view of God as a father figure, both firmly establishing laws and compassionately loving and forgiving. Theism is distinct from pantheism, in which the divine spirit is seen in nature in many forms. The meaning of life is to live in harmony with the beliefs of the faith, seeking to express God's love and justice.

Monotheism

Christians also adopted the Jewish theology of one God, as opposed to many gods (polytheism). This principle raised the divine from many local tribal deities, such as Mars the Roman god of war, to a universal, cosmic force of order and goodness, pictured in the heavens. God surpasses all of creation, because God created the universe. Thus creation is not in itself evil, but good, for God assures that ultimately life is good, no matter how painful it may seem at times. Monotheism was also a forerunner of the basic concept of a unified universe, logically consistent throughout.

Original Paradise

In the biblical tradition of Genesis, the first humans, Adam and Eve, lived in a garden paradise, the Garden of Eden. They were like innocent children, naked and unaware of evil, able to live off the fruit of the garden. But they disobeyed God, gained knowledge, and were thus expelled from Eden (the Fall). Some Christians believe that human moral flaws are explained by Adam and Eve's "Original Sin" that is inherited by all humans.

Law

Christians respected the Jewish law, but because Jesus had taught the importance of sincere motivation, rather than simple obedience to religious rules, Christians abandoned most of the Jewish laws, such as male circumcision. Most of the 613 Jewish laws, beginning with the Ten Commandments, were written for a specific historical period, such as the laws about sacrifice and for regulating slavery, so they were not seen as binding for later Christians. But Christians did see some of the Laws, especially the first Ten Commandments, as having lasting validity, so they were adopted into Christian tradition. Some branches of the later church emphasized law and obedience to higher church authority, such as the Eastern Orthodox and Roman Catholics, and others, such as most Protestants, minimized it.

The Nature of Jesus

In the ancient world, many religions had divine figures appearing on earth as human, such as the divine pharaoh in Egypt and heroes in Greece whose father was Zeus. So Christians needed to clarify their understanding of Jesus's divinity and his humanity. The Gospel of John reports that Jesus said, "I and the Father are one" and that for this he was thus almost stoned for blasphemy (John 10:30). This line of thought led to a conflict as the church developed, when some believers emphasized that Jesus was to

Mary holding crucified Christ in her lap in "Pieta," altar sculpture at Santa Maria in Piano Roman Catholic Church, Loreto Aprutino, Pescara, Italy. Courtesy of the author.

be seen as not fully human, not really feeling human desires, but primarily divine, just seeming to be human. This tendency was called "Docetism." But other Christians emphasized the opposite: Jesus's full humanity and suffering, especially "Arianism," which saw Jesus as a human subordinate to God. Arianism was widespread among newly Christianized medieval invaders into Europe. The conflict between Jesus's divinity and his humanity was called the problem of "Christology" and was theoretically solved at the council of Chalcedon in 451 CE, where Christ was proclaimed to be paradoxically both fully human and fully divine. This doctrine saw Christ fulfilling both extremes of knowing the suffering of human existence and being the divine power to overcome it through faith, sincere motivation, social justice, and eternal life. Jesus Christ the Savior was interpreted as God's Son come to earth, experiencing the full range of human life (except sin) and overcoming its sinfulness and suffering by bringing the fullness of God's redeeming spirit to believers.

Trinity

Another theological problem for early Christians was the relation of Jesus to the one God and how his continuing spiritual presence was possible. The Gospel of Matthew says that Jesus spoke to his disciples about the Father, the Son, and the Holy Spirit. Just how there could be one God in heaven who appears on earth as the human Jesus? Does this subordinate Jesus to God? Others reflected on the continuing invisible presence of divinity before and after Jesus's death. This led to the formation of the doctrine of the Trinity: the Father, the Son, the Holy Spirit, paradoxically one essence and three persons.

Nicene Creed

The Church's early disputes over issues such as Jesus's nature culminated in the Nicene Creed, whose formulation began at the first Church-wide council in 325 in Nicaea, just south of Constantinople. It was finally accepted at the council of Chalcedon in 451 CE:

> We believe in one God the Father All-Sovereign, maker of heaven and earth, and of all things visible and invisible;
> And in one Lord Jesus Christ, the only-begotten Son of God, Begotten of the Father before all the ages, Light of Light, true God of true God, begotten not made, of one substance with the Father, through whom all things were made; who for us men and for our salvation came down from the heavens, and was made flesh of the Holy Spirit and the Virgin Mary, and became man, and was crucified for us under Pontius Pilate, and suffered and was buried, and rose again on the third day according to the scriptures, and ascended into the heavens, and sitteth on the right hand of the Father, and cometh again with glory to judge living and dead, of whose kingdom there shall be no end;
> And in the Holy Spirit; the Lord and the Life-giver, that proceedeth from the Father [and the Son], who with Father and Son is worshipped together and glorified together, who spoke through the prophets;
> In one holy Catholic and Apostolic Church;
> We acknowledge one baptism unto remission of sins. We look for a resurrection of the dead, and the life of the age to come. Amen

The words in brackets, "and the Son," above indicate a division between the Eastern Orthodox Churches (which exclude them) and the Western churches (which include them). These words are called the *filioque* ("and the son"). They were not in the original short Nicene Creed, approved at the Nicene Council in 381, then supplemented and approved at the Council

of Chalcedon in 451. The *filioque* was slowly added to the Western liturgy
and approved by Popes between the eighth and eleventh centuries. The
difference hinges on the question whether in the Holy Spirit the Father is
the source of the whole divinity (East) or whether the Son is believed to be
necessarily included (West).[8]

Original Sin

Considering human behavior, the question arises: Is human nature basically good or predominantly sinful? Should believers be optimistic or
pessimistic about human nature? This is answered in the Genesis creation
account, where God planted two trees in the Garden of Eden: the tree of
life and the tree of knowledge. He told Adam and Eve not to eat of the tree
of knowledge, lest they die. Tempted by a serpent, Eve ate the fruit (not
"apple," but "fruit") and persuaded Adam also to eat. God was angered and
expelled them from Eden, telling Eve that she must bear children in pain
and that her husband would rule over her. Adam was punished by being
forced to work hard for a living. Their "Fall" from paradise is an allegory for
the loss of childish innocence, the sanction for patriarchal domination of
women, and the source of human tendencies to evil, or sin. This supports a
pessimistic view of human nature, although not all Christians accept such
pessimism.

Paul said that by Adam's fall, sin entered the world. Paul also made a
clear distinction between spirit and flesh. The medieval theologian Augustine interpreted this to mean that Adam's "guilt" was transmitted to all
humans descended from Adam and Eve. This view is a rather pessimistic,
harsh belief in the inherently wicked tendencies of each human that may
require strict discipline to control but can be overcome in sincere believers by God's grace. Perhaps Augustine's stress on original sin came from
his early life, when he fathered a son out of marriage. This led him not into
marriage but into the priesthood. He saw pride and lust as major negative
forces in the human soul.

Those Christians who see sexuality as a major sinful tendency can trace
their belief back to Paul's distinction between spirit and flesh and Augustine's view of original sin with sexuality high on the list of sins. The celibacy later required of Roman Catholic priests is based on this belief that
one must suppress the flesh, including sexuality, to get close to God. God's
grace can overcome original sin, but Christians must still work to suppress
it. Another more optimistic Christian view is that no original sin is literally

inherited from Adam and Eve by subsequent humans. Rather, the tendency to evil is a potential in humans that can be encouraged or suppressed by one's environment and faith.

The early days of Christianity were filled with a variety of basic doctrinal disputes. From the first century a group called the Ebionites argued that Christians should follow the strict practices of the Jewish Law. At another extreme, the Antinomians taught that because Christians were saved by faith alone, they should not have to follow any behavioral rules.

Evil, God, and Church: Augustinian Theology

Augustine (354–430 CE) formulated several fundamental tenets of Christianity. As a young schoolteacher in the Roman city of Carthage, North Africa, he took a lover. They lived together for 14 years, and she bore a son, Adeodatus. But Augustine's devoutly Christian mother, Monica, demanded that he reject his lover and marry. Augustine sent his beloved back to "Afric," and as he said, "this was a blow which crushed my heart to bleeding."[9] But instead of marriage, he turned to the quest for spiritual wisdom, which he described in his *Confessions,* the first surviving autobiography to record such an intense self-awareness. He moved to Rome, then Milan, where he discovered the immaterial realm of God and the infinite realm of divinity, concluding that he had found the unchangeable and eternal Truth beyond his changeable mind. He embraced Christianity and eventually became Bishop of Hippo, North Africa.

Augustine became a most important early Christian theologian. He wrestled with the question of why there is evil in the world, which is called the problem of "theodicy." Initially he believed that there are two equally strong opposing cosmic forces of good and evil, which was taught by the Manichaeans. Instead, he concluded that, because God is the all-powerful ultimate reality, evil is due to a lack of good (Latin: *privatio boni*). Influenced by the Neo-Platonists, he came to believe in a cosmic hierarchy descending from an immaterial, eternal, unchangeable, intelligible God, down to earth. He experienced the intellect as illuminated by the divine that enriches both reason and meditative introspection.

Augustine saw the divine in a Platonic way, as the supreme being, "true being," unbound by space and time, present everywhere, rather than as a personal being, like a father. A group of Christians in North Africa taught that the church must be holy and pure, and that sacraments administered by imperfect bishops were ineffective. They won many converts, but Augustine argued against them that, due to God's grace, the sacraments are valid, even if administered by a priest of questionable morality, and this became church doctrine. He also promoted the idea of the church as universal and hierarchical. He wrote *The City of God* in 426 CE as a defense against those who blamed the fall of Rome on the Christians. In it he contrasted self-centered "pagans" following false gods and demons with devout, God-centered Christians seeking immortal grace.

Augustine stressed the need for God's grace given through Jesus to motivate moral behavior, for human nature is not free to be moral on its own, due to its flawed, sinful nature driven by desires. He emphasized the original sin of Adam and Eve as sexual and transmitted through the generations by sexual desire. He thus moved sexuality into a central place in Christian views of sin.

Augustine's view of original sin was opposed by the British monk Pelagius and others, who argued that there is no such thing as original sin, for all people have a tendency toward goodness. He argued that Adam may have set a bad example of disobedience, but no necessary, inherited moral weakness has been handed down to his descendants who need God's grace to save them. This more optimistic view stresses human freedom and basic goodness that, with a good environment and faith, can be cultivated by God's grace and good works. Some pessimistic, conservative Christians tend to stress original sin and the need for strict controls, such as firm child discipline (e.g., spanking), while liberals tend to be more hopeful and optimistic about basic human goodness and trust individual freedom and God's grace to guide toward the right moral choices.

The Role of Images

The second commandment against bowing down to images may have been a Jewish reaction to the elaborate paintings and sculptures of gods in Egypt, from where they escaped. But the imagination is hard to stifle, and although Jews honor few carved images, except the ark of the covenant, their literature is full of verbal imagery, from parting seas to family dramas, heroes, battles, and sacrifices. For centuries most Christians believed that images are important expressions of the faith, so they developed elaborate visual images in the Middle Ages—paintings and carvings of Jesus, Mary, and saints. Orthodox churches are still lavishly decorated with mosaic and paintings (icons) of Jesus, Mary, saints, and other scenes. Saints are vener-

Statue of Mary in a Roman Catholic church.
© Corbis.

ated, and Mary is especially honored as the "Theotokis" (God-bearer). Ancient Eastern Christians had continued pre-Christian practices of burning incense before sacred images, kneeling before them, kissing them, washing them, and clothing them, because they pictured the power of the holy persons in the icon to be present in the image. Many believed that icons had miraculous powers, such as healing, raising the dead, or intervening in war. Orthodox worshipers to this day kiss the icons. Roman Catholics use images widely in artistic expressions, from Michelangelo's Sistine Chapel ceiling pictures of God as an old bearded man in the clouds, to local church statues of Mary.

Protestants believe that visual art can distract from the verbal and intellectual expressions of the faith, and so they are generally much more restrained in their use of visual art. They objected to elaborate church art during the sixteenth-century Reformation and even tore down some stained-glass windows and other church art. Their churches today tend to be rather plain, expressing their belief in the impossibility of picturing God, the ultimate reality.

Theosis

A belief strong in the Orthodox Church is that the descent of God in Jesus has made possible the human ascent to the Father through the work of the Holy Spirit. Each Christian is involved in a movement toward God called *theosis,* or deification. It is seen as a movement of love toward God, a pilgrimage toward increasing holiness, coming to participate in the divine nature. This is not a union with the always hidden essence of God, but with the energies of God. The human and divine retain their unique characteristics, but *theosis* is the true fulfillment of human life within the Church.[10]

Arguments for the Existence of God

Medieval intellectual life in the new universities, as in Paris, re-shaped the Classical tradition, blending Christian theology with the ancient philosophers, such as Plato and Aristotle. This philosophical and theological development was called medieval "Scholasticism," and it explored both rational thought and revelation in its search for religious truth. One of its main efforts was to articulate rational arguments for the existence of God.

Anselm of Canterbury (1033–1109) developed one of the logical arguments that medieval scholastics explored. His "ontological argument" (ontology means the study of Being, or ultimate reality) is a typical rational argument for the existence of God. It has three steps: (1) The greatest and most perfect being that one can think of is God, (2) Perfection must include existence, therefore (3) God must exist.

Critics such as the German philosopher Immanuel Kant (1724–1804) responded that existence is no more proven by the concept of perfection than the existence of any money is proven by the concept of money in one's mind. This kind of argument depends solely on logic, not experience. Rational analysis of faith experiences and statements is an essential component of religion, helping clarify, purify, and prevent errors. But spiritual experience is obviously also an essential component of theology. Subsequent versions became not an argument but a question, the ontological question: "What makes existence itself possible?" which is meant for contemplative reflection on experience, rather than logical proof.

Reason and Faith: Thomas Aquinas's Theology

Thomas Aquinas (1224–1274) was an Italian theologian who taught mostly in Paris and blended Christian beliefs with the thought of the an-

cient Greek philosopher Aristotle, along with influences from Greek Neo-
platonism, Augustine, the Jewish Maimonides, and Arabic philosophers.
He was a creative thinker with a systematic theology and philosophy. He
argued in his *Summa Theologica* in 1274 that human reason is an independent ground for seeking truth. This was a new development in Christian thought, which opened the world to early scientific study. Through
Aquinas, Aristotle's focus on reason and the world's nature was absorbed
into Christian theology. This was partly so Christian thinkers could discuss
religion with non-Christians, especially the Jews and Muslims. Muslims
had been responsible for bringing Aristotle's texts back to Europe after the
collapse of Rome, through translators in Spain. Whereas Augustine had
proclaimed: "I believe in order to know," now Aquinas said, "I know in
order to believe." Faith and reason are ultimately in agreement, Aquinas argued, because God made them both. Some things can be known by reason
alone, such as the existence of God, the immortality of the soul, and some
moral principles. Other truths require revelation, because they transcend
human reason, such as the mysteries of the Trinity, the resurrection, or the
Incarnation of God in Jesus. This "two-levels of truth" philosophy became
the hallmark of scholasticism and was the culmination of medieval theology. Much medieval scholasticism became too speculative, but Aquinas
encouraged study of the natural world as well as the divine. Drawing from
earlier thinkers, Aquinas developed five classic arguments for the existence
of God:

1. Since things in the world are always changing or moving, there must be one
    first cause of motion, or "prime mover."
2. Since all the world's things are produced, there must be a "first cause."
3. Since all things in the world are contingent and do not have to exist there
    must be a different kind of being that has to be a "necessary being."
4. Things show gradations of goodness, truth, and nobility, so there must be a
    "highest Being" that is most good, most true, and most noble.
5. The orderly character of worldly events is all directed toward one final goal.
    This universal order points toward the existence of an intelligent source of
    universal order, called "teleology."

Aquinas concluded that each of these demonstrates the existence of
the ultimate reality called "God," not in time, not in place, not changing—
immaterial transcendent Being, yet knowable to some extent by humans in
time and space. Toward the end of his life, however, Aquinas had a mystical experience that led him to call his carefully constructed life's theology

nothing but "straw" compared with the direct experience of the divine that he was shown. His thought has continued to be an important part of the official doctrines of the Catholic Church.

Grace and Works

Christians believe grace to be God's gifts to humanity, such as love, justice, care, salvation from suffering, happiness, guidance, forgiveness, healing, law, inspiration, wonders, the incarnation of Christ, and the Eucharistic body and blood of the Savior. All Christians believe grace to be freely given, with varying amendments, and that good works are also necessary. Medieval doctrine came to emphasize the importance of believers regularly partaking in the Eucharist to receive God's grace and using their free will to perform good works. Partaking in the sacraments, such as Baptism and reconciliation, came to be seen as "works" or actions required for one to be allowed to take Communion, belong to the Church, and receive God's gift of eternity in Heaven. Traditional Orthodox and Roman Catholic churches emphasize this doctrine, having had for centuries to strengthen the faith in the context of competing religions. Current liberal Orthodox and Catholics may recommend rather than require such preconditions for Communion. Most Protestants take from Augustine a different view of grace as not earned, but freely given and (usually) unmerited, stimulating good works from right motivations. Therefore, Protestants are less restrictive about who takes Communion.

Faith

Faith is trust in God's reality and power, loyalty to God's guiding laws, hope, and confidence in God's power in daily life. New Testament faith means belief in Jesus's teachings, his power to save from suffering, and his assurance of eternal life. For some, faith stresses accepting the authority of Bible and tradition; for others it is more a matter of conviction based on experience, study, and self-awareness. It should not be "blind" faith, but it should be accompanied by study and understanding using reason, even skeptical questioning. The body of Christian beliefs is the collective faith. The basic meaning of faith is confidence that God is the strongest force in the cosmos, and its goodness will ultimately overcome evil. Personal faith ranges from an intellectual assent to doctrines such as God's grace to a more personal feeling, belief, and trust.

Sacraments

The sacramental principle is a very important theological focus of the church. It means that everything is capable of embodying and communicating the Divine, for God is everywhere and all-powerful. The mysterious dimension of life is openly affirmed, and the Divine can reach believers through the finite, just as believers can, in turn, reach the Divine through the finite world—cosmos, history, persons, nature, art, and ritual. The Orthodox do not limit the number of sacraments, because they see the church and all of Christian life as having a sacramental character, although the traditional seven are primary in practice. Thus there is no need to debate how bread and wine become the body and blood of Christ, for this is a mystery. A sacrament grants the believer a power to participate in and progress toward the Kingdom of God. The Eucharist is the most prominent Orthodox sacrament, the focus of the Divine Liturgy, the presence of the risen and glorified Lord in the midst of his faithful.[11]

For Catholics today, Christ is the central sacramental encounter with God, and the church is the "sacrament of universal salvation." For them sacraments are the means of God's freely given grace, present everywhere, to be channeled through the church insofar as they signify grace and the presence of Christ. The priest or Eucharistic minister need not be morally perfect in order for the sacraments to be effective. The sacrament has no impact if the recipient has no faith in it or the reality that it symbolizes, or is morally unprepared for it. The sacraments are empowerments for the faithful to carry out the mission of the church in the world. Since Vatican II the sacramental grace is conveyed through both the congregation and the priest simultaneously in Mass. There are seven sacraments in the Catholic Church. For Protestants, the sacraments are simply the two biblical sacraments: Baptism and Communion. They are "outward signs of an inward grace."

Eternity

Early Christians, like the Jewish Pharisees, emphasized belief in the theology of resurrection. Belief in resurrection stresses body-soul unity at the end of time and entry into paradise, thus promoting burial rather than cremation. Belief in immortality, which came into Christianity through the Platonic Greeks, is belief in the soul's endless existence, before birth and after death. The Greek version found in Plato, also known in many Asian cultures, was introduced later in the Middle Ages (when Jesus's expected second coming and believers' mass resurrection did not happen) and was blended with belief in later resurrection. It envisioned separation of the immortal soul from the body at death, like a butterfly rising heavenward.[12]

Judgment after Death

Christians believe that their faith and works in this mortal life will determine their judgment after death. Many world religions believe this. Reward for goodness is being sent to a metaphysical Heaven, a paradise of bliss in the presence of God. Punishment for evildoing is being sent to Hell, a fiery realm of miserable torture. One problem with this schema is the question whether anyone is purely good or purely evil. Thus Roman Catholics believe in Purgatory as an in-between process where one's sins are purged before going to Heaven. The medieval belief in indulgences developed as a way for people to cancel their sins by good works, including contributions to church finances and property.[13] Crusaders were offered "plenary" (full) indulgences. Reactions against abuses of this practice, such as selling indulgences, were a major cause of the German theologian Martin Luther's protest. Roman Catholic indulgences are still offered for piety and good works, for living people or souls in Purgatory. These beliefs are highly speculative but do help solve the problem of "theodicy," that is, when good people suffer unjustly on earth, they are still rewarded in the afterlife. Similarly criminals who remain unpunished on earth are believed to be punished, ultimately. Afterlife judgment was a strong theme in chaotic times such as the European Middle Ages, when law enforcement was weak, ignorance and misery were normal, and moral behavior was not taken for granted. Today few people believe in Hell, though many believe in Heaven.

Contemporary Tenets

Today in many ways Christian tenets have divided along a continuum of conservative to liberal beliefs that often cross other organizational lines. Some conservative beliefs can be found in all churches and some liberal beliefs in all churches.

Eastern Orthodox Conservatives

The Orthodox Church sees itself as the authentic Christian Church, having maintained closest identification with the earliest Church's apostolic witness of Jesus's times. Orthodoxy generally deemphasizes the individual and stresses a strong collective church tradition to which individuals are expected to conform. It emphasizes less a legal reading of the Bible and more the importance of the early church councils, such as Nicaea, and its continuity with those traditions. Orthodox believers emphasize liturgy and the pictorial tradition of the icons. The incarnated Christ is seen more immediately in Orthodox icons than in the Word of the Bible, especially in contrast with Protestants. For conservative Orthodox, the Old Testament is simply the ancient Septuagint, translated from Hebrew into Greek about 240 BCE. Orthodoxy is hierarchical, although no single member of the church hierarchy holds highest authority, because councils are regarded as most authoritative. No particular council may be doctrinally infallible, but the Orthodox Church overall is believed to be infallible in its doctrines. The Church's mission is not to adapt to contemporary society but to protect the Church's unity and continuity since apostolic church times.

Catholic Conservatives

Catholic conservatives emphasize belief in the Pope's authority to establish doctrines. They accept biblical literalism, as opposed to historical-critical scholarship. For example Jesus's words in the New Testament are interpreted as having been actually spoken by him. This view believes that Jesus left his apostles a blueprint—seven sacraments, the papacy with a supreme and universal jurisdiction, and the monarchical priestly organization with its doctrines, laws, and liturgies. Nineteenth-century popes usually condemned more scientific and socially democratic modernism. Some conservative Catholics today object to new Vatican II ideas and still believe that Latin is the only suitable language for the Mass. Similarly Catholic conservatives strongly endorse the celibate clergy and oppose abortion and birth control, based on belief in Jesus's celibacy and the need to strictly separate one's spirituality from the "flesh." They also firmly oppose the ordination of women as priests, because Jesus and his apostles were all male. Human sinfulness is also emphasized, and Jesus's death is seen as a necessary sacrifice to pay God for, or "atone" for, human sin.

Protestant Conservatives

As the influence of modern scientific thought spread, in Darwinism especially, conservative believers reacted against this by affirming their biblical doctrines more rigidly. Between 1900 and 1915, a group of Protestant fundamentalists published a list of beliefs, entitled *The Fundamentals,* that they believed were necessary to preserve amid modernism's growth. Distinctive beliefs of Protestant fundamentalism are:

- The omnipotence of God, the all-knowing, all-powerful, perfect deity who created the universe and maintains it today.
- The inerrancy of the Bible, as against historical-critical biblical scholarship. Human language is sufficient to express God's authority, and the Bible's revelation accurately records the events of world history and God's saving grace. Thus, events such as creation are accurately described in the Bible, and Darwinian evolutionary theory is wrong. The Bible provides believers with absolute truths to guide life.[14]
- The deity of Jesus. Jesus is the only Son of God, who must be accepted as one's personal savior to go to heaven. His is the only valid religion.
- Humans are radically sinful and need Jesus's redemption to save them.
- The physical resurrection and bodily return of Christ to earth. This proves eternal soul.
- Believers are part of a cosmic struggle between good and evil, and God's will conflicts with atheism and the materialistic, individualistic, rationalistic scientific worldview and its values.
- The Bible reveals God's will that males have "headship" over females, so men must respect their wives in love, and women are to serve their husbands and are not to be church ministers.
- The end of the world is coming anytime, so believers must behave morally to be admitted to heaven at Jesus's apocalyptic second coming.
- Obedience to authority is important, so children's misbehavior may be physically punished by some fundamentalists.

Protestant evangelicals are conservative, but not as strongly as fundamentalists. They stress above all a personal relationship to Jesus based on the Bible. Evangelicals are firmly opposed to secular industrial-commercial society's materialistic and consumerist worldview that dismisses God. They oppose communism, and they reject the utopian capitalist optimism of technological "progress." They also oppose what they see as moral decline in practices such as abortion and homosexuality.[15] They often promote the "Gospel of Prosperity," encouraging believers to seek wealth. They also see salvation coming only through Christ but try to be humble rather than intolerant about such exclusivism and strongly promote missionary activities worldwide. Distinctive beliefs of evangelicals are:

- Inerrancy of the Bible, or belief in the literal, factual accuracy of the Bible as a worldview and guide to ethical behavior, which is strong, but not complete in scientific matters.[16]

- Acceptance of Jesus as a personal savior is required for one to go to heaven; Jesus Christ lived a sinless life on earth and his death atoned for human sins.
- Jesus is the exclusive way to salvation from eternal damnation. Fundamentalist exclusivism resists accommodation to the larger culture. But evangelicals stress the humility needed with exclusivism. A few are carefully opening to more liberal ideas that other religions may have some valid beliefs.
- Creation science. God created the world literally in six solar days, as the book of Genesis states. "Creation science" is a conservative movement that attempts to prove that Darwinian evolutionary theory is wrong and that God created the world as described in the Bible. Creationists argued that the universe and life were recently, suddenly created—they did not slowly evolve from nothing. More left-wing evangelicals reject this theory and accept more scientific conclusions. God's creative sovereignty is the point to be preserved, the latter would say, not the literal details of the Bible.
- Humans are radically sinful. Humans are thoroughly, if not totally, sinful and need Jesus to be their savior from afterlife punishment. Christians need to be made anew and born again.
- Faith precedes works. Faith, not just moralistic behavior, is expected of evangelicals, as an inner orientation that guides behavior.
- Missions to other cultures are a strong commitment of evangelical churches, which seek to have each local church support a missionary program. The "G12" and "Great Commission" are evangelical missionary movements. Conservatives focus on personal conversion, rather than social service. More liberal evangelicals also take Jesus to the world in social action programs, such as disaster relief, self-reliance food programs, medicine, and education.
- End-of-world beliefs. Conservative evangelicals are drawn to apocalyptic beliefs about the impending end of the world, in which Jesus will come again in the "Rapture." God will save believers from the wicked Anti-Christ, they expect, and punish nonbelievers. No one knows the exact time that the world will end. But popularized fictional media portrayals of this belief are seen by left-wing evangelicals as an unnecessarily pessimistic fearfulness and a despairing escape from commitments to heal the world's sufferings.

If not perfectly inerrant, liberal evangelicals believe, the Bible is infallible, meaning true in matters of faith and practice but not true in matters of history and science. Theologian Carl F. H. Henry, the first editor of *Christianity Today,* wrote a six-volume evangelical theology *God, Revelation and Authority* (1982) that explores many important evangelical doctrines. He rejects the image of evangelicals as "wooden-headed" literalists and argues that the Bible's various literary genres include poetry. Biblical statements such as "the eyes of the Lord are in every place" are obviously metaphors for God's omniscience. For Henry, human language is capable of conveying infinite truths, and unless it is obviously metaphorical, we can assume that all biblical language, such as the words of Jesus, is literal, inerrant, and objective and not just additions by later editors,.[17]

Orthodox Liberals

Among the Orthodox, the modernists, or liberals, seek strengthened roles for women in the form of deaconesses, ranking just below a priest. They also welcome ecumenical relations with other Christian churches, as in the World Council of Churches. They share some beliefs with Protestant and Catholic Liberals, such as the importance of social justice.

Catholic Liberals

Catholic liberals also seek broader roles for women, such as the acceptance of previously married Catholic women whose marriages were annulled who become nuns and administrators of spiritual and social programs. The Catholic Worker movement has long nourished those who protest social injustices and war. Dorothy Day was a founding journalist of this movement (see Chapter 6, "Major Figures"). The priest brothers Dan and Phillip Berrigan, for example, were prominent leaders in the 1960s antiwar movement and openly protested war by pouring blood over war records and hammering warheads. They share some beliefs with Orthodox and Protestant Liberals, such as ecumenical outreach.

Protestant Liberals

Protestant liberals, or progressives, believe that God is the sovereign creator of the universe but share open-minded religious discussion and worship with nonbelievers who are seeking to understand religion. Key beliefs of liberals are:

Inclusiveness. They welcome people of all races, cultures, and sexual orientations. Women are believed to be equal to men and are welcomed as ministers and church leaders.

Tolerance. They reject the exclusivist notion that one religion or denomination has the absolute truth. They may see Jesus as providing a path to religious truth, but not the only one, so other faiths are respected. Liberals value the search for spiritual truth over creedal certainty. Their churches are more likely to have an "open table" communion, where any sincere person can partake, and cooperate with ecumenical and interfaith organizations.

Education. Liberals value wide-ranging, open-minded education, not limited by religious doctrines.

Science. Liberals welcome the contributions made by science to human welfare and, short of believing that science can answer all questions, are open to adjusting religious beliefs to new knowledge, such as biological evolution. New technologies, such as birth control, are more easily considered consistent with the faith.

Historical-critical biblical analysis. Liberals welcome the application of new linguistic, archaeological, historical, and literary knowledge to biblical interpretation. Thus ancient cosmologies, as in the creation account, or miracles are read as part of ancient cultures that need not be accepted literally in view of new knowledge about the world. Comparative studies of other religions and their similarities to Christianity are considered seriously.

Biblical symbolism. Liberals easily acknowledge the value of symbolic, poetic language in religion, such as "I am the resurrection" or "living bread" as serious, meaningful images of spiritual realities. Literalism is seen as a naïve way of reading religious texts, so efforts to read texts such as the Creation account literally are rejected. Ancient biblical texts about slavery and oppression of women have long been too misinterpreted, they say.

Social justice. Liberals tend to stress social justice and critiques of institutional injustices, such as racism, poverty, and patriarchy, rather than simply personal conversion and conformity. Thus they more easily criticize governmental flaws than promote simple patriotism. The struggle for human rights, as in racial and gender issues, is seen as an expression of God's call for justice. The Protestant support for the rise of the middle class should not be interpreted as a self-indulgent "Prosperity Gospel," they say.

Optimism. Liberals are optimistic about human nature and progressively improving the world, believing not in a Calvinist "depravity" doctrine, but a hopeful stress on God's compassion and mercy. Children are to be treated patiently and compassionately and not authoritatively disciplined or spanked. Thus they also reject pessimistic withdrawals from the world, angry end-of-the-world apocalypticism, and harsh, self-righteously judgmental views that others are going to Hell for disagreeing.

Creativity. Liberals are more open to creative, new explorations in culture, theology, and worship, and look to the future, not just the past, for guidance.

Democracy. Strongly liberal Christians tend to shy away from church hierarchy and authoritarianism in favor of individual and congregational freedom. But liberal-thinking believers can be found in all branches of the church, Orthodox, Catholic, and Protestant. And conservatives can be found in nonhierarchical, independent churches. Mainstream churches blend various conservative and liberal ideas.

NOTES

1. Alex Heidel, Chapter IV, "The Story of the Flood" in *The Gilgamesh Epic and Old Testament Parallels* (1949; reprint, Chicago: University of Chicago Press, 1971), pp. 224–69.

2. The Jewish Publication Society in Philadelphia published a new authoritative English version of the *Tanakh* in 1985.

3. Paul Achtheimer, ed., *The HarperCollins Bible Dictionary* (San Francisco: HarperSanFrancisco, 1996).

4. Burton Throckmorton, ed., *Gospel Parallels*, 4th ed. (Nashville: Thomas Nelson, 1979).

5. James M. Robinson, ed., *The Nag Hammadi Library* (San Francisco: Harper and Row, 1977).

6. Geza Vermes, ed., *The Complete Dead Sea Scrolls in English* (New York: Allen Lane/Penguin, 1997), p. 115.

7. For the Jesus Seminar, see Weststar Institute http://www.westarinstitute. org.

8. *The Catechism of the Catholic Church* (New York: Doubleday, 1995), Sections 243–48.

9. Saint Augustine, *Confessions*, Trans. R. S. Pine-Coffin. (New York: Penguin, 1979) Ch. VI, Part 15, p. 131.

10. Rev. Thomas Fitzgerald, "Spirituality," http://www.forministry.comUSNY GOARCSCGOC/vsItemDisplay.

11. Fairbairn, Donald. *Eastern Orthodoxy Through Western Eyes* (Louisville, KY: Westminster/John Knox Press, 2002), sections 25–27.

12. Plato, "Phaedrus," in *The Collected Dialogues of Plato*, ed. Edith Hamilton and Huntington Cairns (Princeton: Princeton University Press, 1978), pp. 250–51.

13. Dante Alighieri, *The Divine Comedy*, 3 vols. Trans. John D. Sinclair (New York: Oxford University Press, 1961).

14. The Chicago Statement on Biblical Inerrancy, http://www.iclnet.org.

15. Defining Evangelicism, http://www.wheaton.edu/isae/defining evangelicalism.html.

16. The Barna Group, http://www.barna.org.

17. Carl F. H. Henry, *God, Revelation and Authority*, 6 vols. (Waco, TX: Word Books, 1982), vol. 4, ch. 5.

3

BRANCHES

Three major branches of the church have emerged in the history of Christianity. For its first thousand years, the original church was simply the "Christian" Church. When the city of Rome decayed in the Middle Ages, Byzantine Constantinople became the center of Christendom. Medieval Rome increasingly gained a stronger leadership role as missionaries spread across Western Europe, and the Pope gained authority. The Western Roman church developed a rather legalistic, Latin, and practical style, while the Eastern Byzantine church moved in a more philosophical, Greek, and mystical direction, stressing the immediate experience of the divine. The Roman Catholic and the Byzantine Churches separated in 1054 CE.

The Roman Catholic Church expanded north from Italy into Europe through missionaries such as Ireland's St. Patrick. It slowly gained strength and authority through the Middle Ages. In 1517 in Germany, Martin Luther began the tumultuous Protestant Reformation that expanded across northern Europe in Lutheran, Anglican, Calvinist, and Free Church branches that split into numerous denominations. After Christopher Columbus came to the Americas in 1492, all branches spread across the world. The differences between branches have to do with factors such as the historical context of their origins, their relationships to governments, their preferences for hierarchical church structure or more democratic congregational independence, their views on gender and sexuality, their inclinations toward formal liturgy or informal spontaneity and simplicity, their ways of interpreting the Bible, and their views on issues such as whether God's revelations continue after biblical times.

THE EASTERN ORTHODOX CHURCH

History

As Rome slowly collapsed, Byzantium became the major early medieval Christian Empire. Its capital city was Constantinople, which became the largest and wealthiest city in the European Middle Ages. It began when the Roman General Constantine (c. 274–337 CE) had a vision of a cross that inspired him to win a battle. He admired Christianity's promise of immortality, so he announced his conversion to Christianity and called himself a bishop. When he became Roman Emperor, Constantine ordered the freedom of religion in the Edict of Milan (313 CE), thus stopping the persecution of Christianity. He made Sunday a public holiday in 321. Constantine moved the Empire's and the church's capital from crumbling Rome to Byzantium in 330 CE, which was renamed "Constantinople" after him.

Byzantium (324–1453 CE) expanded its territory and collected fabulous wealth, developed powerful royalty, and cultivated elaborate art. Much of the wealth was gold sent as required tribute by defeated tribes and cities. Byzantine armies fought "barbarian" tribes invading Europe as the Roman Empire collapsed, such as the Vandals, Germans, Arabs, Slavs, and Turks. Constantine ended much of the earlier anarchy in the East and established a huge elaborate bureaucracy, so the word "byzantine" has since implied a recalcitrant maze of rules-bound officials.

Church and State

The Orthodox Church has always seen the Emperor as the ruler anointed by God, a semi-divine protector of the church, like the biblical King David was for Israel. So Byzantine Emperors followed in the Roman tradition of serving as church leaders. Thus Christianity became the official religion of Byzantium, a theocracy. In 380 CE Emperor Theodosius proclaimed Christianity to be the official religion of the Roman Empire. Emperor Justinian I (427–565) forbade all "pagans" from holding state office, teaching, or from offering sacrifice to their gods, on pain of death. He closed the philosophical school in Athens and forced baptism on non-Christians in Constantinople. This theocratic practice was not unusual at the time but later became a point of dispute among Christians. Justinian ordered the codification of Roman law, soon called "Justinian's Code." He also built the monumental church of Saint Sophia in Constantinople in 532–537.

Orthodox-Catholic Schism

Long-standing cultural and political differences between Rome and Constantinople finally led to a schism. In 1053 CE, invading Normans captured the Roman Catholic Pope Leo IX. Leo sent a delegation to Constantinople in 1054, requesting support. The Roman leader Hubert was rude, and when ignored by the Orthodox Patriarch Cerularius, Hubert excommunicated him. Then the Orthodox Church rejected Rome. Both sides finally lifted their mutual condemnations (*anathemas*) in 1965.

Western Crusaders, intent on capturing Jerusalem from the Muslims, attacked Constantinople in 1204 for not supporting them with money and soldiers. Joined by Venice and the Normans, they devastated and looted the city for its famed treasures. St. Mark's Church in Venice is now decorated with marble pillars, bronze horses, and gold treasures from that raid on Byzantium. The Byzantine government was exiled south to Nicaea (now *Isnik* in Turkey) until 1261. This further deepened the chasm between the Western and Eastern churches. The weakened Empire lost much territory, but survived. The Byzantine Empire was finally defeated by the Muslim Ottoman Turks in 1453. The city then became Muslim and was renamed Istanbul, St. Sophia was converted to a mosque, and four tall minaret towers were added at each corner. But the Byzantine missionaries had established the Eastern Orthodox faith with its cupola-domed churches and passed its law and religion to the Russian, Greek, and Balkan states. Orthodox Church leadership shifted to the Russian Czar, Russia's Ivan "the Great" (1440–1505).

The Russian Orthodox Church

Christianity in Russia is rooted in a long tradition going back to the Rus Prince Vladimir of Kiev, who in the tenth century sent emissaries to study various religions to find the one to adopt for his country. They visited synagogues, mosques, and churches in nearby countries. When they attended the Holy Liturgy in Saint Sophia Cathedral in Constantinople, they wrote back to Vladimir that God must dwell with these people, for they felt like they were in Heaven. So in 988 CE, Vladimir adopted Orthodoxy for his nation. Before this, Vladimir was insatiable in his vices. But after his conversion to Christianity, he showed new compassion for the ill, orphans, and the poor. Palace gates were opened to the hungry, and he prohibited the torture and execution of criminals.

Orthodox monks in monasteries have played an important part in Russia's history, providing education, recording Russian history, painting icons, and translating foreign literature. During the violent Mongol Tartar invasion in the thirteenth century, the church was a stabilizing, comforting force that helped keep Russia together. Sometimes the Church aided the Russian state. St. Sergius of Radonezh (1314–1392), the first noted Russian Orthodox mystic, inspired and blessed the national opposition that began the liberation from the Mongol Tatar invasion. At St. Sergius's Holy Trinity Monastery, begun about 1334, the artist Andrei Rublev developed his outstanding talent for icon painting. In the seventeenth century, the Poles and Swedes invaded Russia from the west, and the Orthodox Church again served as a patriotic unifier and support for the war against the invaders. But the Patriarchs of Moscow were subordinated to the Czars for centuries. The church's goal was at times overrun by the despotic rule of Russian Emperors such as Ivan "the Terrible" (1530–1584), crowned the first Czar in 1547. He was a good ruler at first, helping the common people and the merchants, but in 1560 he went insane and killed many people, including his son. In remorse, he entered a monastery.

Czar Peter "the Great" (1672–1725) expanded and modernized Russia and made St. Petersburg the new capital. He cut off the symbolic beards of stubborn aristocrats and forbade them to wear their old-fashioned costumes. He forced the Orthodox Church to reorganize under a government department that made him head of the Church and executed rebels. The modernizing Czarina Catherine "the Great" (1762–1796) confiscated monastic properties, reducing the number of monasteries in Russia from 881 to 385 (318 men's and 67 women's). Despite this, new religious communities were formed that ran schools, orphanages, and hospitals, with inspiring leaders such as the war-widowed Margarita Tuchkova (see profile in Ch. 6).[1] Orthodox missionaries from Russia in the 1700s converted some Alaskan natives. In the late 1800s and 1900s immigrants from Eastern Europe took the Orthodox Church to the United States.

Europe's nineteenth-century liberal democratic revolutions, then Marxism, led to the violent overthrow of the Czar and Russia's aristocratic social structure in 1917. This was followed by the fiercely atheistic Communist Soviet Union. Thus began a violent repression of the Orthodox Church, which was seen as part of aristocratic Czarist society. The Church was almost completely destroyed by the Communists, who saw it as an ideological enemy. Thousands of believers and priests were killed, exiled to Siberian prison camps, or forced to change occupation. The Communists confiscated

Russian Orthodox Cathedral of the Mother of
God "Joy of All Who Sorrow," San Francisco.
Courtesy of the author.

Church buildings, made them into warehouses, or destroyed them. They
dynamited Moscow's prominent Church of the Savior in 1931. Museums
and University Professorships of Atheism promoted harshly critical and
one-sided attacks on religion based on Marxist materialism. During World
War II the Church supported the war effort against the Nazis, patriotically
helping fund many war needs, even army uniforms. Some Church leaders,
their thought immersed in centuries of totalitarianism, even praised Stalin.
From 1917 until their fall in 1989, the Communists killed more than 50,000
priests and more than 50 million believers and closed 1,000 monasteries
and about 85 percent of Russian Orthodox churches, reducing them from
about 50,000 to about 7,000.

A New Era

In 1988 Soviet President Mikhael Gorbachev spoke to Orthodox leaders, saying that religious believers have the right to express their convic-
tions without restrictions, which he saw as helpful in strengthening morals.

In 1989 Gorbachev's *perestroika* (restructuring) and *glasnost* (openness) began a new era of religious freedom. The 1997 "Law on Freedom of Conscience and Religious Organizations" in theory opened Russia to religious freedom, although many local governments passed laws restricting non-Orthodox church growth.

Though some old-fashioned communist-leaning functionaries resist the changes, new churches are being built and old churches reopened. Seminaries are opening to train priests, and radio, television, and newspapers can now have religious content. Churches are sending volunteers to understaffed hospitals and orphanages, where they are allowed to read the Bible to patients and are often welcomed gladly by patients and staff. People are lining up to buy Bibles and standing up when a choir sings the "Lord's Prayer." Although the Orthodox Church remains the largest church in Russia, other churches are sending missionaries and emigrating from abroad (notably the Catholic, Baptist, Adventist, and Armenian churches), although their numbers remain around 1 percent of Russia's population. Immigrant groups are strong abroad and sending help to rebuild Russia.[2]

The Orthodox Church of Greece

In Greece, famous Orthodox monasteries have long been perched on high cliffs, notably on Mount Athos, where icons are painted and no females are allowed. Theological schools have produced leading scholars. The Greek Church suffered when the Muslim Ottoman Turks conquered Byzantium in 1453. Many Orthodox priests and believers were killed and the Church was suppressed until the war of Greek independence, ending in 1832. Early in the twentieth century, Greece passed laws making illegal any attempts by Protestant missionaries to convert any Orthodox.

The largest division of the Orthodox Church is the Greater Eastern Orthodox Communion, which includes Constantinople, Jerusalem, Russia, Greece, Serbia, the Czech Republic, and American churches. A smaller group includes the Russian Old Believers, and a third group includes the Armenian and Coptic Orthodox churches. Today the fairly independent churches elect their bishops and district leaders called "Patriarchs," centered in Egypt, Syria, Jerusalem, Moscow, Georgia, Serbia, Romania, Bulgaria, Cyprus, Athens, Poland, Prague, Spain/Portugal, and North America. Orthodox churches in Israel and Palestine are important Christian shrines, as in Bethlehem. The liturgical language, originally Greek, now includes Slavonic, Arabic, Romanian, and Georgian. The Orthodox belong to ecumenical groups such as the modern World Council of Churches, since 1948, and were observers at the Second Vatican Council.[3]

Beliefs

The Eastern Orthodox Church stands in direct historical continuity with the communities created by the apostles of Jesus. Today Orthodox Churches are independent; they elect a regional bishop, archbishop, metropolitan, or patriarch, and are governed by councils, or synods of bishops. Informal leadership belongs to the Patriarch of Constantinople. They do not accept the authority of Rome's Pope, but today there are cordial relations between the Catholics and Orthodox. Priests must be male, and they may marry before ordination, although bishops come from the ranks of celibate monks or widowed priests. The Christian Church developed many of its central doctrines during the period of the early Byzantine councils. For example, Athanasius (296–373 CE), Bishop of Alexandria, insisted on the full humanity and divinity of Jesus. Orthodox Churches are guided by the first seven councils, up to the one in Nicaea in 787 CE.

The Orthodox Church absorbed much Greek theology, such as the Platonic principle of participation of a pictorial image (such as Jesus) in its heavenly archetypal energy. Orthodox theology stresses the mystical experience of the divine rather than intellectual assent to a dogma. A God rationally comprehensible and exhaustively understood by the reasoning brain is not God but is an idol, the Orthodox believe, fashioned in a human likeness. The divine is simultaneously "wholly other" (transcendent "essence"), immediately present (immanent "energy") in a personal way and in love, and evident from the wondrous beauty in the world and cosmos. Faith involves a personality transformation and repentance.

For the Orthodox, God is the Trinity: one "essence" in three "persons," Father, Son (Jesus Christ), and Holy Spirit. God creates the world continually, and God is present in all creation, not just a heavenly entity. The capital sins are pride, covetousness, lust, anger, gluttony, envy, and sloth. The fruits of the Holy Spirit are charity, joy, peace, patience, kindness, goodness, forbearance, mildness, faith, modesty, self-restraint, and chastity.

The Orthodox believe that each believer has existed from eternity in God's love and plan. Humanity is not depraved, for the divine image in humans is obscured but not lost, so Orthodox are optimistic about human nature. Free will has been restricted but not destroyed. Humans were created when God planted the seed of life in the world and then guided its development, which is somewhat consistent with evolutionary theory. Jesus's incarnation in the virgin birth shows that his birth is due to a unique divine initiative, not a human act. Jesus's suffering and resurrection are a victory over earthly sinfulness, and his loving sacrifice brought human salvation from sin and suffering. The resurrection shows the reality of immortal life through Jesus's conquest over death.

For the Orthodox, the Holy Spirit is present in and among believers as a conscious awareness of the divine love, joy, and peace. Prayer and silent contemplation can carry the soul from darkness into the divine light. Orthodox reject the Catholic theology of Purgatory and the Immaculate Conception. Decisions of Orthodox synod councils, not the Roman Pope, are considered infallible.

The Orthodox celebrate the biblical Wisdom of God (Sophia), as found in the book of Proverbs. Popular devotion to Mary as the pure mother of Jesus was widespread from the early days of the church. She is called "Theotokos" (God-bearer), "Ever-virgin," and "Mother of God," who grieved for him at the cross.

Orthodoxy is moderately hierarchical, blending a system of bishops and higher officials with the autonomy of various regional churches. They prefer a highly structured, traditional liturgy, with icons, chanting, elaborate priestly robes, and richly decorated buildings. They believe in the Platonic principle that beauty leads one to God. The Orthodox view of gender is traditional in requiring priests to be men, but liberal in encouraging priests to marry.

THE ROMAN CATHOLIC CHURCH

History

In the early church, Constantinople was the informal central city of the faith, and then the Bishop of Rome claimed priority above other bishops, because the tombs of Peter and Paul were in Rome. Bishop Damasus (366–384 CE) began to claim Rome as the successor to St. Peter and to call the Roman church the "apostolic see" (seat or throne). By 400 CE, when the Roman Empire faded away, the Roman Church claimed the right to central church authority in the West and began to enforce liturgical uniformity in Latin in all local churches. The Papacy acquired vast tracts of farmland and helped alleviate hunger. Whereas the Eastern Orthodox Church in Constantinople was protected by the Emperor and often had to submit to political control, the Roman Church saw itself as separate from imperial rule and attempted to provide moral guidance for rulers from outside the government.

The many medieval tribal invasions destroyed much of Roman culture. Tribes such as the Huns repeatedly crossed the Danube River, and sailors such as the Vikings attacked shorelines. The Persians attacked from the east. At first the Roman military had to expand, weakening the economy by increased taxation. Inflation then weakened the value of money, overtaxed peasants fled their land, and then the Vandals sacked Rome in 455. Living conditions and hygiene sank to a miserable level. Literacy disappeared with schools, so that the clergy were typically the only educated ones. Society remained a strict division between the feudal land-owning aristocracy and serfs or slaves who worked the land. National languages developed—Spanish, French, Italian—blending Latin with tribal languages. Latin, which helped unify Europe, was preserved only in church documents and in the Mass. Personal blood vengeance and clan feuds continued. Often the medieval believers could only retreat from this violent chaos, so hundreds of new monasteries became centers of refuge and church activity, slowly expanding to rebuild society with schools, hospitals, orphanages, then cathedrals.

Missionaries such as St. Boniface in Germany traveled to spread the Gospel. The Visigoths in Spain were slowly Christianized, as were the Celts of Gaul and Ireland, and the Angles and Saxons in Britain. The king of the Franks, Clovis, converted to Christianity in 496 and led his people to conquer most of Germany and parts of Gaul, including Paris. He also fought the Visigoths and kept them south of the Pyrenees mountain range. The Roman Pope from 590 to 604, Gregory "The Great," founded more monasteries and strengthened the papacy. When Rome was in chaos, he took responsibility for the city's administration, finance, and welfare.

Appointing Priests

A major problem for the integrity of the growing church was the question of who had the authority to officially appoint (ordain) a priest. Too common were the ancient worldwide problems of "simony," the practice of buying and selling religious offices or pardons; "nepotism" or appointing family members to official positions; and "lay investiture," the ordination of priests and bishops by rulers rather than by church authority. These practices easily led to corruption, because a local tribal chieftain, such as a Visigoth king, would traditionally appoint family or sell offices to sympathetic political allies who would of course bless the king's every action, no matter how corrupt. As the church Christianized these violent invading tribes that were often contemptuous of the meek, the high spiritual tone of the church was sometimes dragged downward. Bishops were frequently also barons who were married with family and had large land holdings that conflicted with a genuine religious vocation. This became a scandal, and the Popes struggled to resist corrosive secular control of the church.

Pope Nicholas II led a Roman synod (a regional council of clergy and laity for policy making) meeting in 1059 that put the election of the Pope in the hands of clergy, rather than kings. This reform sparked a struggle and came to a head when Emperor Henry IV of Germany (1050–1106) defied the Pope and called a council 1076 in Worms, where the Pope was denounced. The new reform-minded Pope Gregory VII (c. 1020–1085) struck back by excommunicating Henry and releasing his subjects from allegiance to him. This gave his subjects license to rebel, endangering his rule. So Henry repented in 1077 CE, standing barefoot in the snow for three days in Italy before the castle gates until the Pope inside forgave him. After some struggles, this bold move distinguished the authority of the Pope from kings and separated the church from the dangers of excessive political control. This was called the Lay Investiture Struggle, and it gave the Pope increased authority.

Crusades

The Crusades began in the 1000s as a Christian movement to regain Jerusalem from Muslim conquerors. Emperor Alexis of Byzantium in Constantinople sent a letter to the Pope in Rome asking for aid in fighting invading Turks. In southern France in 1095, Pope Urban II spoke to a large crowd, urging them to aid Eastern Christians attacked by Turks and Arabs now advancing north. He promised forgiveness of sins to any crusaders who lost their lives. Amidst crop failures, wood fuel shortages, and population growth, many took the vow to fight, put on red crosses, and prepared for the long journey east. This fever to fight to reclaim Jerusalem, long a well-known pilgrimage journey, was encouraged by popes for 200 years (1096–1291).

Several waves of crusaders took their religious and military fervor east, beginning in 1096. Even before the first official Crusade, a "People's Crusade," numbering tens of thousands, left Europe for Jerusalem without de-cent military planning. Crying out *"Deus vult"* (God wills it), thousands of poorly armed pilgrims, a barely Christianized rabble, mostly poor and inexperienced, set out in advance of the knights and army. Some began massacring Jews along the Rhine River. Poorly prepared and ignorant of the land, weather, and food and water needs, many died along the way, and Muslim warriors slaughtered the rest in Asia Minor.

Then a serious army of about 30,000 mostly French and Norman knights captured Jerusalem in the First Crusade, after a bloody battle in 1099, leaving mounds of corpses and rivers of blood. But they squabbled among themselves, rejected Byzantine authority, and scrambled for booty, thus weakening their position.

In the Second Crusade, the Muslim hero Saladin reconquered most of Palestine, including Jerusalem, in 1187. In the Third Crusade, Richard the Lionhearted, King of England, and others managed to capture a few fringe territories such as the coastal city of Acre and the island of Cyprus. The Fourth Crusade began with a crude attack on Constantinople in 1204 by the Crusaders, because the weary city refused them financing and reinforcements. Another tragic crusade was the Children's Crusade in 1212, led by foolish, unprepared youths into disease, slavery, and death before they even reached the Holy Land. Finally, a fierce Muslim army from Egypt put an end to Crusader remnants in the Holy Land. The Crusades ended in disaster for Christians.[4]

The Council of Trent

Some councils have marked major turns in church history. One was the Council of Trent (1545–1563) called the Catholic Reformation, or Counter-Reformation, summoned by Pope Paul III to Trento, Italy, to respond to the Protestant Reformation. The hierarchy gathered, and the worst church abuses were condemned, but no concessions were made to new Protestant theology.

The Pope maintained control of the council. Contrary to the emerging Protestant belief in justification (or salvation) by faith alone, the Catholic statement of justification by faith was stated so that a Catholic could still aid in his salvation by accumulating works, or merits. Belief in Purgatory was maintained, and tradition was placed on a par with the authority of scripture. The Vulgate Latin Bible was declared the only valid Bible, not to be questioned. Translated by Jerome in 404 CE, the Vulgate remained the Catholic Bible until 1943.

Rules on celibacy were to be enforced, bishops were given greater control, and clergy were to be better educated. The doctrine of indulgences, by means of which one could earn salvation by service to the church, was upheld, but its worst abuses were abolished, such as the sale of indulgences. Humanist critical scholarship was not to be applied to the Bible. The seven sacraments (Baptism, Confirmation, Communion, Penance, Anointing the Sick, Holy Orders, and Matrimony) were retained, against the new Protestant two (Baptism and Communion). Saints could still be invoked, and the censorship of books was instituted. These positions hardened the conservative stance of the Catholic Church, which continued its monarchical organization and later opposed developments in science and democracy until the nineteenth century. The medieval character of the Catholic Church was affirmed, emphasizing the divine authority of the Church and its priests who convey the necessary grace from God through the sacraments. Trent sharpened the impossibility of reconciliation with the Protestants.

The New World

By 638 CE, Muslims had conquered Jerusalem, Egypt, and many formerly Christian lands. They conquered most of Spain beginning in 711 and left a strong influence. The Christian "reconquest" of Spain took centuries. Fighting from north to south, the battle against the "Moors" (Muslims from North Africa) slowly reconquered the regions and cities of Spain until 1492, when Muslims were finally expelled from Spain. The war fever was so great that Jews were also expelled the same year. Once attention to the war was relaxed, King Ferdinand and Queen Isabella of Spain could afford to invest some money in the proposal of a persistent sailor, Christopher Columbus, who had been proposing the wild project of sailing west to China and India, to gain the wealth of the East that the Arab traders had long controlled.

After Columbus began the spread of European society into the Americas in 1492, Pope Alexander VI assigned Spain most of the new lands, and Portugal gained Brazil in 1494. Catholic missionaries accompanied the conquistadors. Greedy for gold, silver, land, and exportable wealth, the conquistadors spread out across Latin America with their powerful horses and guns and conquered the Mayans, Aztecs, Incas, and other tribes. Some missionaries struggled to tame the violent excesses of the conquistadors.

Northward, French Catholics controlled Quebec, often trading for beaver skins to be made into European men's top hats. Moving up from Mexico and along the west coast, Spanish Catholics built many missions in the western regions. After the 1776 Revolutionary War, Catholics occupied much of Maryland and New Orleans.

Heretics: Cathars/Albigensians and Waldensians

Church history is filled with accounts of groups who developed beliefs and practices that challenged the essence of Christian faith. They were called "heretics," and the church's response clarified and defended Christian faith. For example, late medieval believers disagreed over the question of whether God was equal to a cosmic power of evil, or was more powerful than evil. One such group, the Cathars, aroused opposition from the Church. The Cathars in the Languedoc region of southern France were also known as the Albigensians, because Albi was a major center.

Basic to Orthodox Christian faith is the belief that ultimately, no matter how bad the world may seem at times, goodness will triumph, because the ultimate power of the universe, God, is good. The Cathars disagreed and believed, like some ancient faiths such as Manichaeism, that goodness is not guaranteed to overwhelm evil in the cosmos, and evil is a strong power that threatens God's benevolence. This theology is called dualism, where two opposing divine principles or gods fight in open warfare forever. By 1200, the Cathars had gained the allegiance of much of southern France.

The leading Cathars were known as the "Perfect," because they practiced a severe asceticism, rejecting marriage and avoiding oaths, war, property, meat, milk, cheese, and eggs. To them the greatest of sins was sexuality, and the purest Cathars would oppose the evil god by abstaining from its worldly influence in reproduction. These "Perfect" were known for their black robes, their gaunt bodies, thin from constant fasting, and incessant repetition of the "Lord's Prayer." They preached, consoled the dying, and were entitled to a special greeting from others of three deep bows. Women were among the Perfect, although they were not admitted to the circles of bishop or deacon. These high moral standards impressed many French.

Ordinary Cathars were permitted to marry, own property, eat meat, and even outwardly conform to the Christian church. They believed in reincarnation, rather than Heaven and Hell, so this world was seen as a vast Purgatory. Some Cathars rejected the Old Testament as the work of Satan. And since they regarded the body as evil, they believed that Jesus did not have a real human body, die a real death, or experience resurrection. The sacraments, too, as material elements, were seen as the creation of the evil power.

Another major heresy was the Waldensians, founded by Valdès (died 1217), in Lyons, France, who rejected the authority of the Pope and church, claiming that only the Bible is the valid religious authority for Christians. They also granted women the right to preach. In 1184 Pope Lucius III condemned all such "heresies" and excommunicated the Cathars and Waldensians. Perhaps the violence of the Middle Ages had convinced them that the world was full of a strong evil force not overcome, as the church taught, by God's cosmic goodness. The Church saw this theology as a serious threat to the basic Christian faith in life's goodness. In 1209 a 20-year war in southern France shattered the Cathars and sent Waldensians into hiding.[5]

The Inquisition

The Inquisition was instituted by Rome to combat conflicting beliefs of earlier tribal invaders, then Cathars and Waldensians, and it spread to other areas of religious war, such as Spain, where Christians fought with Muslims. In 1233 Pope Gregory IX appointed special inquisitors to combat opposing faiths. The crude legal methods of the medieval era were rooted in Roman law, which had little concept of human rights and did little to protect the accused. But the Inquisition went even further in denying judicial fairness. Informers were planted in jail cells to spy on prisoners. Convicted heretics were forced to wear identifying clothing, imprisoned, sent on pilgrimages, or burned at the stake.

The Inquisition spread across Europe, and its purpose broadened. Joan of Arc (1412–1431), a visionary young woman who dared to dress as a man and take up war, was burned at the stake (see profile in Ch. 6). In Spain, trials persecuted Jews, Muslims, and mystics. The Inquisition then spread to the Americas, where many were burned in Mexico for sorcery or hanged for witchcraft in Protestant New England. The Inquisition quickly degenerated, and its cruelty was clearly one of the darkest stains in Christian history. Catholics now think that the disregard for human rights and intolerant, distorted judicial tactics of the Inquisition were an un-Christian horror.

Beliefs

The Roman Catholic Church is centered in Rome because that is where the apostles St. Peter and St. Paul preached and, Catholics believe, were buried beneath what is now St. Peter's Basilica in Vatican City. The Church regards itself as the only valid inheritor of an unbroken succession of apostolic church leaders, beginning with St. Peter. This is symbolized by the image of the key to heaven, in tradition given to Peter by Jesus (Matthew 16:18).

Basic Catholic beliefs include: God is the Supreme Being, self-existing, benevolent, omniscient, omnipresent, and almighty Spirit, above all creatures; God can be known through natural reason (inferring the world's creator), the Bible (inspired by God), and divine traditions. Theologians such as St. Thomas Aquinas (1225–1274) clarified the role of reason, such as arguments for the existence of God. The Bible contains both history and symbolic expressions, such as the parables. The Bible's authority is great, but church traditions are also important, such as writings of the Church Fathers and the Pope's official proclamations. Only twice has the Church called the Pope's decisions infallible, in the cases of the doctrines of Mary's Immaculate Conception (1870) and her Assumption into heaven (1950).

The Trinity of God the Father, Jesus the Son, and the Holy Spirit, is one Divine nature in three persons. The gifts of the Holy Spirit are wisdom, understanding, counsel, fortitude, knowledge, piety, and fear of the Lord. Sins are of two kinds, mortal (serious, depriving the sinner of God's grace and eternal life in Heaven) and venial (less serious sins).

St. Peter's Basilica, the Vatican, Rome. Courtesy of the author.

Catholics believe that God redeems, or saves, believers from sin through his son, Jesus, fully God and fully man, sent into the world. Jesus, born of the Virgin Mary, taught God's loving grace and prophetic call for justice. He died as the last sacrifice to God for the sins of humans (atonement) and regained for them the right to be children of God and heirs of heaven. Thus, Catholics usually portray Jesus on the cross to remind them of his suffering for them but may also display an empty cross, emphasizing his resurrection. According to the New Testament, Jesus was resurrected from the dead after three days to show his divinity and that all people will also rise from death at the end of time. Jesus will judge and grant eternal reward or punishment to all. Faithful believers will join Christ in heavenly glory. God's grace is bestowed on humanity through Christ, and can be resisted by free will, but its channel from God to humanity is through the church, via prayer and the sacraments, especially the Eucharist bread and wine.

The sacrament of matrimony is seen as a divine, not human institution, so humans are called to love each other, since God is love itself to Christians. Marriage is the sacred bond supporting the well-being of individuals and society. God encourages humans to be fruitful and multiply, and this is the goal of marriage. It is meant for men and women to leave the parents and unite in an unbreakable union. The couple should seek to help each other to attain happiness and holiness, and welcome and educate their children into the world. Natural conjugal love is a deeply personal unity that demands faithfulness and is open to fertility. Children are the supreme gift of marriage, but couples without children can, of course, have a conjugal life full of charitable meaning. And, of course, single people are also close to Jesus's heart.

In response to modernism, nineteenth-century Catholic leadership generally reacted negatively, taking a traditional, literalist view of the Bible and opposing scholarly historical-critical biblical interpretation. Later, Vatican II (1962–1965)[6] opened many doors, even consideration of the potential for religious truth in other religions. Conservative Catholics in groups such as *Opus Dei* stress traditional allegiance to the Pope and strictness on issues such as the virgin birth, celibacy, abortion, and the exclusive validity of the Catholic Church over others. Liberals are more open to the new scholarly approach that seeks to distinguish historical from mythic, instructive elements, since Pope Pius XII in 1943. Openness to dialogue with other religions was encouraged in 1927. Scholars are pointing to papal advocacy of social ethics, questioning strong papal authority, and promoting discussion of priestly marriage and the ordination of women.[7]

Modern Catholicism

The large church built at the center of the Catholic Church in Rome is St. Peter's Basilica, situated in the modern independent state called the Vatican, founded in 1929, that houses the papal offices. The First Vatican Council (1869–1870), called by Pope Pius IX, resisted many modern trends and proclaimed the infallibility of official *(ex cathedra)* papal proclamations. By 1891 Pope Leo XIII showed a more liberal openness to modern problems, especially a concern for social justice. While industrial society was growing, workers were too often exploited, and the church took a position against this in his *encyclical* (papal letter) *"Rerum Novarum"* (About New Things). This encyclical has had great influence and has been reaffirmed by subsequent Popes. It argued that workers and employers should come to agreement on wages fair to the workers, and mothers should not be compelled by their husband's low wages to work outside the home.

The Second Vatican Council, called by Pope John XXIII, was held in 1962–1965. The role of the laity in church liturgy and administration was increased. This "bringing up to date" allowed for the celebration of the Mass in the local vernacular language, as well as in Latin. The priest could now face the congregation, and reading scripture and the homily were given a more prominent role. The dignity of individual conscience was heightened. The importance of the Virgin Mary was reaffirmed as advocate, helper, and mediator with God. New scientific thinking such as evolution was carefully considered. The separation of church and state was declared necessary to assure religious freedom.

Vatican II also promoted a dialogue with other faiths, especially the Jewish and Muslim traditions, and rejected "nothing of what is true and holy" in Eastern religions. Baptized Protestants were recognized to be part of the Body of Christ and Jews to be a people of God. The Council deplored all persecution, hatred, and anti-Semitism and rejected accusations that Jews in general could be held responsible for the crimes committed that led to Jesus's crucifixion. After the fascist and communist tyrannies in the twentieth century, the Church spoke up for freedom of religion as a human and civil right. Social discrimination was rejected and equality for all men and women affirmed, regardless of race, color, social conditions, language, or religion. Women are not to be denied educational and cultural benefits and should be free to choose their husbands. The modern weapons of mass destruction were also abhorred. Vatican II had a major impact.

Modern Catholic thought has developed some old and some new

themes. Mysticism is still encouraged by some. Social ethics is promoted in service to the world's poor. Struggles for and against church hierarchical authority continue. Some have urged an environmental ethic. But the most contentious Catholic issues are about gender and sexuality. Feminists such as Mary Daly (see profiles in Ch. 6) have challenged the male-only priesthood and called for the ordination of women. Many women have been legally appointed parish administrators, and Catholic women are calling for the right to control their own reproductive decisions.[8]

THE PROTESTANT CHURCH

History

Protestantism was a protest against medieval church and society. Late medieval European society, beginning about 800 CE, was feudal, structured as an aristocratic, land-owning upper class and a landless, poverty-ridden class of peasant serfs with few rights, who farmed the nobles' land and paid them heavy taxes in agricultural produce. Nobles usually scorned work and engaged in war, adventure, and sport, glorified and refined by the idea of chivalry, while the peasants farmed and sweated. Thanks to donations of land, the medieval church owned about half of France and Germany at one point, so it was fully invested in aristocratic feudalism. The Roman Catholic Church adopted this model of society with its hierarchical structure, seeing the Pope as a monarch and cardinals as princes.

But at its peak the feudal system began to break down. The Black Death was a horrible plague that swept across Europe in 1347–1349, killing perhaps a third of Europe. This resulted in a shortage of peasant labor and enabled surviving serfs to demand more rights. The Crusades also eliminated a number of nobles. Consequently, strong national monarchies, such as England and France, grew and reduced the power of local nobility. Traders expanded into a more middle-class part of society, replacing some rural aristocratic structures. Urban universities and artists promoted new thinking. Gold imported from the Americas stimulated a larger money economy that weakened the aristocratic view of the priority of inherited property and wealth. Europeans provided a rising demand for imported products such as spices and silks, so more middle-class merchants grew wealthy. By the thirteenth century, Paris had a population of about 250,000 and London about 45,000. Many towns bought their freedom from local nobles, so no longer did everyone feel loyalty to rural, feudal, hierarchical society and the Catholic Church. As the middle class grew, so did new ideas about religion and its blessing of the social classes.

By the thirteenth century, the Catholic Church had helped stabilize Europe, so beliefs such as Italian Renaissance poet Dante's pessimistic, frightening view of Hell seemed outdated. Now life in this world was more optimistically valued for its own sake, not just as preparation for the afterlife. Human nature was no longer seen as so wicked, and humans could cooperate with God to build a better world. Cathedrals and universities in enlarged cities bustling with trade were signs of a more stabilized society. Individual initiative was now more fruitful without the restraints of a rigid, feudal class structure. People began to seek egalitarian goals, different from the feudal hierarchy. College had been a privilege limited to the nobility, but now more middle-class boys went to college.

Protestantism was an important part of this historical rise of the middle class, because it gave its blessing to the middle-class values such as self-improvement through education, hard work, thrift, social equality, and democracy. Protestant beliefs emphasized the priesthood of all believers, thus supporting a more egalitarian society. Protestant stress on the authority of the Bible gave religious blessing to literacy, education, and the authority of the individual to interpret scripture. In contrast to cloistered monastics and priests who sought spiritual goals, Protestants elevated economic work into an ethical vocation by which one can serve God. Being more worldly, they also saw little point to celibacy. Protestants approved of new capitalist business practices, such as interest on loans (previously banned as immoral "usury"), which promoted business growth and social mobility.

After Johann Gutenberg refined the printing press with movable type in Germany and printed a Bible in 1456, books spread. Literacy increased, and more informed Christians came to believe that individuals had the right to interpret the Bible, rather than passively accepting the Church's interpretation, which had long assumed an illiterate laity. Also, the humanistic Renaissance rejected the validity of pilgrimages, indulgences, relics, and saints. Protestant northern Europe developed a strong early industrial economy, more dynamic than the old agricultural one.

Innovative ministers, such as Martin Luther in Germany and John Calvin in Switzerland, saw the early Reformation not as an innovation, but as an effort to restore the early Church. Any Protestant could start a new church, so protesters splintered into numerous denominations. Reformation churches are still generally more democratic than hierarchical, more Bible-oriented rather than Rome-oriented, and encourage their clergy to marry. Political shifts promoted confiscation of Catholic property. The boldness of the Protestant revolt infuriated the authoritarian nobility of Catholic Europe and provoked bloody wars. Northern Europe's growing, more educated middle class welcomed the Protestant faith and developed many elements of the early industrial revolution. This economic theme is still strong in Protestantism, notably in the "Prosperity Gospel" that encourages the acquisition and display of wealth.[9]

Beliefs

Protestants believe that all people have direct access to God and do not have to go through a church. The Bible is the highest authority, rather than a church, Pope, or tradition. They stress faith as a sincerely felt belief freely given by God that naturally leads to good works, rather than focusing on the priority of good deeds. They encourage their ministers to marry rather than be celibate, because they do not believe that one needs to severely restrict the body's natural desires to be close to God. Protestants also have rather democratic forms of church governance, with a congregational emphasis on deciding matters such as selection of a minister, rather than a strongly hierarchical, top-down rule. Some Protestants also prefer believers baptism rather than infant baptism, so the newly baptized person understands the meaning of baptism. Some branches cooperate with their government; others reject any government actions that they do not believe in such as war. More democratic and educated, with more Bible study and local congregational control, Protestants stressed sincere faith and social advancement through and education and business, rather than just good conventional behavior and a strong priesthood.

The four major branches of Protestantism are the Lutheran, Calvinist, Anglican, and Free Churches. There are many denominations of Protestants, because anyone may start a church, and some split or blend elements of various branches. This radical shift in Christianity was not simply a rediscovery of the gospel, or an heretical apostasy from the Catholic Church. Rather, it was a major paradigm shift in the beliefs and practices of Christianity.[10]

Lutheranism

Christianity began to flourish in what is now called Germany when an Anglo-Saxon monk named Boniface (680–754) traveled to Frisia, Saxony, Bavaria, and Hesse. Boniface was so influential that he dared to cut down an oak tree sacred to the ancient god Thor. He founded a monastery and was named Archbishop of Mainz. The Catholic Church became the church of the German kingdoms until the Reformation.

In 1517 Martin Luther (1483–1546), a professor of the Bible at the University of Wittenberg, Germany, openly expressed a growing protest that was "in the air." This protest culminated in the Protestant Reformation. Luther had visited Rome in 1510 as a Catholic monk and was shocked to find corruption, even in high church offices. And his studies increasingly led him to disagree with the traditional teachings of the church. The Pope was raising funds to build St. Peter's in Rome by encouraging the sale of "indulgences," or releases from time in Purgatory, the afterlife realm for "purging" souls of sins so they can go to Heaven. So, in 1517 Luther stepped up to the great wooden church door in Wittenberg and nailed up a sheet of "95 Theses" or ideas for discussion. Some were:

- Those who preach indulgences are in error when they say that man is absolved and saved from every penalty by the Pope's indulgences.
- There is no divine authority for preaching that the soul flies out of purgatory immediately [when] money clinks in the bottom of the chest.
- Christians should be taught that one who gives to the poor, tends to the needy, does a better action than if he purchases indulgences.

Luther's critique, shared by others, cut to the heart of papal authority.

Copies of Luther's protests quickly spread around Europe and released a storm of debate, challenging the Roman claim that God's grace comes only through the church's priests. Thus, for those who agreed, the Pope lost authority. In the Mass there is no sacrifice offered up by the priest, Luther argued, and no mystical transformation of bread and wine into the holy body and blood of Christ (transubstantiation). The material world created by God is a suitable vehicle for communion with the divine, whether in the Eucharist (church Communion with bread and wine) or in marriage. Luther defended his ideas but was accused of heresy and called before a papal court, where he refused to retract his arguments. The movement spread across northern Europe. Many monasteries were abandoned or confiscated. His books were burned, and he was excommunicated from the Catholic Church in 1521. Undeterred, Luther translated the Bible into German and wrote new theologies. Luther's main ideas were:

- The priesthood of all believers. Christians are not required to receive God's grace through the sacraments dispensed by any church. This dismantled the crux of Catholic social control and focused on democracy and the faith of the individual's personal relationship to God. It also allowed anyone to start a new church.

- Justification by faith. Sincere faith in God and Jesus would lead one to good works, in contrast to the traditional Catholic emphasis on the priority of works, such as church activity and moral behavior. This reduced the influence of the church's rules and put trust in sincere faith. Luther said: "Good works do not make a man good, but a good man does good works."
- Scripture is the only church authority. Biblical scriptures have authority over church tradition. This challenged the Roman church's authority based on non-biblical traditions, such as the seven sacraments and clerical celibacy. It also assumed the increasing literacy of the masses.
- Grace before works. The Roman Church has no authority to eliminate sin by administering sacraments, or by prescribing behavior (works), such as prayer, pilgrimages, and financial support. God's grace, which alone can free one from sin, is freely available to all, not restricted to church channels.
- Celibacy is unnecessary. Luther opposed the idea that celibate priests were closer to God because they suppressed bodily desires and were able to reach higher in the spiritual realm. The flesh is not a realm of moral impurity, he taught, but includes the entire self, body, senses, soul, and reason and is a suitable location for the life of the spirit. Marriage for ministers is good. (Luther married a former nun, Catherine Bora, and they had six children.)
- Simpler liturgical arts. Luther protested against excessive church art, because so many churches were richly decorated with expensive art and gold. Instead he added more Bible reading, preaching, and congregational singing.
- Two sacraments. Luther reduced the sacraments from the traditional seven to the two in the Bible: Baptism and Communion. Lutherans understand the change in wine and bread into the body of Christ as "consubstantiation" with the divine next to the material realm. Children are still baptized as infants. The church is not primarily a sacramental agent, but rather a community of believers. Luther considered private confession very desirable, but not required.

Luther was called by the Pope to recant at the Diet of Worms in 1521 but replied saying: "I cannot and will not recant anything. . . . On this I take my stand. I can do no other. God help me. Amen." His life was in danger, but Luther was protected in the Wartburg castle by Frederick the Wise (1463–1535), King of Saxony, who had founded Luther's Wittenberg University. Luther was horrified when a number of peasants rebelled against their aristocratic rulers, however, and defended the nobility as valid rulers of the state. He was not prepared for the intensity of the impact of his revolt.[11] His ideas were soon welcomed by priests in other countries, such as Ulrich Zwingli (1484–1531) in Switzerland.

Philip Melanchthon (1497–1560), an influential early German Lutheran theologian, drafted the Augsburg Confession in 1530 that remains the creed of the Lutheran church. It focuses on the importance of faith over works. That means that doing good works, as a church may prescribe, such as attending church, taking Communion, and aiding the poor, are not enough. More important is faith in God's goodness and Jesus's power to save from suffering and death, and from that follows good works. As Luther also emphasized the priesthood of all believers, this allowed anyone to start a church, which began immediately.[12]

Lutherans first united under this 1530 Augsburg Confession. They condemned another emerging branch, the Anabaptists, who believed that the Holy Spirit came to them outside the Bible and who rejected the baptism of infants. Lutherans affirmed that the church is a congregation of saints who need no strong ecclesiastical hierarchy and whose liturgies need not be everywhere alike.[13] The German Lutheran Church continued to accept the principle of a state church that Luther advocated, which is still strong in Scandinavia, but now less so in Germany, and rejected in the United States. Since the Peace of Augsburg in 1555, which allowed each prince to determine the religion of his kingdom, northern Germany has been largely Lutheran and southern Germany largely Roman Catholic (neglecting Calvinists and Anabaptists). But the Thirty Years war (1618–1648) erupted between Catholic and Protestant princes and brought a bloody devastation to Germany. The population was reduced from 16 million to 6 million; intellectual life and commerce were demolished. The final Peace of Westphalia in 1648 again affirmed the right of princes to decide the religion of their subjects, and the Reformed churches with Calvinist beliefs were also accepted.[14]

Pietism and the Moravians

Emerging seventeenth-century rationalism seeped into religion by influencing theologians to organize systematic, dogmatic interpretations that became too rigid. In Germany, Lutheranism developed a dogmatism that was criticized for making religion largely a matter of formulated beliefs, rather than of heartfelt celebration. In reaction, Pietism emerged as an assertion of the primacy of feeling in Christian experience and an ascetic view of the world. It expanded into the "Evangelical Awakening." Pietism's central figure, Phillip Spener (1635–1705), became chief pastor of Frankfurt, developed home Bible study groups, and criticized the immorality around him. He valued a genuine spiritual transformation over a "lukewarm," passive church attendance and urged a rather Calvinist, Puritan view of moderation in food, drink, dress, and rejection of theater, dance, and cards. In London, John Wesley was influenced by heart-warming Pietist worship. Pietists were praised for their sincerity and missionary work but criticized for being irrational.

A second leader of Pietist tendencies was the German Count Nikolas von Zinzendorf (1700–1760), who founded what came to be known as the Moravian Church, which cultivated a "heart-religion." Zinzendorf established missions in the West Indies, Africa, and the United States. Bethlehem, Pennsylvania, is the headquarters of the Moravian Church today.

The Church of England (Anglicans)

The Church of England has its roots in the missionary work of Augustine of Canterbury, who was sent to England by Pope Gregory the Great. When the Romans withdrew, the Angles, Saxons, and Jutes invaded England. Little Christianity had flourished until Augustine arrived on the shores of Kent in 597 and was welcomed by King Ethelbert. The French Queen Bertha was already a Christian and eager to convert her husband. Ethelbert converted and organized mass baptisms of his subjects. Augustine was consecrated Archbishop of Canterbury, which has remained the honored center of the Anglican Church. Some Christians preferred Celtic customs that conflicted with Rome, until a council at the Whitby monastery in 664 united them under Roman customs.

The Church of England began when King Henry VIII of England (1491–1547) was determined to have a male heir to his throne to end civil war, to prevent a foreign king from marrying a princess, and thus to provide a strong government. This led him to marry six wives. When unable to provide him with a boy child who lived past childhood, each of his wives was dismissed in a series of dramatic scandals. He loved all but one, but was driven by political necessity. First was Catherine of Aragon, a daughter of Spanish royalty, whom Henry married in 1509. Her son lived only a few weeks, and her daughter was Princess Mary. When Catherine became too old to bear children, Henry wanted her to enter a nunnery and thus annul their marriage, but she declined. The Pope refused to do so also, so in 1533,

16 years after Luther's revolt, Henry severed links with Rome and his marriage was annulled.[15]

William Tyndale translated the New Testament into English in 1526, but for his efforts was burned at the stake near Brussels. In 1535 Miles Coverdale translated an English Bible. Another translation by John Rogers soon appeared. In 1536, in response to a need for some definition of the New Church of England's theology, King Henry himself drafted the "Ten Articles," including these principles:

- The Bible was now the prime authority for the faith
- Three sacraments were defined: Baptism, Penance, and the Lord's Supper
- Justification implies faith in Christ alone, but confession, absolution, and works of charity are also necessary
- The Saints are honored, but not because they hear prayers before Christ
- Christ is physically present in the Lord's Supper
- Images may be honored, but in moderation
- Masses for the dead are desirable, but the "Bishop of Rome" cannot deliver a soul from Purgatory.

Seriously fearing Catholic military attacks on England, Henry sought to show his Catholic principles, except for loyalty to the Pope. So he drafted the "Six Articles" of 1539 that retained the Eucharist's transubstantiation, repudiated priestly marriage, ordered permanent priestly vows of chastity, as well as Communion with both bread and wine (instead of the old custom of bread only for the laity), and encouraged private masses and confessions.

Henry again fell in love with and married his second wife, Anne Boleyn, in 1533. She gave birth to Princess Elizabeth, but miscarried a son. Henry was becoming increasingly tyrannical. He believed the apparently untrue rumors of her infidelity and had her beheaded in 1536. Ten days later he married his third wife, Jane Seymour. In 1537 she gave birth to the longed-for son, but then she died of the too common "childbed fever," and Henry mourned her loss deeply. Their son, Prince Edward VI, was scholarly and delighted Henry, but he was sickly. Henry then married number four, Anne of Cleves, a Lutheran ally, but he was not attracted to her and divorced her after six months. Next came Catherine Howard, who revived the King's spirits in 1540, and they married. But the obese, moody king soon found that she was having love affairs. Furious, he had her beheaded. Finally this line of tragedies ended in 1543 with his sixth marriage to Catherine Parr, who was not expected to bear a child in Henry's old age. She cared well for the young Elizabeth and Edward and comforted the aging king, who died in 1547.

The English people resented the Catholic Church's heavy financial requirements, as well as its rule over property. Anti-clericalism and humanism flourished, stimulated by the Dutchman Erasmus (c. 1469–1536), who called for church reform and return to its biblical roots. But humanists were soon overshadowed by Luther's new ideas, adopted by some university students who grew up to become Anglican bishops.

Upon Henry's death, Edward VI took the throne at age 10 and allowed many Protestant innovations. He repealed most heresy laws and the Six Articles, removed all restrictions on Bibles, ordered giving wine to the laity in Communion, and authorized a new Prayer Book, which was required in Church of England services in 1549. More Catholic property was confiscated, images were ordered removed from churches, and the marriage of priests was made legal in 1549. In 1552 a more Protestant Prayer Book was written that dispensed with some Catholic practices: prayers for the dead, special wafers in communion, exorcism, anointing the dying, and medieval priestly vestments. In 1553 Edward ratified a new set of Forty-two Articles, opposed to both the old Catholic and the new Anabaptist movement.

When Edward died of tuberculosis in 1553, a period of Catholic rule under Henry's daughter, the Catholic Queen Mary, brought a time of severe persecution of Protestants and an attempt to restore Catholic rule in England (1553–1558). Protestants fled to Geneva or were burned. Mary brought a Cardinal back from Rome and married Philip II, son of the King of Catholic Spain. But by then Protestantism had deep roots in England, and these persecutions sparked resentments against Catholics. King Philip did not love his wife Mary; she bore no children and died alone in 1558.

Mary's younger sister, Elizabeth (1533–1603), became the next Queen, but she refused Philip's marriage proposals. She decided to marry no man, so as to avoid political domination and potential religious wars. Elizabeth's Protestant allies managed to reverse most of the Catholic legislation enacted under Mary. She ruled from 1558 to 1603 and proved to be a brilliant queen, quelling rebellions, strengthening the Church of England, supporting New World explorations, and promoting cultural achievement. From the right, the Pope urged her subjects to depose her, and from the left Puritans wanted to take the English Reformation even further. Elizabeth steered a middle course between Catholics and Protestants to avoid civil war or invasion.

Elizabeth reissued the Prayer Book in 1552 with some amendments and appointed a moderate Archbishop of Canterbury to lead the Church of England. Gradually, religious uniformity in England was sought, and the first version of the "Thirty-nine Articles," finally defining the Anglican faith, was issued in 1563. The Catholic Spanish sent a massive Armada of ships to attack England in 1588, but storms and the more nimble English naval tactics defeated the Spanish and prevented England from becoming Catholic again. In summary, Anglicans in the Reformation took six basic positions:

- For a minimal sense of the "priesthood of all believers" and a moderately strong priesthood, retaining bishops and archbishops
- Against a radically simplified liturgy and church arts, retaining a formal, prescribed liturgy that resembled the Catholic liturgy
- For justification by faith and grace, not works alone
- For seeing the Bible as the primary authority in faith
- Against required celibacy for priests
- For only two sacraments: Baptism and Eucharist.

The Puritans

The other Protestants in England were called Puritans, Dissidents, Separatists, or Nonconformists, who combined Calvinist and Free Church principles. The Bible was their final authority, excluding any church interpretation. They rejected the idea of a state church. They urged the purge of Catholic "superstitions" lingering in the Church of England, such as prescribed clerical dress that implied the priesthood was a higher calling than other Protestant views of an egalitarian priesthood of all believers. They rejected kneeling at the altar rail for communion and the marriage ring as the remnant of seeing marriage as a sacrament. They preferred simple, egalitarian dress for ministers, sincere, spiritual sermons, and local church governance. Pastors, bishops, and presbyters were to be seen as equal in rank. Puritanism emphasized local congregational rule and simple dress for all, as distinct from elaborate aristocratic costume. Puritans also objected strongly to excessive church art, and some Anglican churches suffered damage from rampaging mobs that destroyed stained glass and other church art. Many Dissenters were imprisoned or hanged for denying the Queen's supremacy in church matters. Puritans rejected use of the Prayer Book, and some fled to Holland. One Puritan request was granted in the form of the new "King James" translation of the Bible in 1611.

John Smyth, a former Anglican clergyman, began the English Baptist church in exile in Amsterdam about 1609. Other Puritans founded the first Congregational Church in 1616. Puritans argued over Anabaptist issues such as infant baptism, congregational rule, and Calvinist issues such as whether Jesus died for the elect only or for all believers. In their Calvinist and Anabaptist suppression of sensory pleasures, Puritans opposed King James I's support for popular games, sports, and dances on Sunday. Despairing of ever gaining religious tolerance in England, Puritans began to immigrate to the colonies in 1620. Soon at least 20,000 Puritans resided in Massachusetts and Connecticut.

The English Toleration Act of 1689 finally granted religious freedom to the main Protestant Dissenters most strongly influenced by Calvinist theology: the Presbyterians, Congregationalists, and Baptists, then called the Free Churches (free of state control). Those who rejected the Trinity or were Roman Catholics were not granted tolerance. In 1707 Scotland and England were united as the United Kingdom, and the Presbyterian Scottish Church was protected. Catholics finally gained tolerance in 1778.

Methodism

In 1738 an Anglican priest who became a dissenter, but never wanted to leave the Church of England, started a new movement that became a major

Protestant minister giving a third-grade girl her Bible at St. Paul's United Methodist Church, Ithaca, New York. Courtesy of George Gull.

denomination. John Wesley, his brother Charles, and their friend George Whitefield began what became the Methodist Episcopal Church. They rejected Calvin's pessimistic view of human nature as depraved and stressed the "Arminian" view of a strong human free will and God's love and salvation for all, not just the elect. Wesley retained the Anglican structure of bishops but with a much weaker role. He rejected the formal liturgy of the Anglican tradition and traveled widely by horseback to preach to crowds outdoors.

Calvinism

John Calvin (1509–1564) was a French lawyer who left the Catholic Church for emerging Protestantism. Forced to flee France, he traveled, published, and settled in Geneva. He eagerly adopted Luther's ideas and in addition emphasized congregational rule, whereby each congregation is fairly autonomous in selecting a minister, breaking with Luther's practice of government oversight and bishops appointing ministers. He also sought to have the church lead the state, so he worked to institute laws for both church and state in Geneva. Among Reformation leaders, his thought was the most legalistic. Geneva attracted many Protestant refugees from other countries who took Calvin's principles home.

By 1541, Geneva under Calvin became a religious oligarchy, where the Congregation of the Clergy prepared all legislation and submitted it to the city Consistory to be ratified. Calvin ruled with an iron fist, stubbornly convinced of the rightness of his ideas. He imposed a creed on each citizen of Geneva and staffed schools with teachers trained in his doctrines. He succeeded in achieving a church governance that could excommunicate the unrepentant. Such power had not been granted to churches by any other Reformation countries' governments. He seemed to some to be a severe man. He was married for nine years, until his wife died. He wrote the influential *Institutes of the Christian Religion* (1536). Its unique principles are summarized in the "TULIP" formula:

- Total depravity of humanity—no human by himself is capable of goodness, so no good works are valid before God. Only through Christ are some "elect" saved, if they show repentance and faith. Then their good works will flow naturally from their faith.
- Unconditional election of individuals to heaven, despite any flawed actions. They would be exemplary figures, due to being God's chosen.

- Limited salvation; reconciliation with God for sinfulness was limited only to a few. Jesus did not die to save everyone (as the Anabaptists believed), only the chosen: the predestined elect.
- Irresistible grace from God for the elect, who cannot refuse being chosen, but must work to bring God's kingdom to earth.
- Predestination to heaven for the elect; this is all in God's plan, restricting human freedom. This gave a sense of cosmic destiny to the reformers in the battle.

Calvin had a powerful and widespread influence in shaping the Reformation. He saw the church, the sacraments, and the civil government as divinely established. John Knox (c. 1513–1572), a Scottish priest who became Protestant and studied in Geneva, took Calvinism back to Scotland, where it became the state Presbyterian Church in the 1560s. Ulrich Zwingli led a Calvinist reformation in Switzerland from his cathedral in Zurich. Calvinism was established in the Netherlands and shaped the English Puritans. Calvin influenced the rise of the Reformed churches in Poland and Hungary. In France the Calvinists were called "Hugenots." When the devastating Thirty Years War ended in 1648, many kingdoms gained new rulers, and the Calvinists were finally granted more rights. France, Spain, Italy, and some of Eastern Europe remained largely Catholic, but northern Germany, Holland, Scandinavia, and England remained largely Protestant.

More than early Lutherans and Anglicans, Calvinists have always wholeheartedly participated in the rise of the middle class. This meant encouraging hard work, self-discipline, thrift, helping each other in business matters, and supporting education as an essential means to rise out of poverty into middle-class life. The Westminster Catechism of 1647 was adopted by almost all Presbyterian and Congregational churches. It is considered the best statement of Calvinism in English. It emphasized God's greatness and humanity's sinfulness, Christ's sacrifice and exaltation, justification by God's freely given grace, the importance of the biblical and preached Word, and the effectiveness of the sacraments, not from those who administer them, but from Christ's blessing. The Presbyterian Church spread from Scotland to Northern Ireland and the American colonies.[16]

When the Calvinist Puritan Congregationalists immigrated to the Americas and founded colonies around Massachusetts Bay, they attempted to establish a holy commonwealth, a theocratic state based on the Bible, which they enacted in 1631. They founded the first colonial college, Harvard College, in 1636, to educate their ministers. They were stubbornly intolerant toward Baptists and Quakers, who had to flee to other areas.

But their Calvinist policy of integrating church and state did not last long. Liberals at Harvard, at Boston's Brattle Street Church, and in Connecticut rejected such intolerance.

In the Netherlands a strong Calvinist Reformed Church survived Catholic occupation by Spain's King Phillip II until a Dutch revolt against Spain succeeded in 1609. The former minority of Calvinists helped form the northern independent Dutch Republic now called The Netherlands, while the south continued to be Catholic and was called Belgium. The Calvinists agreed upon the Belgic Confession in 1619, which accepted many Calvinist dogmas, such as the depravity of humanity due to original sin and God's election of saints who can be saved only by Christ. The early Dutch Reformed Church was seen as the union of the saved, and all were obliged to join it and separate themselves from unbelievers. Yet the true church should not persecute those who criticize it. The officers of the church should be elected by its members. All ministers should hold equal power, with no bishops above them.

However, the Dutch government should remove any obstacle to the preaching of the Reformed Church's Gospel or worship; it should uphold the sacred ministry, destroy all idolatry and false worship, and promote the Kingdom of Christ. All citizens (not excluding nobility) should be subject to its laws and pay taxes. The five points of Calvinist theology (TULIP) were affirmed against the Arminians, who denied original sin and stressed free will. The *Solas* or "onlys" that became a cry of the Reformation were affirmed: Belief and Teaching in salvation by Faith Alone *(Sola Fide)*, through Scripture Alone *(Sola Scriptura)*, by way of Christ Alone *(Sola Christus)*, because of Grace Alone *(Sola Gratia)*, all for which to God Alone be the Glory *(Soli Deo Gloria)*.

The Dutch sent immigrants to America who founded a Dutch trading post called New Netherlands in 1624. By 1628, the first colonial Dutch Reformed Church was established in New Amsterdam on Manhattan Island, where it continues as Marble Collegiate Church. The Reformed Church unsuccessfully attempted to prevent other churches from settling there, as did the Church of England, when the English took over in 1664 and renamed it New York. But American tolerance of other churches soon became the norm. Today's descendants of the Calvinist tradition include the Reformed churches, the Presbyterian churches, and Congregational churches with several names—such as the United Church of Christ, Churches of Christ, Christian churches, and Disciples of Christ. Most Baptists have a strongly Calvinist theology, but because their focus on independence from government and adult baptism is a defining practice, they are grouped with the Free Churches with Anabaptist backgrounds. England proved to be fertile ground for the origin of several Protestant denominations.[17]

Today Calvinism shows its wide influence in its continuing support for the rise of the middle class and its business culture. Conservative Calvinist churches stress a pessimistic view of human nature, the depravity of humans and their need for Jesus's salvation from sin, the theology of a salvation limited to a predestined few elected by God, rather than for all. It appears in some church denominations in rather strict practices such as spanking disobedient children. In the more mainstream and liberal Calvinist churches, his influence remains in the stress on congregational autonomy, although the old idea of the church leading government has faded as religious tolerance has spread. Predestination and depravity have faded away in most liberal churches as well. Calvin had a fear of idolatry in the church, so simplicity in worship has always been a strong Calvinist principle. But now music and drama, which he restrained, have regained their place in many Calvinist churches. The importance of preaching and congregational singing, that Calvin adopted from Luther and amplified, continues in all Protestant churches.

The Free Churches

Still a number of Protestants thought that the Reformation did not go far enough. They formed the radical left wing of the Reformation. Most important was their belief that revelation did not end with the Bible but could come through to any sincere believer anytime. Like Lutherans, they stressed the authority of the Bible and the priesthood of all believers but took these ideas further. They went beyond Luther's belief that each person has the right to follow his or her own conscience and developed strongly individualist traditions. Some deny the necessity of any priesthood at all, because every individual should follow the guidance of their "inner light," although most do develop an educated clergy. Believing that each of the faithful is a channel of the Holy Spirit, not just priests, many encourage lay members to assist ministers in serving the Lord's Supper. Like Calvinists, they are congregational, having fairly autonomous, self-supporting churches that call their own ministers, and reject much church visual art. Going further, they see the church as an egalitarian Calvinist community of saints, where anyone can speak in worship when moved by the Spirit, rather than a hierarchy. They reject strongly Calvinist ideas of limited salvation or predestination. Some have optimistic views of human nature, and some pessimistic. "Free Church" became the term used to identify non-Anglican churches in England, not affiliated with the government.

Unlike early Lutherans, early Calvinists, and the Church of England, most Free Churches clearly separate church and state, because they perceived too much abuse from the mixture of religion and politics. Inevitably, however, politics gets mixed with faith, as when churches split over the slavery issue in the nineteenth century, or when some conservative church groups openly supported right-wing politicians in the twentieth century. Some Free Churches are conservative, some mainstream, and some liberal or radical. Like the Calvinists, some support the rise of the middle class. Others take more radical, utopian positions by sharing communal property, separating from mainstream society, and opposing war. Some of the more radical Free Churches, such as the Quakers, are called the "peace churches" because they advocate nonviolent resistance to injustice, refuse military service, and serve as conscientious objectors in alternative ways during wars, such as in hospitals.

The early events of the Radical Reformation that emerged in Switzerland, the Rhine River valley, and Holland focused on the issue of Baptism. Infant Baptism was required by some states for citizenship and had governmental agents in church hierarchies, which closely tied church and state together. But the Free Churches, amid bloody religious wars, wanted to separate church and state, as well as baptize only believers old enough to understand their commitment. So they were called the "Anabaptists," or "re-baptizers," because they had likely already been baptized as infants. There were several leaders of the Anabaptist movement around Zürich and Strassbourg. In 1523, Balthasar Hubmaier, a doctor of theology at the German University of Ingolstadt, was influenced by Luther and began to doubt the biblical basis for infant Baptism. He became a minister in Waldshut, Switzerland and gained a following around Zürich.

Defying the Zürich city council, Dissenters began baptizing adults in prayer meetings. They denied the validity of infant baptism on the basis that an infant has no understanding of the meaning of Baptism and that it had become a way of securing church membership with "cradle members" rather than by a sincere spiritual awakening. Thus they were nicknamed "Anabaptists," even though they recognized only believers' Baptism to be valid. Zürich's Calvinist minister Zwingli opposed them.

The original Dissenters, now called "Swiss Brethren," emphasized, as distinct from the state-administered churches, that the faith should be experienced as a genuine spiritual rebirth at an age of understanding and demonstrated in a life of saintliness. Religion should not just be a matter of citizenship or conformity, but a statement of nonconformity if necessary, they firmly believed. Thus they were the first to practice the complete separation of church and state. Authentic faith to them is voluntary, and any coercion or automatic membership in a national church is unacceptable. Thus outsiders saw Anabaptist separatism as a threat to ordered society. This was exacerbated by their emphasis on the authority of the individual conscience that led them to reject swearing oaths in court or serving in the military. To them this was a restoration of primitive Christianity, but to others it was a threat to social order. Thus many Anabaptists were persecuted; four were drowned in 1527 in Zürich, and thousands of others died.

Jacob Hubmaier published and gathered a large Anabaptist community. He participated in a failed peasants' revolt, so he was forced to flee to Moravia, where he spread the new Anabaptism. The movement expanded into Holland, Austria, and Hungary. Strasbourg was an Anabaptist center until 1533. Both Catholics and Lutherans proclaimed Anabaptists to be heretical and subject to death penalties. This type of law was enforced severely in Catholic territories. Many in Switzerland suffered the "blood-judgment." One fringe group of radicals who joined the Anabaptists captured the German city of Münster in 1534, established polygamy and communal property, and slaughtered opponents. They were soundly defeated by Catholic and Lutheran troops in 1535 and rejected by other Anabaptists.

The Anabaptists needed a less radical and violent leader. A Dutch Catholic priest who became an Anabaptist minister in 1537, Menno Simons (1496–1561), inspired many with his gentle, tolerant, and reasonable leadership. His followers became the Mennonites, who live a humble, peaceful life. He traveled around Holland, Switzerland, and Germany, urging the education of the poor. He immigrated to Pennsylvania and was joined by Russian immigrants escaping religious persecution.

Articles of the Anabaptist Faith were affirmed at a meeting of the Swiss Brethren in 1527, in the Schleitheim Confession, including:

- Believers' Baptism replaces infant Baptism
- The church is seen as local associations of Christians, united by the Lord's Supper
- Absolute rejection of "self-indulgence of the flesh" was required, since Münster
- Worship practiced by Catholic, Lutheran and Zwinglian churches was disavowed as unchristian
- Pastors can discipline, even excommunicate (ban), problematic members

- Civil government is a necessity, but Christians should neither partake in it, nor join the military, nor take oaths

Thousands of Anabaptist refugees gathered in Moravian aristocratic estates in 1526 and began sharing property communally. But the Lutherans had their leader, Hubmaier, burned at the stake. Communities abolishing private property continued in Moravia, and Jakob Hutter took leadership in 1533. Debates among Anabaptists emerged over participation in civil government, paying taxes, military service, and capital punishment. Outsiders saw their communal societies as a threat to "ordered society." Yet they continued to expand in Switzerland, Holland, Germany, Prussia, and Poland. As the movement expanded overseas, they called themselves "Christians," "Brethren," "Apostles," "Mennonites," or "Evangelicals." Their most numerous offspring are the many branches of what became the more mainstream, more Calvinist Baptist church, which now supports hardly any radical practices, such as nonviolent resistance to war.

Free Churches today range from conservative fundamentalists with numerous names, such as "Bible Church," to mainstream and conservative Baptists. The more radical churches in varying forms reject many mainstream values. They advocate not only opposition to violence and war, but also individualism, materialism, commercialism, industrialism, church hierarchy, and formalism, and so some of them separate themselves from mainstream society. Liberal churches today with Free Church roots can be identified as the Brethren, some Baptists, Mennonites, Hutterites, Amish, Quakers, Shakers, and many other independent churches with various names.

Denominations Today

The Reformation fragmented Christianity with the theology of the priesthood of all believers, which permitted anyone to start a new church. Lutherans and Anglicans retained their distinctiveness, although splinter groups emerged from each. Calvinist and Free Churches splintered into many different denominations in Europe, such as the Puritans in England and the Brethren in Switzerland. Many blended Lutheran, Calvinist, and Free Church theologies.

Methodists

John Wesley (1703–1791), a Church of England priest, along with his brother Charles, and friend George Whitefield, had a spiritual awakening at Oxford University, and sought a "method" of pious spirituality. Once when visiting Pietist Moravians on Aldersgate Street in London, he felt his heart "strangely warmed" and sensed that God removed his sins. He taught an optimistic view of human nature, as distinct from the stern, pessimistic Calvinist view of human nature. He adopted the theology of Jakob Arminius (1560–1609), a Dutch reformer who rejected Calvin's doctrine of predestination, and instead stressed human free will and God's love and salvation for everyone, not just the elect. This is called "prevenient grace," the doctrine that God actively seeks to transform people through grace.

Wesley also stressed the importance of social responsibilities of believers and the need for social improvements for the workers and poor. He traveled about 8,000 miles a year on horseback in England to preach widely. He was denied pulpits, so he preached outdoors to large crowds. He wrote many popular, comforting hymns. He ordained new ministers, which forced an unwanted break with the Church of England. At his death there were 294 Methodist preachers in England and more than 70,000 Methodists.[18] Methodism grew into a major American denomination.

Congregationalists (United Church of Christ)

The emphasis on self-governing congregational rule, stressed by Calvin and the Free Churches, led to the founding of the Congregational Church in England. A major early advocate of congregational rule in England, Robert Browne (c. 1550–1633), who taught, against the Church of England's loyalty to the Queen, that the true church is a local body of believers with an experience of God, united voluntarily, not by law, having no authority over another congregation. He founded such a "separatist" congregation in Norwich in 1581, was briefly imprisoned, and had to flee to Holland. His congregational autonomy idea preceded any Anabaptist influence in England by many decades, and he did not reject infant Baptism. The turbulence of his movement pressed him back into the fold of the Church of England in 1585, where he served in its ministry until 1633.[19]

Persecuted by the established churches, more Calvinist Puritans sailed the Mayflower to America in 1620. They formed Congregational churches, but also Calvinist "established" state churches, in Massachusetts, Connecticut, and across New England. Such Congregationalists also developed liberal tendencies. They led the Boston Tea Party protest against unjust taxation, which was the first U.S. act of civil disobedience. They were among the first Americans to oppose slavery and ordained the first

African-American Protestant minister, Lemuel Haynes, in 1785. In 1853 in upstate New York, a Congregational church ordained the first woman minister since New Testament times in a mainstream denomination, Antoinette Brown Blackwell (see Ch. 6). Mergers with other churches led to the United Church of Christ in 1957. In 1972 in England Congregational Unions merged with the English Presbyterians to form the United Reformed Church. In 1972 the United Church of Christ's Golden Gate Association ordained the first openly gay minister.[20]

Presbyterians

Calvinist Presbyterian churches originated as the state church in Scotland founded by John Knox (1513–1572) after the Catholic Queen Mary of Scots left. During her reign he had fled to Geneva, where he absorbed Calvinist principles, then returned to Scotland to apply them. Presbyterianism (rule by elders) grew in England and then spread to North America in 1683. They have split over issues such as slavery and reunited several times. Today there are several branches, but largest is the Presbyterian Church USA formed in 1983, reuniting the southern and northern branches. Their catechism today affirms that God's maleness in the Bible does not mean God is actually male, but is beyond gender, thus women and men are equal and women can be ordained ministers. It also affirms the importance of ecological responsibility.[21]

Reformed

The Calvinist Dutch Reformed Church developed in the Netherlands, despite Spanish repression for a time, and then took root in America in 1628 in New Amsterdam. Services were held in the Dutch language until 1764. The Reformed Church in America was formed in 1867. This example of a liberal Reformed Church has long been concerned with peace, justice, poverty, race, and ethnicity and more recently with violence, capital punishment, climate change, socially responsible investing, stem cell ethics, and developing nations' debt. The first woman Reformed Church of America minister was ordained in 1973.

The Protestant Reformed Church of America today represents the conservative side of the Reformed spectrum. They emphasize strongly Calvinist doctrines such as the total depravity of humans, who need Christ to save them from sin. They oppose divorce and remarriage, and believe that one cannot do any good in this world without God's grace. They affirm the predestination of only an elect number of believers to heaven. They believe that Christ is only for the elect, never for the "reprobate," and that God does not offer salvation to any except those elected by him.[22]

Baptists

Baptists combined some Calvinist theology with Free Church local autonomy and baptismal practices. They have multiplied into many varieties and divided over issues such as the U.S. Civil War (1861–1865). Baptists in the more northern, liberal American Baptist Church today accept the Bible as their final authority, and follow few creeds. They tolerate individual differences of theology, seek ecumenical relations with other churches, and focus on care for the needy, week, and oppressed. Their ecological concern stresses the need to care for the earth and all its creatures. They are inclusive and diverse, embracing a pluralism of race, ethnicity, and gender and ordaining women as ministers.

The conservative U.S. Southern Baptist Convention, the largest U.S. Protestant denomination, today teaches that the Bible was authored by God alone without any error and is thus totally true. God is seen as an all-powerful Father. Christ died for human sins and now dwells in all believers. Humans fell from innocence and thus are inevitably sinners. There is no salvation from sin and suffering apart from Christ. While both men and women are gifted to serve in the church, the role of ordained pastor should be limited to men, as directed by the Bible. Southern Baptists believe in the full dignity of every person and every race in God's eyes. Therefore Christians should oppose racism, selfishness, vice, greed, and sexual immorality, including homosexuality, adultery, pornography, and abortion. Marriage should be the union of a man and a woman. God values husband and wife equally, and husbands must provide for and lead the family. The wife's role is to respect her husband and serve as his helper in managing the household and children.[23]

Holiness and Pentecostal

As early as the 1860s in New Jersey, the Holiness Movement split off from Methodism, and leaders such as Phoebe Palmer in the 1870s led them toward an emotionally charged style of worship that stressed sudden conversion, sincere change of character, speaking in unknown tongues, and emotional baptism by the Holy Spirit. Holiness camp meeting preachers emphasized moral strictness and opposition to liberalism. The Church of the Nazarene was the largest of the early Holiness churches. The Salvation Army is also a Holiness church that has a strong program for helping the poor.

Out of the Holiness church emerged the Pentecostal Church in Kansas in 1901. They believed the Bible to be inerrant, they rejected the Trinity, and emphasized the oneness of God as Father. They advocated strict morality, faith healing, and end-of the world beliefs. They continued belief in the "descent of the Holy Spirit," expressed in speaking in foreign tongues and spiritual healing. This phenomenon was also called the "charismatic" experience. Some also taught the goal of financial prosperity. Pentecostal membership soon exceeded the Holiness churches. William Seymour, a black evangelist, gave this movement a boost beginning 1906 on Azuza Street in Los Angeles, with many black and white worshipers feeling that the Holy Spirit had visited them. They became the Assemblies of God International Fellowship.

Today the Assemblies of God Church is the largest, most widespread international pentecostal denomination, and it is growing. Most members live outside the United States. It was founded in 1914 in Arkansas, and in 2004 it claimed about 2.6 million worshipers in more than 12,000 churches across the United States. They believe that the scriptures are inspired by God, infallible, that there is only One True God, revealed in three persons (Father, Son, and Holy Spirit), the deity of Jesus, human sinfulness, and salvation through Christ only. They believe in the end of the world—the Rapture—when all believers, living and dead, will meet Christ in the air, and join him forever. Those who have rejected Christ will be judged and consigned to eternal punishment in fire.

Brethren

The Free Church Brethren also grew out of the Reformation Anabaptist movement, at a baptism of seven people in the Eder River in Schwartzenau, Germany, which was illegal, because they had been baptized as infants. Due to persecution and economic difficulty, they immigrated beginning in 1716 and settled in Germantown, Pennsylvania. They spread across the country, divided into three branches, and sent missionaries abroad. They subscribe to few formal creeds or rules. They simply try to do what Jesus did. Brethren look to the scriptures for direction rather than to doctrine.

They emphasize compassion, simplicity, and peacemaking. Brethren live a simple life, refuse military service, refuse to swear legal oaths, and simply affirm the truth of what they say. Early Brethren did not go to court to solve problems.

Mennonites

Free Church Mennonites, grew out of the church begun by the Dutch minister Menno Simons, who was ordained Anabaptist in 1537. They believe that God established the state to promote the well-being of all people, so Christians should cooperate with others in society to care for the weak and poor and promote social justice. They pay taxes and obey all laws that do not conflict with the Word of God but will witness against corruption and injustice. They pray for social order, but deplore the violence and death resulting from national military actions. They give their allegiance to God above the state, so they would not say "God bless America." They refuse to swear oaths in legal transactions, but simply affirm the truth of their statements. They seek reconciliation rather than conflict, so in times of national conscription or war, they offer alternative service where possible. Mennonites treat people of other faiths with respect, but lovingly and urgently proclaim Christ as the only way of salvation for all people. There are many branches of the Mennonite church. The Mennonite Central Committee (MCC) is a relief, service, and peace agency of the North American Mennonite and Brethren in Christ churches.[24]

Quakers

George Fox (1624–91) founded the Friends, or Quakers (who "quake" before the Lord). He began his ministry in England in 1647 after a transforming mystical experience. He organized the first community in 1652. From this came his conviction that direct experience of the divine is available to every person, who also carries a portion of the divine "inner light." Thus revelation is not confined to the Bible, he believed, but God speaks directly to believers who are then stimulated to service. As the inner light can be awakened in any man or woman, no professional ministry is needed, and women naturally rose to leadership positions along with men, although sometimes men and women sat separately. Friends have few formal creeds. They stress simplicity, equality, and thrift. Fox converted Margaret Fell

(1614–1702) and married her when she was widowed. Her home, Swarthmore Hall, provided a headquarters for his preachers.

Hundreds of English Friends were imprisoned for their radical views. The English Toleration Act of 1689 finally stopped persecution. Meanwhile Friends began immigrating. William Penn welcomed them to his colonial land, and so many Friends settled in and around Philadelphia. Friends promoted education and opposed slavery early, so by 1787 no Friends in the United States owned slaves. The leadership of both the antislavery abolition movement and the women's rights movement included a number of educated Quaker women, such as Lucretia Mott. Quakers were active in Nantucket Island's whaling. Today Friends can be found on the continuum from conservative, evangelical Christian to liberal and universalist (believing that all world religions have some truth). The1990's Quaker Tapestry pictures Quaker beliefs and history.[25]

Amish

The Amish originated when a group led by Jacob Amman broke away from the Mennonites in 1693 and became known as "Amish," but many Amish today maintain good relations with Mennonites. Beginning in Switzerland and France, they fled persecution in the 1700s to the United States, where they settled first in Lancaster County, Pennsylvania. Today there are about 22,000 Amish in Lancaster County, and they are well known for the quilts, pies, and woodwork that they sell, so tourists often visit the area. Other Amish communities can be found across North America with some variations in practice.

Seeing the problems of modernism as divisive for the family, meaningful work, and religion, most Amish reject cars, electricity, and formal education after eighth grade in favor of traditional rural farms, a quiet life, and close communities. They retain a strong attachment to nineteenth-century rural culture, driving horses and buggies rather than cars. Their clothing is old-fashioned. Instead of buttons most clothing has hooks and eyes. Men wear beards and wide-brimmed hats. Women wear long dresses and a white "prayer covering" hat. A resident male bishop in each community serves the Lord's Supper, performs Baptisms and marriages, ordains ministers, and carries out church discipline. Some Amish later accepted telephones, tractors, and electricity, which remain taboo for Old Order Amish. They speak English, German, and a German dialect called Pennsylvania Dutch.

Like early Anabaptists, the Amish maintain their communal discipline by "shunning" those who leave their path, although some have protested that this practice is too severe.[26]

Black Protestant Churches

Many early Christians in the United States attempted to justify slavery with biblical texts. Some tried to convert slaves to save their souls from their indigenous African "paganism" and made them sit in church balconies. Others would not baptize them, for that would make them more human. In response, some black slaves absorbed enough Christianity to form independent, secret churches. They quietly slipped off into the woods and held secret Christian services or "camp meetings," that rejected the justification for slavery and instead emphasized Christianity's core message of justice, compassion, and freedom.

Some African-Americans were drawn to the Methodist and Baptist churches. Missionaries sent to southern plantations brought 118,000 to 200,000 African-American members into the Methodist Church by 1861. Baptists counted about 400,000 African-American members at the same date. In the Caribbean, some merged Christianity with their indigenous African traditions into new religions, called Voodoo in Haiti, Santeria in Cuba, Shango in Trinidad, Rastafarianism in Jamaica, and Macumba in Brazil.

Choir singing, Calvary Baptist Church, Ithaca, New York. Courtesy of George Gull.

The African Methodist Episcopal (AME) Church protested the dehu-manizing treatment of Africans brought to America for cheap labor. Keep-ing the doctrines and structure of the Methodists, the AME Church was founded in Philadelphia by Richard Allen in 1787. Today it reports about 3.5 million members in about 8,000 congregations worldwide. The AME Zion Church now numbers about 1.2 million members and about 3,000 congregations.

As the Baptist Church expanded with missionaries from Rhode Island, African-Americans were drawn to its principle of the equality of all mem-bers. By 1758 Black Baptist churches had been formed in Virginia and South Carolina. The largest African-American pentecostal denomination was formed by Charles Mason in 1896 and was named the Church of God in Christ. Recognition of the spontaneous power of the Holy Spirit (rather than a strong dogmatism) allowed women to rise to leadership in these churches. For example, Arenia Mallory (1905–1977) founded a private school, a health center, and a religion school. The Rev. Martin Luther King, Jr., was a Baptist minister and based the 1960s civil rights movement on Christian principles. Today, the largest U.S. Black Baptist churches are the National Baptist Convention (3.5 million members), the National Baptist Convention USA (5 million members), the National Missionary Baptist Convention of America (2.5 million members), and the Progressive Na-tional Baptist Convention (2.5 million members). They increasingly work in close affiliation.

African-American theologian James Cone challenged racism in his 1969 *Black Theology and Black Power* and subsequent books. Black Gos-pel music has had a far-flung impact. It shaped "white" gospel music, as well as Protestant choir music as far away as Barcelona, Spain. "Womanist Theology" is the voice of Black women Christian feminists who focus on the needs of Black women and men. Always strong in the Black Church, they are now speaking up with critiques of white middle-class culture that has suppressed the Black woman. Womanists fight for survival and build community, rather than separate from their men, compete with each other, or forget to love themselves. Mothering and nurturing are important to them.

In Africa, Africans began many contemporary churches independent of missionary churches. They are called AICs, which can stand for African In-dependent Churches, African Instituted Churches, or African Indigenous Churches. They range from churches similar to missionary churches, to those really practicing African indigenous traditions, but using Christian language. They are most numerous in Nigeria, Kenya, and South Africa. Most AICs are Protestant, as the Catholic churches have maintained their ties to Rome, and the Protestants allow anyone to start a new church. They stress the authority of the Bible, in most cases with a literal reading. Many arose from disagreements with missionaries about the use of traditional African practices, notably polygamy, which many AICs permit. They also have a worldview more like the biblical worldview than the modern Western industrial perspective. They see the world as spiritual, a cosmic battleground populated by demons and witches. Diseases thus have spiritual causes and cures, they believe. Prayers can also cause God to affect the weather, they believe. Most of them, however, clearly reject the traditional African religious belief in witchcraft as a tool to fight demons and witches. AICs believe instead that demons must be resisted in the name of Jesus. Also many AICs forbid traditional dancing and ceremonies. Many distinguish themselves from traditional culture by wearing white robes and distinctive headgear. They have firm dietary laws, and some abstain from beer and tobacco. AIC membership numbers more than 100 million.[27]

NOTES

1. Brenda Meehan, *Holy Women of Russia* (San Francisco: HarperSan Francisco, 1993).

2. Russia: Christian Persecution in Russia, http://www.persecution.org/Countries/russia.html; Jim Forest, *Religion in the New Russia* (New York: Crossroads, 1990); Russian Orthodox Church, http://www.russian-orthodox-church.org.ru/hist_en.htm; Russian Orthodox Church Outside Russia, http://www.russianorthodoxchurch.ws/English.

3. Demetrios Constantelos, "The Historical Development of Greek Orthodoxy," http://www.myriobiblos.gr/texts/english/constantelos.html; Greek Orthodox Church, http://www.greekorthodoxchurch.org; Greek Orthodox Church of America, http://www.goarch.org.

4. Of the many studies of the Crusades, see W. B. Bartlett, *God Wills It!* (Gloucestershire: Sutton, 1999).

5. Williston Walker, et al. *A History of the Christian Church.* 4th ed. (New York: Scribner's, 1985); and "Cathares: Les Fortresses de l'Hérésie," *Pyrénées Magazine Special Edition,* ed. Jean-Paul Bobin (Toulouse: Milan Presse, 2002).

6. Vatican II was the major Catholic council that modernized the Church somewhat. See Walter M. Abbot, ed. *The Documents of Vatican II* (New York: The American Press, 1966).

7. On Catholic history and doctrine, see Richard McBrien, *Catholicism,* 2nd

ed. (New York: Harper and Row, 2001); and Hans Küng, *Christianity: Essence, History, and Future* (New York: Continuum, 1995).

8. Andrew Greeley, *The Catholic Myth* (New York: Collier/Macmillan, 1990).

9. Max Weber, *The Protestant Ethic and the Spirit of Capitalism* (New York: Scribner's, 1958); and Roland Bainton, *The Reformation of the Sixteenth Century* (Boston: Beacon, 1952).

10. Paul Tillich, *A History of Christian Thought* (New York: Simon and Schuster, 1968), Ch. 5; John Dillenberger and Claude Welch, *Protestant Christianity* (New York: Scribner's, 1954); and Hans Küng, *Christianity: Essence, History, and Future* (New York: Continuum, 1995), p. 524. The basics of various branches' creeds that follow are collected at the Creeds of Christendom, http://www.creeds.net.

11. John Dillenberger, ed., *Martin Luther: Selections from His Writings* (Garden City, NY: Doubleday Anchor, 1954).

12. John Dillenberger and Claude Welch, *Protestant Christianity* (New York: Scribner's, 1954).

13. Clyde Manschreck, *A History of Christianity: Readings in the History of the Church from the Reformation to the Present* (New Jersey: Prentice-Hall, 1964).

14. David Barrett, "Germany," in *World Christian Encyclopedia,* 2nd ed. (New York: Oxford University Press, 2001), I:298–308.

15. Anglican Timeline, http://Justus.Anglican.org/resources/timeline.

16. The Presbyterian Church USA, http://www.pcusa.org.

17. Walker, et al., *A History of the Christian Church,* pp. 498, 546, 577; and the Reformed Church of America, http://www.rca.org.

18. United Methodist Church, http://www.umc.org.

19. Walker, et al., *A History of the Christian Church,* pp. 546–47.

20. United Church of Christ, http://www.ucc.org.

21. Presbyterian Church USA, http://www.pcusa.org; and the Church of Scotland, http://www.churchofscotland.org.uk.

22. Reformed Church of America, http://www.rca.org; the Protestant Reformed Church of America, http://www.prca.org/prc.html; and the World Alliance of Reformed Churches, http://www.warc.ch.

23. American Baptist Churches USA, http://www.abc-usa.org; and the Southern Baptist Convention, http://www.sbc.org.

24. Mennonite Church USA, http://www.mennoniteusa.org; and the Mennonite Central Committee, http://www.mcc.org.

25. *Pictorial Guide to the Quaker Tapestry,* Friends Meeting House, stramongate, Kendal, Cambria LA94BN, England, 1998.

26. Steven Nolt, *A History of the Amish* (Intercourse, PA: Good Books, 1992).

27. Anne Pinn and Anthony Pinn, *Fortress Introduction to Black Church History* (Minneapolis: Fortress Press, 2002); James Cone, *Black Theology and Black Power* (New York: Seabury Press, 1969); Lucas Johnson, "Black Baptists Hope to Tackle Social Issues with Unified Voice," *Ithaca Journal/Associated Press*, 28 August 2004, B4. Delores Williams, *Sisters in the Wilderness: The Challenge of Womanist God Talk* (Maryknoll, NY: Orbis Books, 1993). AICs are explained at African Christianity, http://cas.bethel.edu/cas.bethel. edu/%7ELetnie/AfricanChristianity/SSAAICs.htm; and African American Publications, http://www.africanpubs.com/Apps/bios.

4

PRACTICE WORLDWIDE

Christianity developed various practices, from worship to youth groups, both formal and informal. At the formal end of the continuum are the structured liturgies of "episcopal" churches with bishops, a strong priesthood, and a fairly uniform liturgy worldwide, such as the Catholic Church. At the informal end are the many Protestant traditions of strong local "congregational" church autonomy and minimal formal leadership, such as the Quakers. This chapter explores these developments and gives statistics. Traditional practices, such as worship, monasticism, celibacy, and mysticism, will be discussed. Current practices and issues, such as the major conservative—liberal dichotomy, are reported as well. The new development of worldwide regional churches resulting from missionary work, and immigration, notably the massive expansion of Christian churches in Latin America, Africa, and Asia, are also overviewed.

Many churches strive to develop strong youth group programs, such as weekly meetings for lessons, recreation, and charitable activities. Youth groups typically organize fund-raising events such as luncheons after church to help pay for trips to sing as a choir or do charitable work, such as renovating old churches and schools in impoverished regions in their nations or abroad. Retreat centers are supported by most denominations for individuals or groups to focus on spiritual growth. Private schools and colleges are supported by larger denominations. Seminaries to train clergy are supported by specific denominations, and a few seminaries are interdenominational.

Church choirs vary with the size of the church, from a small group of Orthodox cantors or chanters, to a large Protestant gospel choir, a Catholic youth choir, and children's choirs. Special music may include orchestral presentations, bell choirs, or folk music. Anglican schools usually support a formally trained choir (or "quire"). Many recordings of choir, instrumental, or solo church music are available. Women's and men's groups frequently organize to support their concerns. Women's groups may welcome baptized babies into their local church with a hand-knitted blanket, or organize food, blanket, and emergency supply collections. Men's groups may organize building and renovation projects, or educational programs for disadvantaged youth.

STATISTICS

The Christian Church is the largest church in the world. Christians number 2 billion, about 33 percent of the world's approximately 6 billion people. According to a United Nations survey, in 2002, Europe had the most Christians—about 559 million, which is about 27 percent of the world's Christians. In Latin America, about 492 million are Christians (24 percent); in Africa, about 376 million (18 percent); in Asia, about 323 million (16 percent); in North America, about 263 million (13 percent), and in Oceania, about 26 million (1 percent). For the number of Christian affiliated with specific churches worldwide, the Orthodox make up about 12 percent, the Protestants about 29 percent, and the Roman Catholics about 59 percent. There are about 37,000 various denominations worldwide, 3,663,000 congregations, 25,000 service agencies, 4,200 Christian radio or television stations, and Bibles translated into about 2,800 different languages. Not counted are some believers unaffiliated with churches or in marginal groups with variant beliefs, such as the Christian Scientists or Mormons. Church memberships anywhere are fluid, difficult to collect, and come from different sources, so numbers may vary in different surveys and in various years.[1]

The nations with the highest percentage of Christian populations in 2000 were Italy: 47,690,000 (98 percent), France: 44,150,000 (98 percent), Mexico: 95,169,000 (96 percent of the total population), Brazil: 139,000,000 (93 percent), Philippines: 63,470,000 (93 percent), United Kingdom: 51,060,000 (88 percent), The United States: 224,457,000 (85 percent), Germany: 67,000,000 (83 percent), Russia: 80,000,000 (60 percent), Nigeria:

38,180,000 (45 percent). China's large number of Christians is a small percentage of its population: 70,000,000 (5.7 percent).[2]

The diverse Christian churches in the United States in 2003 with the most membership (more than 1 million) were Catholic (65,270,000), Southern Baptist Convention (16,052,920), United Methodist (8,298,145), Church of God in Christ (5,499,875), Evangelical Lutheran Church in America (5,099,877), National Baptist Convention, USA (5,000,000), National Baptist Convention of America (3,500,000), Presbyterian Church USA (3,455,952), Assemblies of God (2,627,029), Lutheran Church—Missouri Synod (2,540,045), African Methodist Episcopal Church (2,500,000), National Missionary Baptist Convention of America (2,500,000), Progressive National Baptist Convention (2,500,000), Episcopal Church USA (2,333,327), Churches of Christ (1,500,000), Greek Orthodox Diocese of America (1,500,000), Pentecostal Assemblies of the World (1,500,000), African Methodist Episcopal Zion (1,447,934), American Baptist Churches of the USA (1,442,824), United Church of Christ (1,359,105), Baptist Bible Fellowship International (1,200,000), Christian Churches and Churches of Christ (1,071,616), and The Orthodox Church in America (1,000,000).[3]

CHURCH ORGANIZATIONS

Interdenominational Councils are umbrella organizations promoting cooperation between various branches of the church. The World Council of Churches, founded in 1948 and centered in Geneva, Switzerland, is the world's most inclusive ecumenical organization seeking Christian unity. Its members include more than 340 church denominations in more than 100 countries, representing 400 million Christians—Protestant, Anglican, and Orthodox. World Council of Churches charitable activities include efforts to combat racism, oppose violence, and promote human rights under dictatorships. Founded in 1950, the U.S. National Council of Churches is the major organization facilitating ecumenical cooperation among Christians in the United States. It includes 36 Protestant, Anglican, and Orthodox member denominations and about 50 million people in more than 100,000 local churches. The World Evangelical Alliance organizes 200 million evangelicals in 123 countries. In 2004, a New Ecumenical group, "Christian Churches Together in the U.S.A.," brought together an unprecedented combination of Roman Catholic, Orthodox, evangelical, and Protestant churches.[4] The largest interfaith organization is the global Parliament of

World Religions, which met first in 1893 in Chicago and most recently in 2004 in Barcelona.[5]

Christian churches organize on a spectrum of principles. At one end is the strong Catholic hierarchy, in which three factors establish uniform doctrines and practices for all Catholics: the Pope's official word, scripture, and tradition. Cardinals and archbishops supervise Catholic bishops, who have a strong authority over regional dioceses, placing priests in local parishes, and managing finances. The Anglican/Episcopal churches and some other Protestants have archbishops and bishops with less authority.

The Eastern Orthodox Church is moderately hierarchical, for each regional unit is autonomous. Councils, archbishops, metropolitans, patriarchs, and bishops guide the Orthodox Church, with the Patriarch of Constantinople having a special place of honor.

Among Protestants, the Church of England is supervised by and supported by the King or Queen, Parliament, the Archbishop of Canterbury, and regional archbishops and bishops. Globally, Anglican Churches, such as the U.S. Episcopal Church, have various structures, according to local laws, but within are organized by archbishops and bishops. Methodists have bishops and district superintendents. Calvinist Presbyterians have regional Presbyteries and larger Synods with more democratic-elected structures. Calvinist Congregationalists (such as the United Church of Christ) are strongly democratic and communal in structure. At the most democratic extreme, Protestant Free Church "congregationalism" in many denominations allows for the autonomy and independence of each local church to call clergy and manage finances. Regional denominational conventions, synods, or fellowships form umbrella support groups that may cooperate on doctrinal statements or programs such as ordaining clergy and sending charitable missions.

SUNDAY WORSHIP

All Christian churches worship on Sundays. Much of Christian worship was modeled on early Jewish synagogue ritual: psalms, prayers, music, scripture reading, and a sermon or homily. Sunday morning is the traditional time of Jesus's resurrection. So "Eucharist," also called "Communion" or the "Lord's Supper," is central and is celebrated daily, weekly, monthly, quarterly, or less often, according to the branch of the church.

Many traditional church buildings have bells in steeples. They may be rung to call believers to worship on Sunday morning, to mark the high point of the Sunday worship when the wine and bread are presented, or to call the community's attention to an important situation.

The Orthodox service is called "Divine Liturgy," the Roman Catholic service is called "Mass," and the Protestant service is usually called "Sunday worship." Christian services vary greatly in style. "High church" formal Orthodox Liturgy worship is structured, following a written text, with elaborate priestly robes, chanting, iconic art, and incense.

More informal Protestant churches worship with less prescribed liturgical structure, less church ornament, more congregational singing, and a longer sermon. Anglican churches are closest to Roman Catholic in style, but with less art, such as statues of Mary and saints. Calvinist-influenced churches have churches rather bare of art, stressing instead simplicity and the Word—Bible and sermon. Pentecostal churches worship with spontaneous emotional expressions of praise and joy, such as clapping with songs. Most Quakers have minimal church art and music and no regular order of service, and they sit in reverent, meditative silence until someone is moved by the Spirit to speak. Around the year 2000, many Christian congregations spontaneously moved into an informal style of dress during services. Although Orthodox and Catholic services are fairly prescribed and uniform, there is some room for variety, especially on holidays. Structured, formal, Roman Catholic Mass now includes more women assisting priests, or even leading Mass if a priest is not available and had blessed the sacraments beforehand.

EUROPE AND NORTH AMERICA

Eastern Orthodox Church

The Orthodox Church worldwide is comprised of about 217,522,000 members, mostly in Europe; this is about 12 percent of affiliated Christians and 3.5 percent of the world's population. In Europe there are about 158,648,000 members, in Africa about 36,790,000, in Asia 14,326,000, in North America about 6,458,000, in Latin America, about 571,000, and in Oceana about 230,000.[6]

Sunday Worship: Divine Liturgy

Orthodox worship is seen as the manifestation of God's presence and action in the midst of God's people and the congregation's response of

Greek Orthodox deacon and priest carrying the liturgical containers for Eucharist bread and wine at St. Catherine Greek Orthodox Church, Ithaca, New York. Courtesy of the author.

thanksgiving for God's presence and saving actions. Four types of worship are practiced: the Eucharist or Divine Liturgy, the seven sacraments, special services and blessings, and Daily Offices—public prayers throughout the day.

Orthodox services are always sung or chanted. They are long, solemn, and elaborate. They focus on belief in the resurrection of Christ and the deification of humanity. As in many Christian churches, the "antiphon" is frequently part of the liturgy—short verses said or sung in response to other phrases by the leader or choir (such as: Priest: "In peace let us again pray to the Lord." People: "Lord, have mercy."). Prayers, recitation of creeds, scripture readings, and processions are common. There is a prescribed order to maintain collective consistency and continuity with the past. The Divine Liturgy may be celebrated each day. Priests or a bishop must lead the service, but the active participation of the congregation is required. The congregation frequently stands, kneels at solemn moments, sometimes sings hymns, concludes prayers saying "Amen," bows, makes the sign of the cross, and receives Communion. Originally in Greek, early services were adapted to the vernacular language of local regions.

Orthodox believers typically enter a church, bow, kiss an icon, light a candle, cross themselves on the forehead, shoulders, and chest, and stand or sit while a choir is chanting. Priests wear elaborate robed liturgical vestments and hats. Orthodox altars have a "sanctuary light," a continually burning lamp. The Orthodox altar is placed behind a screen of icons called the "iconostasis." A central doorway called the "Royal Door" is just in front of the altar. Only the priests and attendants go behind the iconostasis to the altar area.

An icon is a uniquely Orthodox painting of Jesus, Mary, John the Baptist, and other biblical or church leaders. Icons are seen not simply as the work of human hands, but as liturgical creations, mystical manifestations of heavenly archetypes, sacred windows to heaven. Greatly revered by the faithful, icons are painted by monks in a medieval style.

In preparation for liturgy, the priest prays, then puts on his vestments—an ornate robe decorated with crosses (brocaded silk, in Byzantine times), a stole over both shoulders, and over it a chasuble, like a cape. A bishop also wears a crown-like mitre and carries a crozier or staff.

The Divine Liturgy of St. John Chrysostom is the traditional Orthodox service read from the liturgy book. It includes the Nicene Creed (an early basic statement of faith—see Chapter 2) and readings from the Bible, with specific texts added for each holy day. (The annual calendar includes many special holy days.) Ushers hand out a bulletin program with calendars, announcements, and reminders of church etiquette. (Orthodox ask worshipers to not enter or leave during the Gospel reading or "Lord's Prayer"). A choir leads chants before and during the service, often in response to the priest's readings. Commonly the liturgy begin with a procession from the back of the church with priests and altar boys or "acolytes" who assist the priests carrying candles or candle lighters, the Bible or Gospels, and perhaps incense in a container called the "censor."

The Divine Liturgy begins with a Service of Preparation, followed by a Liturgy of the Catechumens (for those still being educated in the faith), and then the Liturgy of the Faithful. The priest offers prayers for the gifts of life and the Church, with congregational responses such as "Lord have mercy" (kyrie eleison). Then the Liturgy of the Faithful begins with the Great Entrance—the priest carrying the bread and wine through the congregation up to the altar table. Then the faithful are invited to pass the kiss of peace or shake hands. Then they recite the Orthodox Nicene Creed. The Communion begins with the priest focusing attention on the holiness of the moment and saying: "Let us lift up our hearts," to which the people respond: "We lift them up to the Lord." The Eucharist begins with the priest holding up the leavened bread, saying "Take, eat, this is my Body which is broken for you for the forgiveness of sins," and likewise for the wine. The priest asks God to send down the Holy Spirit to make the bread and wine into the body and blood of Christ.

After more prayers, including the "Lord's Prayer," the priest adds water to the wine. Those who are baptized, chrismated (ritually crossed on the forehead with perfumed oil), and practicing members of the Orthodox Church say prayers of preparation clarifying the meaning of Communion. Adult Orthodox Church members are not supposed to take Communion unless they have undertaken a recent serious effort at prayer, repentance, forgiveness of others, confession, and fasting. The priest partakes of the bread and wine at the altar, then comes out the Royal Door and administers the Eucharist to the believers who have come forward to receive the Eucharistic bread and wine. The wine is administered with a spoon. The congregation sings a hymn during this time. Afterward, the priest blesses all, who give thanks, and are dismissed with a Benediction. Then the congregation may come forward to receive from a bowl remaining cubes of the leavened bread that were not used in Communion. A coffee time or meal is usually offered after the service for socializing.[7]

Children may sit with their families for the entire liturgy, or leave part way through to go to a separate room for Sunday school lessons in the faith, or may spend the entire service in Sunday school. Infants are left in the care of a nursery for the entire liturgy. If language lessons are taught during the week among immigrants, such as Greek or Russian, the children may wear national costumes for special days and, after church in the social hall, recite passages they have learned.

The Liturgy of St. Basil is celebrated 10 times a year, such as on Christmas Eve. The liturgy is written in books in the pews. Typically Greek, Old (Slavonic) Russian, or a region's traditional liturgical language is on the left page, and English or the local modern language is on the right page. Congregational singing is secondary to liturgical chanting. Crossing one's legs, going in or out during important moments, or talking during the service are considered disrespectful, and modest dress is expected.

Orthodox liturgical music is primarily the ancient Byzantine form of chanted psalms sung in simple antiphon form, in response to the priest's words. Hymns using biblical passages and more harmony were developed in medieval times, influenced by monastery choirs. Some large churches supported larger choirs. In a large church in Athens two choirs may face each other and sing responsively. In Russia, the "St. Petersburg" style of singing was developed in the nineteenth century, with its sonorous harmonies. Perhaps the greatest music for the Russian Orthodox Liturgy was composed in 1878 by Tchaikovsky. His "Liturgy of St. John Chrysostom" is a powerfully moving blend of the priest's deep, bass chant with the choir's higher-pitched harmonies.

Church Organization

The organization of the Eastern Orthodox Church is mildly hierarchical. Fairly independent churches elect regional bishops and other leaders and are governed by councils, or synods, of bishops. They do not accept the authority of Rome's Pope, but today there are cordial relations between the Catholics and Orthodox. The international church today is a federation of patriarchal, autocephalous (self-directed), and autonomous (independent) churches. Each church is independent in customs and organization but all share the same faith and order. "White" priests, in charge of a parish, are first deacons and marry before becoming priests. A deacon is an assistant to a priest, ranking just below the priest. "Black" priests are unmarried, monastic priests, eligible to become bishops. Orthodox priests retain the Byzantine custom of wearing a beard.

The Church has always held monastics in high esteem. They are the primary painters of icons. The famous monasteries on Mt. Athos in northeastern Greece house about 1,000 monks, who take vows of celibacy, obedience, and poverty. Monasteries across Russia have cultivated education, the arts, and charity. On gender issues, Orthodox Christians oppose the ordination of women as liturgical clergy. While the Orthodox Church in America did not support an Equal Rights Amendment, they did agree that no law should deny rights to anyone because of sex. Women are now being educated in Orthodox seminaries. Some favor inclusive, nongendered language in liturgy. Strengthening the roles of deaconesses is being discussed. The Church opposes same-sex unions.[8]

Nationalism

Ethnic distinctiveness, such as the Russian and Greek cultures, is strong in Orthodox Churches, although it appears in other Christian churches as well—Italian, Spanish, and French Catholics, German Lutherans, Scottish Presbyterians, and the Church of England. The Russian branch is the largest Orthodox Church, claiming 80 million members (about 60 percent of Russia's population). Like other religions, Orthodoxy at times has spread because entire kingdoms were baptized by rulers who adopted the faith, as with Russia's Vladimir in 988 CE. Nationalism may have a very compelling rationale. In Greece, for example, during the period when the Muslim Ottoman Turks conquered and controlled Greece (1453–1832), Orthodox Church priests were often leaders of the underground efforts to preserve Greek culture and language by teaching Greek to children in secret. When Greece regained its independence, the people were grateful and further identified the church with their nationality. Yet some have criticized religious nationalism in all branches of Christianity for drawing attention away from Christ and for being a distortion or contradiction to true Christianity. In some nations closely identified with a particular church, religion is for many more a matter of national history and identity than a motive for frequent church attendance. Conversely, in the United States, mixed marriages and converts have made many Orthodox congregations more ethnically diverse.

Orthodox Charities

Among the world's numerous charities, religious and secular, the International Orthodox Christian Charities, founded in 1992, with headquarters in Baltimore, is a leading international charity. Its mission is to assist the poor, both in emergencies and with long-term needs, to foster public awareness of problems, and to develop local leadership. International Orthodox Christian Charities does not support church programs but purely humanitarian needs. Its major programs include community development, refugee assistance, youth development, business development, agriculture and food programs, disaster relief, education, social welfare, and shelter construction. Orthodox Churches also support local and regional charities such as food banks.

Roman Catholic Church

A typical Catholic church is a version of the Gothic style of church architecture common in Europe that began in France around 1200 CE, or later in Spain and Italy. Often three front doors enter into a "narthex," or entry hall, where people may hang coats, gather information booklets, and receive a bulletin program from an usher. Doors then enter into the main hall full of seating, called the "nave." Up front is the raised platform ("chancel") commonly with an altar close to the congregation, a lectern or two for reading, and candles. Older churches may have railings or high gates in front of or around altars. Churches usually have high ceilings, often with decorative art, such as timber posts and beams, arches, or paintings, to express the search for transcendence. A parish hall for meals and social events is often in the basement or an adjacent building.

Roman Catholic Worship: Mass

Mass is the Catholic name for the central liturgy of worship. Mass may be daily, always includes Eucharist, and follows traditional texts, with biblical readings and traditional prayers. Priests wear elaborate, colorful robed vestments. Crossing oneself is part of the service at certain times, such as upon entry. Kneeling (genuflecting) is also a respectful traditional gesture when in front of the altar, even at the back of the church.

At the beginning of Mass, worshippers gather quietly in the pews or chairs and may pray, and the priest may prepare the front area, where the altars and lecterns are. Modest, respectful dress is expected, and, in St. Peter's in Rome, this is strictly enforced. Crossing oneself means moving one's hands in a cross shape over one's chest. First one places the fingers of the right hand over the forehead, then down to the center of the chest, then to a shoulder, then to the opposite shoulder, then perhaps down over the abdomen, then back to the center of the chest, or to the lips. This may be done

Medieval Roman Catholic Cathedral of Notre Dame in Paris.
© Getty Images.

several times during the service, often following the priest. People also do it as a mark of spiritual attention on their own, as when facing a statue of a saint, or praying privately.

The guide to the order of a Mass is in a book called the "Missal" that is stored in a bookrack in front of each pew (on the back of the pew in front of it), along with the songbook or hymnal. Those not familiar with a Mass might want to first get acquainted with the Missal's organization, which is by dates, and find the current day's "Order of Mass," which follows the particular Sunday's special prayers.

An organist may play a preliminary song, and then musicians will play and sing an entrance song to accompany the processional. The choir may be up front or in a rear balcony. The processional is the ritual entry of the priest behind the acolytes and other liturgical participants, who carry images such as a tall cross, candles, and a Gospel book. On holidays or in large churches and cathedrals this processional may be grand, with echoing chanting and incense. Incense is a fragrant smoke coming from a "censor," or container carried or swung to distribute the incense. This is an ancient tradition originally intended to cleanse the church with smells offensive to evil spirits. The priest(s) wear robes of a color indicating the season of the church year. Green, for example, is the Catholic liturgical color of "Ordinary time," which is the time between the holiday seasons around Christmas and Easter (see Ch. 5, Rituals and Holidays). The same color may appear in banners and other decorations. The congregation stands for certain events, such as the processional, and kneels for others, such as prayers. A prayer kneeling bench may fold or slide out as one needs it from beneath the pew in front of one's seat.

Candles are placed in brass candleholders and may be lit before the processional or afterward by acolytes. One large, tall, decorated candle for is a "Paschal" (Easter) candle. A "high" altar farther from the congregation behind the front altar in the "apse" supports the "tabernacle," a small cabinet where the bread and wine of communion are traditionally stored. In cathedrals, the high altar is commonly far more decorated with fine art than the front altar. Before 1965, most priests stood at the high altar only and faced with their back to the congregation, as an intermediary between them and God. Now the front altar serves to let the priest face the people and join with them in welcoming the divine presence, while the high altar is more symbolic. Flowers are usually placed up front, perhaps poinsettias for Christmas and lilies for Easter.

One lectern is commonly used for reading the Bible, and another for the priest to give the "homily" or sermon message. The priest begins the Mass with a prayer, typically an "antiphon," which means a liturgical form in which the leader recites a short saying, and the congregation responds with a second saying, such as: Priest: "The Lord be with you." "Response: "And also with you." After biblical readings or prayers, the congregation may also sing a short antiphon.

Roman Catholics divide the Mass into the Liturgy of the Word and of the Eucharist. Congregational members usually read passages from the Old Testament and New Testament at a lectern, which are followed by an antiphon, longer song, Psalm, or "Alleluia." The priest's homily then interprets the biblical text's meaning for contemporary times. For example, the New Testament passage "You are the Light of the World" may be interpreted to be a call for social justice. Then a profession of faith follows, in which the congregation, led by the priest, recites creeds, usually the Nicene Creed ("We believe in one God") and the Apostles' Creed ("I believe in God, the Father almighty.") (See also chapter 2, Texts and Major Tenets.) These are followed by prayers and antiphons. The voluntary financial collection is taken at some time by ushers who extend a basket on a long handle to people in each pew. Donations are all collected in the back of the church and taken forward to the altar. Special offerings may also be requested, such as disaster relief funds.

The Liturgy of the Eucharist (Communion or Lord's Supper with the bread and wine) follows, which is the high point of the Mass. Only Roman Catholics who have celebrated the sacrament of Reconciliation (including Confession and Repentance) at least once in the past year are supposed to partake of the Eucharist. Non-Christians and non-Catholics are welcomed to the Mass (but not the Eucharist) in a note in the Missal and encouraged to pray for peace and unity during the Eucharist. This begins with the preparation of the gifts of bread and wine being carried from the congregation up front to the front altar, where the priest, altar boys and girls, and Eucharistic ministers (men and women) or deacons (men) prepare the communion elements. The priest washes his hands before Eucharist. The altar boys and girls take the Gospel, the cups, and the wine and bread to the altar, where the priest mixes the wine with a little water, signifying Jesus's blend of the divine with humanity. Eucharistic prayers give thanks and consecrate the elements, ritually bringing Christ's body and blood into the bread and wine, with the people praying in responses (such as: "Dying you destroyed our death") and singing brief prayers (such as: "Holy, Holy, Holy"). After the elevation of the "host" or circular wafer of compressed unleavened bread and the chalice of wine, the priest partakes, then serves those assisting him. Catholics then walk forward in lines to those serving Eucharist. If a priest is not available, another qualified celebrant may serve Eucharist using wine and host elements blessed ahead of time by a priest.

The priest or Eucharistic minister places a special circular wafer of pressed wheat bread on the believer's outstretched hands, then holds a cup of wine for then to drink a sip. The server then wipes off the edge of the cup for sanitation. Sometimes people instead take the bread and dip it in the wine (intinction). Most people respond by saying "Amen" and crossing themselves. Sometimes an altar rail is up front where some recipients may kneel. Other times people stand while receiving. For Catholics, the Eucharist takes away sins, unifies the mystical body of the Church, commits believers to serving the poor, and is a pledge of the glory to come in the heavenly kingdom. Following the Eucharist is a Eucharistic prayer, with antiphons and songs, commonly including the saying "Christ has died, Christ has risen, Christ will come again." The people sing hymns such as the "Lord's Prayer," perhaps holding hands. At various times the people extend the "Peace" voluntarily with a handshake, hug, or kiss, according to local custom and your relationships with the people nearby. This is an ancient Christian custom. After a hymn, the priest or Eucharistic minister concludes with a blessing and dismissal. The priest and other celebrants may recess (reversing the processional) out the central aisle to the entrance, where the priest typically greets people. Sometimes a coffee hour afterward provides a friendly time of conversation and visiting.

Catholics believe in "transubstantiation," the doctrine that the invisible substance of the bread and wine are transformed into Christ's body and blood. Since Christ is believed to be present in both bread and wine, so the Council of Trent (1545–1563) ruled that it was unnecessary to receive both bread and wine. So, for many years the laity received only the bread, and the priests partook of both. Communion with both bread and wine for all has recently been reintroduced, and Vatican II taught that the presence of Christ is also in the minister, the congregation, and the biblical Word, perceived through faith. Vatican II also insisted that the faithful participate not merely through the priest, but along with him. Special masses may be held for a marriage, for the sick, or for many other reasons, such as holidays, meetings, or for the unity of Christians.

Roman Catholic altar with devotional candles. © Getty Images/32245.

The rosary is a private ritual practice of prayer using a circular string of beads for counting prayers. Usually a personal devotional, some people may join in groups to say the rosary together. Rosary prayers include the "Hail Mary," "Our Father," and other prayers, in various numbers of repetitions. The sacrament of Confession, now called Reconciliation, can take place in anonymity in a "confessional" booth, or face-to-face with the priest instead, if they prefer. If the priest were to reveal information from a person's confession, even in court, he could be excommunicated, or expelled from the church.

Early church music was predominantly chants. During the Renaissance, Giovanni Palestrina (1525–1594) was a noted composer in Rome who wrote masses with more elaborate variety and combination of several voice parts. During the eighteenth century, Catholic choirs began to sing elaborate polyphonic Latin versions of the Eucharistic prayers, such as *Kyrie* (Lord have mercy), and *Agnus Dei* (Lamb of God). Today hymns led by a Catholic choir supplement traditional brief songs amid the priest's words. To traditional Christian hymns, many from Psalms, have been added Catholic hymns in Latin, such as "Ave Maria," the "Irish Blessing," St. Francis' "All Creatures", and perhaps Protestant hymns by Martin Luther ("A Mighty Fortress is our God"), John Wesley ("Love Divine, All Loves Excelling"), or African-Americans ("There is a Balm in Gilead").

Sunday school is not a major part of most Catholic churches, as Catholic schools are an important part of Catholicism, and this is where most religious education takes place. Depending on the size of the town, Catholic schools may serve elementary levels, or go up through high school. School children may make posters of stories, prayers, or book reports. So children, if they go, sit through the entire Mass.

Missionaries have always been a strong part of Christian practice since Paul traveled around the Eastern Mediterranean right after Jesus's death. Catholic missionaries, since Patrick and Boniface in the Middle Ages, have long spread the Gospel. Catholic missionaries have spread the faith to Latin and South America, the Philippines, China, and Africa. In 1908, for example, Catholic missions were very active in China, reporting men and women missionaries in more than 18,000 stations, 6,000 churches, 4,000 schools, 140,000 students, and 180,000 baptisms.[9] Today missions are fewer in number. In 2003, missionaries from the United States numbered about 6,500. The largest category is still women—religious sisters—numbering more than 2,800 worldwide.[10]

Catholic churches often organize carnivals to raise funds for schools and

Roman Catholic Pope John Paul II. Courtesy of Photofest.

other programs. Parades on holidays may contain bands and floats displaying saints where people can donate cash. Psychological counseling may be offered by volunteers trained in basic counseling on issues such as job loss, divorce, abortion, disability, self-esteem, financial setbacks, aging, faith issues, and hospital and nursing home visitations by groups such as the "Steven Ministry." Youth groups meet weekly and undertake projects such as learning emergency medical procedures. Retreats to camps offer times for prayer, learning, faith sharing, and fun. Youth group trips commonly undertake social service activities such as building a house for Habitat for Humanity. Bible study is not a common part of Catholic practices, as it is for Protestants.

Church Organization

The Roman Catholic Church is the most structured and hierarchical Christian Church. The Pope in Rome, whose residence and offices are at the Vatican, is the highest authority. Cardinals advise him and supervise archbishops, who supervise bishops, who supervise a diocese, which includes numerous parishes, their priests and monastic monks and nuns, colleges, and schools. The priests, monks, and nuns are organized by orders such as the Benedictines, Dominicans, Franciscans, Jesuits, Augustinians, Paulists, Society of Mary, or Maryknoll Sisters. Lay organizations include groups such as the Catholic Daughters of America, Knights of Columbus, and Opus Dei. Various social services sponsor hospitals, colleges, schools, or orphanages.

Today the community of believers in a church has more priestly duties. There is, however, a shortage of priests, so some serve more than one parish, and Eucharistic ministers, including women, assist more with liturgical, pastoral, and administrative duties. The Catholic priesthood continues to be restricted to men. All the faithful community of believers is a priesthood (similar to the Protestant belief in the priesthood of all believers), and the hierarchical ordained priesthood serves the community. The sacrament of priesthood is indelible and not temporary. Outside the mass, Catholic priests usually wear black clothes with a clerical collar, although some post-Vatican II priests wear regular clothing. Deacons were formerly on the path to priesthood, but Vatican II changed the diaconate to be a permanent Holy Order. They assist the bishops and priests in Mass, distributing communion, they assist in marriages and preaching, they preside at funerals, and they lead charity missions.

The Pope

The Pope or "Supreme Pontiff" (Latin: *pontifex*, priest, bridge-builder) is the Bishop of Rome and highest authority of the Roman Catholic Church worldwide. The College of Cardinals selects him for a lifelong term. The authority of the Pope is based on the tradition of holding the "key" to paradise passed down from Jesus to St. Peter and his successor Popes. This is now seen by some as more a spiritual than a historical tradition. The Vatican is an independent state of 108 acres founded in 1929, with the Pope's residence, offices of the "Curia" or church governing bodies, a large museum, the Sistine Chapel, and the large St. Peter's Church, which by tradition rests on the tombs of St. Peter and St. Paul. It is full of Renaissance and Baroque art. The Pope gives a unity to the Catholic Church that still embraces a wide diversity.

Monastics

Catholic monastics are active in both contemplative quiet and communal social service. Modern contemplative monks such as Thomas Merton (1915–1968) have been well known for their writings. Merton was a Trappist monk in Kentucky, author of *The Seven Storey Mountain* and numerous other inspiring books. Some Catholic nuns have been assassinated for their social activism in areas of conflict such as South America. Numerous sisters serve as teachers, nurses, and administrators of retreat centers and social service agencies.

Sexuality

The influence of mass education and modern contraceptives has brought discussion of sexuality out of the closet into public discourse, notably since the impact of the psychologist Sigmund Freud. Educated women who learn about contraception are far less likely to be surprised by unwanted pregnancies. This development has made celibacy a less urgent practice, and this has had an impact on the Catholic Church. Celibacy has the function of restraining sexual instincts to channel them into spirituality, as well as allowing a priest, monk, or nun to focus more on religion and less on family responsibilities. For potential priests it is inevitably contrasted with much of society's more open views of sexuality. This trend has meant a decline in the number of priests.

Most damaging have been the recent disclosures of priests sexually abusing children in their care in several countries. In a developing crisis for the church, more than 10,000 alleged victims of abuse since the 1950s have come forth to take the church to court. At least forty percent were boys between 10 and 14 years old when the abuse took place. Over 4,000 priests have been accused of abuse (about 4 percent of all Catholic priests), hundreds of priests have been reassigned or removed from duty, over $800 million has been paid to victims in several countries, and about 3 percent of the accused priests have been convicted of a crime. Numerous churches have been closed to save expenses, and a few dioceses have had to declare bankruptcy (such as in Portland, Oregon; Tucson, Arizona; and Spokane, Washington). Many others, from Boston, Massachusetts to Davenport, Iowa, are struggling with the problem and selling property to pay for lawsuits. Suits by Native Americans claiming Catholic boarding school abuse threaten the financial stability of some Canadian churches. The Diocese of St. George in Canada has gone bankrupt. The Diocese of Orange County, CA, paid $100 million to victims in 2005.[11]

Pope John Paul II called the sexual abuse of children an appalling sin in the eyes of God and said that there is "no place in the priesthood and religious life for those who would harm the young." He expressed concern for the victims, urged the most severe penalties for such aberrant crimes, and wanted to defend the good name of the overwhelming majority of priests loyal to the standards of their vocation. The U.S. Conference of Catholic Bishops has expressed profound sorrow for this abuse and developed procedures for removing the offending priests. The church has spent more than $20 million to prevent sex abuse, including police background checks on hundreds of thousands of priests and lay people working with children in Catholic schools and parishes.[12]

Since Pope John Paul II took office in 1978, the number of priests worldwide has decreased by 4 percent, but Catholic membership has increased by 40 percent. More than half the world's parishes do not have a resident priest. Increasingly many priests serve more than one parish, and lay members are taking on more pastoral duties. An estimated 125,000 priests worldwide have left the priesthood to marry, and there is widespread Catholic support for married priests, although most remaining priests express contentment with their celibate lives.[13]

By 2002, the priest shortage and child abuse scandals stimulated questions about the effectiveness of priestly celibacy. The Boston Diocese newspaper boldly asked whether the celibate priesthood attracts too many homosexual men. Priest-sociologist Andrew Greeley replied that celibacy was not the problem. Most (96 percent) of priests are not abusers, he said, and according to surveys, celibate priests are as satisfied as married men on issues such as intimacy, and that in a survey, only two percent of priests were considering leaving the priesthood.[14]

Catholic Charities

Caritas Internationalis is an international confederation of 162 Catholic relief, development, and social service organizations aiding the poor in more than 200 nations. One of the world's largest humanitarian networks, Caritas serves millions of needy people in times of emergency and ongoing urgent problems. Caritas strives to prepare local leaders for independent action. Catholic Relief Services in the United States was founded by the Catholic Bishops to relieve suffering, to promote economic and community development for all people, and to foster justice worldwide.

Catholic Charities is also a large U.S.-based relief agency whose goal is to reduce poverty, support families, and strengthen local communities. It provides social work, health care, and advocacy for the poor across the United States. More than 6 million people were assisted in 2003. It offers aid in the form of food, education, housing, health, counseling, disaster, pregnancy, and adoption services. Local Catholic Churches also support nonchurch charities such as Habitat for Humanity.

Exoteric Saints and Esoteric Mysticism

Religions include a continuum of exoteric and esoteric experiences. An "exoteric" aspect is the outward tradition practiced by most members. Highly exemplary believers may be considered saints. "Esoteric" or mystical experiences may come upon one who mysteriously feels the presence of the divine in moments of beauty, ecstasy, crisis, or pain. Near-death experiences, for example, often awaken a powerful, life-changing sense of the ever-present wonders of the mysterious source of existence and its guiding, healing force.[15] This kind of experience often awakens one to a realization called mysticism. The list of saints includes many mystics.

Mysticism describes a consciousness of what mystics call the ineffable divine mysteries behind all earthly existence and religious beliefs and practices. It can be cultivated and maintained by ritual practices of meditation, contemplation, isolation, monastic communal living, repeating prayers, chanting, fasting, and denial of earthly pleasures in order to allow God's presence to emerge. The mystics have long provided a re-energizing call to the authentic principles of the faith when the church becomes too worldly, theology too academic, or piety too external. Jesus did sometimes speak in mystical language, such as "I and the Father are one." Orthodox mystics include St. Sergius of Radonezh, Catholic mystics and saints include Bernadette of Lourdes, and Protestant mystics include George Fox, founder of the Society of Friends (Quakers).

Christian mystics offer not arguments about God but experiences and images of contemplative reflection. Mystics say they experience the loving presence of the unified ground of Being, the dazzling light of existence itself, before the subject/object split of ordinary consciousness, prior to the imagery of theistic pictures of gods. Five typical stages of mystical experience can be described as: Awakening, Purification, Illumination, Surrender, and Union.[16]

Pilgrimages and Shrines

A pilgrimage is a journey undertaken for a religious purpose, to go to a sacred spot such as a historical mountain, a healing fountain, a sacred shrine, or a cathedral. Often pilgrimages are undertaken by Catholic penitents seeking forgiveness and reconciliation with God. Sacred shrines mark holy places of historical or symbolic importance, and in the past, many held relics traditionally associated with martyrs or saints, such as a bone that supposedly survived from their body. Ancient and medieval pilgrimages and shrines were very popular, and some remain today. Perhaps the most important pilgrimage, difficult, expensive, and dangerous in medieval times, was the journey to Jerusalem. The faithful still go for Christmas or Easter, where processions around the city are led by priests and monks who, for example, follow the path of Jesus's *Via Dolorosa*, where he by tradition carried the cross. Or they may pass the flame to pilgrims' candles at the traditional site of Jesus's resurrection, the church of the Holy Sepulchre. There are pilgrimages to Rome to see its many historical churches, and St. Peter's in the Vatican has always been an important Christian pilgrimage.

Another major pilgrimage is the journey from Paris to the Cathedral of Santiago de Campostela in northwestern Spain. This arduous trip over the Pyrenees mountains follows a well-marked trail from ancient times. Pilgrims wear a symbolic cockle shell (symbolizing their seashore goal), carry a staff, and assemble at the grand cathedral, where a huge incense

"Our Lady of Guadalupe," painting of patron saint
of Mexico. Courtesy of the Art Archive/National
Palace, Mexico City/Dagli Orti.

censor is swung in a large arc inside. In France, at the foot of the Pyrenees
mountains, the village of Lourdes receives about 5 million pilgrims a year.
They come to witness the site of the vision in 1858 of a poor 14-year-old
girl, Bernadette Sourbirous. She said that she saw a vision of the Virgin
Mary in a cave. A fountain there now attracts many sick people who have
left numerous crutches behind when they left. Priests still serve mass to
the crowds.

In Mexico, Guadalupe is the most important place of pilgrimage, attracting 2 million pilgrims a year. Each year on December 12, thousands of
pilgrims arrive from all over Mexico to sing a birthday song *(las mañani-
tas)* to the Virgin, or Black Madonna, for her dark skin. She is the patron
saint of Latin America.

In Ireland, many penitents take the pilgrimage up the stony mountain
of Croagh Patrick on Reek Sunday, the last Sunday in July. This was the site
of St. Patrick's 40-day retreat to fast and pray for the Christianization of
Ireland in 441 CE, according to Irish tradition.

The most popular medieval English pilgrimage was along the Pilgrim's

Way from Winchester to Canterbury, to the shrine of England's most famous saint and martyr, St. Thomas Becket. He was an archbishop who was
brutally murdered in 1170 CE after a quarrel with King Henry II. Several
books have been written about pilgrimages, such as Geoffrey Chaucer's
colorful and bawdy *Canterbury Tales* (c. 1390), and John Bunyan's allegorical *Pilgrim's Progress* (1678), written during a 12-year imprisonment in
Bedford County Gaol.

Pilgrimages in England are not as frequent as during the Middle Ages
but are still undertaken by devoted travelers. Many trails are marked by
ancient wayside shrines and crosses.[17]

Protestant Churches

Lutheran Church

Lutheranism became the state church in northern Germany, Denmark,
Norway, and Sweden, before it spread worldwide. Today, few state churches
remain. In Germany freedom of religion was granted after World War II.
The churches in East Germany were restricted by the Communist regime,
which prohibited religious schools, but continued to receive state subsidies,
primarily for their charitable work. In West Germany in 1970, a 10 percent church tax deducted automatically by the government for registered
church members stimulated a decrease in membership. Although suppressed in East Germany since World War II, church membership began
to grow there after the fall of the Berlin Wall and the unification of Eastern
and Western Germany in 1990. In 1970 the Lutheran *Evangelische Kirche in
Deutschland* (Evangelical Church of Germany) reported 33,417,000 members, and in 1995, 29,205,000, 35.5 percent of the country.

Lutheran Worship   The Lutheran Sunday worship typically begins with
a musical and welcoming invocation, calling God's people to thanksgiving
and praise. As Luther stressed, the church is a singing church, so congregational singing plays an important part. Luther wrote hymns such as "A
Mighty Fortress is Our God." The minister leads a confession of sins and
proclaims absolution, or forgiveness. The introit of the day is the singing
of a psalm or hymn proclaiming the theme of the day. Next the service
of the Word offers readings from the Old and New Testament. The *Kyrie
Eleison* ("Lord, have mercy on us.") may follow, then hymns and the saluta-
tion, or greetings among the congregation and minister. The congregation

may sing a biblical verse before the next reading from the Gospel. The sermon follows, applying biblical lessons to contemporary life. Then typically the Nicene Creed is recited. Ushers collect the offering, and the minister prepares Communion at the altar, while the people sing a hymn of thanks. After the Lord's Prayer, the minister says the words of institution from the Bible said by Jesus at his Last supper, where Jesus broke the bread and said: "Take, eat, this is my body [and] this is my blood of the covenant, which is poured out for many for the forgiveness of sins."

Then those desiring Communion approach the rail before the altar, kneel, and receive the bread and wine with words from the minister and deacons such as "take, eat, for this is the true body of our Lord and Savior Jesus Christ." Communion is open to all Christians. The people return to their seats for a time of private prayer and sing a short canticle or a hymn. During a children's time, the young ones come forward and hear a talk by the minister. Lutherans typically share the Peace with kisses, hugs, or handshakes and sing hymns during communion. The minister blesses the people and dismisses them.[18]

Lutheran Organization   Today, Lutheran denominations worldwide vary from some branches with strong bishops to others with congregational rule. All base their doctrines on the confessional writings in the *Book of Concord.* Many are organized by nation, as with the Mexican Lutheran Church. Three major umbrella groups are: the Confessional Evangelical Lutheran Conference, which includes the Lutheran Confessional Church of Sweden; the International Lutheran Council, which includes the China Evangelical Lutheran Church; and the Lutheran World Federation, centered in Geneva, which reports a membership of 80 million in 150 member churches in 77 countries on every continent. The Lutheran World Relief is a global Lutheran service program devoted to charity and disaster work.[19]

Some European countries still support the Lutheran Church as the state church. Norway, Denmark, Finland, and Iceland support the Church with taxes. In Sweden the Lutheran Church was the state church up until 2000. Church attendance in industrialized northern Europe is small, but people still go to church for baptisms, confirmations, weddings, and funerals.

In the United States, there are more than 20 different Lutheran denominations, such as the conservative Lutheran Church—Missouri Synod (LCMS). Early immigrants, speaking in their native tongue, often German, in church, founded the LCMS in 1847 in St. Louis, which now has about 2,554,000 members in 6,150 churches. It emphasizes biblical doctrine and adherence to traditional Lutheran confessions. It insists on a literalist reading of all passages of scripture and does not ordain women.[20]

In the 1970s, the more liberal Evangelical Lutheran Church in America (ECLA) was founded, which now has about 5 million baptized members. It accepts the canonical Scriptures as the inspired Word of God and the authoritative source and norm of its faith, but it also welcomes modern historical-critical biblical scholarship that sees some passages as symbolic. Thus, the ECLA rejects a literal interpretation of biblical creation, agreeing that God may have used evolution in creation. There are about 17,700 ministers, of which about 2,700 are women, and around 500 are people of color, in 10,721 congregations, with about 5,126,000 members. Trustees and elders govern local churches. [21]

The Lutheran Church began many Protestant rituals that spread rapidly among new sixteenth-century Protestants. Uniformity of all church services was no longer deemed necessary, so Luther replaced Latin with German in worship, and now all Protestants use the vernacular, local language. Local Lutheran ministers are free to shape liturgies to some extent.

Anglican Church

The worldwide Anglican Communion, centered in Canterbury, England, includes the Church of England, the Scottish Episcopal Church, the Episcopal Church USA, and about 50 other branches in many nations. Other

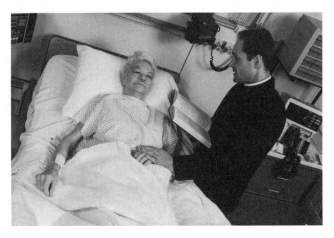

Hospital chaplain reading scripture to a patient. © Corbis/MME 0046E.

Anglican Schismatic or "continuing" Anglican churches not participating in the Anglican Communion include about 12 churches, such as the African Orthodox Church and the Free Church of England. It is the Protestant church closest to Catholicism, seen as the "middle way" between Catholics and Protestants.

The Anglican Church has a worldwide membership of about 81,663,000 members. Africa, has the most members—44,531,000 (17,500,000 in Nigeria), in Europe there are 26,619,000 (24,493,000 in Great Britain), in Oceana, 5,447,000, in North America, 3,217,000, in Latin America, 1,106,000, and in Asia, 742, 000. The Episcopal Church USA reports about 2,311,000 members in 7,359 churches.[22]

Anglicans retain many Catholic practices, except loyalty to Rome, priestly celibacy, devotion to Mary, and strong monasteries. It continues the tradition of strong bishops under the "established" honorary leadership of the Archbishop of Canterbury and a Book of Common Worship. English history has been a long tug-of-war between the highly elaborate style of rich liturgy and simplifying reactions such as the rejection of candles, organs, stained glass, monasteries, vestments, crucifixes, and kneeling to receive communion.

Anglican Worship   An Anglican procession usually begins the liturgy with the celebrants entering from the back of the church down the central aisle, carrying candles and a special Bible or Gospel. In cathedrals this may be a grand entrance, with echoing chanting, music, large candles, billowing incense, and elegantly robed bishops, priests and celebrants. Anglican Prayers are often called a "collect," a term from Latin meaning "prayer of the assembled congregation." Special collects include a "collect for peace." Like other formal churches, Anglicans often sing a "canticle" ("little song"), a song from the medieval church, such as *Te Deum* ("Thee, O God").

The Great Litany, always used on Sundays, includes responsive readings sung or said, such as "O God the Father, Creator of Heaven and Earth," response: "Have Mercy upon us." Special prayers or "Propers" are assigned to each special commemoration Sunday. Someone, perhaps a deacon, says special prayers honoring pastors, theologians, monastics, and those who have died. The ushers collect an offering of financial support. Special liturgies are prescribed for holy days, such as Easter.

A bishop or priest celebrates Eucharist with the aid of deacons and lay people who read and help distribute the sacraments. Various liturgical texts may be followed. Someone reads from the Bible, following the prescribed lectionary (assigned biblical texts to be read each Sunday). This includes a Psalm, an Old Testament reading, and two New Testament readings. Someone makes announcements about church events. The congregation recites a creed such as the Nicene Creed and then spread the Peace of the Lord by greetings, handshakes, hugs, or kisses.

The Holy Communion typically begins with the antiphon: Celebrant: "The Lord be with you." People: "And with thy spirit." Jesus is quoted, as in most all Christian communion services, saying: "Take, eat, this is my Body (or Blood), which is given (or shed) for you. Do this in remembrance of me." All recite the "Lord's Prayer." The celebrant breaks the consecrated bread and says: " O Lamb of God, that takest away the sins of the world, have mercy upon us." The bread and wine are administered with words such as "The Body (Blood) of our Lord Jesus Christ keep you in everlasting life." Recipients reply "Amen." The people are dismissed with a blessing to go in peace, and the Processional concludes with the celebrants walking down the aisle to the back of the church. The priest typically greets worshipers as they exit, and a friendly coffee hour might be offered afterward.

Anglican hymns often highlight Psalms, Gospels, canticles, and hymns carried over from the Catholic Church and its monasteries, often from Latin, such as *Kyrie Eleison* (Lord, have mercy), St. Francis ("All Creatures of our God"), or Mary's "Magnificat." Although Anglicans, like all Protestants, do not emphasize Mary. Many hymns were composed by Anglicans: John Donne ("Wilt Thou Forgive?"), or the Venerable Bede ("A Hymn of Glory Let us Sing"), and John Newton ("Amazing Grace"). George F. Handel's now-famous *Messiah*, written in London, was originally scorned by the Puritans because it was performed in a concert hall, not in a church, in 1742. It was first seen by reformers as an inappropriate use of biblical text in what was an otherwise secular form, the opera-like oratorio. But subsequently it has become a widely used, majestic work sung on Christmas and Easter. Anglican male choirs are traditional, such as in St. Paul's Cathedral in London, but less predominant, as women are welcomed into more choirs.

Anglican Organization The Archbishop of Canterbury now hosts a Lambreth Conference about every 10 years for Anglican bishops worldwide who discuss and advise on current issues. Today the Church of England is the only Anglican Church that is state-established. Parliament still controls its doctrine and liturgy, and the monarch is still the supreme earthly head of the Church. Each Anglican province is divided into dioceses, led by a bishop, elected by parish representatives. Bishops, priests, and lay members vote on major issues in synod meetings. Bishops, priests, and deacons are the three orders of the Anglican ministry.

In the 1970s, when the Episcopal Church USA ruled against ordaining women, a group of qualified American women deacons requested to be ordained, against much opposition. Three bishops ordained them in Philadelphia in 1974 in an "irregular" liturgy. Two years later, the Episcopal Church approved of the ordination of women, and by 1994, 145 women were ordained. By 2000, the Episcopal Church had about 15 percent women priests. In 1992, the Anglicans as a whole voted to ordain women as priests, and in 1994 at Bristol Cathedral, the first 32 women were ordained.[23]

When women's ordination began, some opposing Anglican priests transferred to the Catholic Church in protest and were accepted, along with their wives. Such "high church" Anglicans closest to Rome even reject the term "Protestant," and since 1838 are called the "Anglo-Catholics." In 2003, the worldwide Anglican Communion had a large number of members who opposed the Episcopal Church in the USA when the diocese of New Hampshire elected an openly gay bishop, Gene Robinson. This threatened a split.

Methodist Church

Today the United Methodist Church in the United States reports about 8 million members, in Nigeria, 2,100,000, in Korea, 1,512,000, and in South Africa, 1,451,000 members.[24]

Methodist Worship   Methodist Sunday worship services can be adjusted by the minister and congregation but typically follow this routine: a musical prelude, announcements, a greeting and opening prayer, a time for the congregation to greet each other, and perhaps a confession of sins. Congregational hymns are led by a choir at three or four points in the service, which may be followed by an antiphon, or responsive reading of a scripture passage in which the leader reads a passage and the congregation responds. This may be followed by a time for silent prayer, a pastoral prayer, the "Lord's Prayer" said by the congregation, and a children's message. Then come New Testament and Old Testament readings, the sermon, special music or a choir anthem, an offering, and a concluding benediction. Ministers may wear various robes and stoles for different church seasons, and ordinary clothing otherwise. Communion is served monthly, using grape

Protestant Sunday worship service, St. Paul's United Methodist Church, Ithaca, New York. Courtesy of George Gull.

juice in opposition to alcohol abuse. John Wesley was devoted to music for the common people, sung with sincere hearts. John's brother Charles Wesley wrote numerous hymns, such as "O God our Help in Ages Past."

Methodist Organization   Like the Free Churches, Methodists separated themselves from a state church, but did not separate themselves from society or reject war. Methodist churches are largely self-supporting and self-governing and became a major mainstream U.S. Protestant church. In 1980, the Methodist Marjorie S. Matthews was the first woman in a mainstream denomination to be elected a bishop. By 1992, eight women were elected Methodist bishops. The General Conference is a legislative body and the Council of Bishops resembles an Executive branch of the church.

Calvinist Churches

Calvinist worship today among the several branches of the three largest Calvinist churches—Congregationalist, Presbyterian, and Reformed—is fairly similar. On Sunday morning, after a musical prelude, a minister usually leads a call to worship, several hymns are sung throughout the service, and there may be a congregational confession of sin and assurance of forgiveness by the minister. Then the minister or another leader calls the children forward for a lesson, and then sends them out to their children's education classes. The congregation commonly recites the "Lord's Prayer," someone reads selections from the Old and New Testaments, and the choir sings an anthem or special instrumental music may be played. A sermon is given, usually by the minister but possibly by a deacon, a visiting minister, or a church member. Congregational churches may frequently welcome concerns and prayer requests from the congregation during a service. All may recite an affirmation of faith or creed and perhaps celebrate a baptism or communion. Many Calvinist churches serve grape juice instead of wine in opposition to alcoholism. The bread and cup may be distributed on trays throughout the congregation, or offered from a common plate and cup up front, often by intinction (dipping the bread in the wine, rather than drinking from a cup). Then after a hymn, the minister offers a closing benediction prayer.

Calvinist Organizations   The Calvinist churches are organized under the World Alliance of Reformed Churches, centered in Geneva, Switzerland, and is an international fellowship of about 218 churches in the Congregational, Presbyterian, Reformed, and United denominations in 100 countries with more than 75 million members.[25]

Presbyterian Church   Ministers and laypersons (Presbyters) active in local, regional, and national bodies lead the Presbyterian Church. Each local Presbyterian Church calls its own minister and is governed by an elected Session, which is under the care and oversight of a regional Presbytery, under the care and oversight of a larger Synod. The national General Assembly is composed of one-half ministers and one-half elected lay commissioners.

There are many Presbyterian churches internationally, such as the Presbyterian Church of Korea. The Presbyterian Church USA reports approximately 11,200 congregations, 21,000 ordained ministers, and 2,500,000 members. Most of Canada's Presbyterians merged with Congregationalists and Methodists to form the United Church of Canada, the largest denomination in Canada, which has about three million members and 3,677 congregations.[26]

Reformed Church   The name "Reformed" was originally a synonym for "Calvinist" as distinct from "Lutheran" and "Anabaptist." Internationally, there are about 20 various major Reformed denominations, such as the Dutch Reformed Church, and numerous minor branches. Today names and governance in the various Reformed churches vary, but one is illustrative.

In the Reformed Church in America, each congregation calls its ministers, who are installed by representatives of the larger church. Churches are governed by consistories and classes that exercise oversight of the congregations and ministers in their area. Classes have the authority to form and disband churches and license, ordain, and install ministers into congregations. The highest assembly of the church, the General Synod, assembled the classes into eight regional synods. The Reformed Church in America, with about 240 congregations, has about 300,000 members. The more conservative Protestant Reformed Church in America reports 27 churches and about 6,000 members.[27]

Congregational Church   In the Congregational Church, there is little higher authority than the local congregation's church meeting, but there are regional general assemblies, conventions, or federations to support local churches. In the U.S. United Church of Christ, a group of ministers from different churches assemble to ordain a new minister. In the Congregational Federation of England, each local church calls its own ministers and ordains them, but must seek the advice of the Federation before issuing a call. The Federation recommends a minimum salary to churches for their ministers. There are numerous variations of the Congregational church worldwide with many names. The largest branch, the United Church of Christ in the United States, reports 1,773,000 members.[28]

Free Churches

Baptists   Today Free Churches include the Baptist Church, because they reject infant baptism and insist on adult baptism. Baptists practice total immersion baptism, are active in missions, and see all believers as equal. Each church is autonomous, though affiliated with regional conventions. Baptists have blended Free Church with Calvinist beliefs and practices. Today many Baptist denominations with various names range from fundamentalist to liberal. Of the roughly 50 million Baptists today, 90 percent are American or British. In the United States, the large Southern Baptist Convention numbers about 21 million. The Nigerian Baptist Convention numbers 3,400,000.

Baptists represent the most mainstream of the Free Churches, worshiping in a style similar to many Protestant churches, in fairly plain churches. Ministers may lead a service without a robe and keep worship fairly simple.

A call to worship or confession of sins may or may not be used, although lots of congregational singing is. The ministers or members of the congregation read scripture, say prayers, give a sermon, and collect offering, and the choir sings before a concluding benediction prayer. Some Baptist churches are liberal and welcome new practices, such as women ministers, while others are traditional and retain old ways, such as male ministers. Some are restrained in worship, and some are more evangelical (seeking to convert others) and emotionally expressive. Baptist hymns include many gospel tunes, such as "Blessed Assurance," "The Old Rugged Cross," "I'll Fly Away," "Sweet By and By," "Just As I Am," and "When The Roll Is Called Up Yonder."

Holiness and Pentecostal   Some Free Churches, like the Holiness and pentecostal churches, emphasize the importance of "baptism" in the Holy Spirit, and celebrate this with "charismatic" clapping, singing, dancing, emotional outcries, speaking foreign tongues, hands-on healings, and "altar calls" where those who feel called go up front and kneel at the altar for prayer and perhaps conversion or being "born again." A typical pentecostal hymn is "Down by the Riverside." Like the Pietists, they criticize "lukewarm" believers, and they make other Christians seem rather restrained. Overall, it is estimated that there are more than 20 million pentecostals in the United States, and, in 2000, about 120 million worldwide. The United Pentecostal Church International is now a fast-growing denomination of about 2.3 million members worldwide, including about 600,000 members in their 3,764 North American churches. Attendance at movies, watching television, dancing, wearing jewelry, short hair for women, or long hair for men are not permitted.

There are a number of Holiness, pentecostal, and independent churches, and their general worship style is represented by the large Assemblies of God denomination. A Sunday service may well begin with a half hour of music stressing reception of the Holy Spirit. Traditional readings of the Bible and preaching are common, as well as testimonies of recent influences of the presence of God in one's life.

The large and growing pentecostal Assemblies of God denomination reports 51 million members worldwide. And it is growing; most members live outside the United States. In 2004, it claimed about 2.6 million worshipers in more than 12,000 churches across the United States. They practice two ordinances: baptism by immersion and the Lord's Supper. They reject gay marriage and emphasize aggressive evangelism and missionary work. The

U.S. General Council of the Assemblies of God approves of the ordination of women. The pentecostal revival has spilled over into almost every denomination with the spirit of charismatic renewal.

The Pentecostal World Fellowship is a global communion of many pentecostal churches. A major organizational union occurred in 1994 in Memphis, when the traditionally white-led Pentecostal Fellowship of North America held conferences with traditionally African-American pentecostal leaders, approved a "Racial Reconciliation Manifesto," and united under the racially integrated United Pentecostal-Charismatic Churches of North America.[29]

Mennonite-Related Churches   Quakers, Amish, Hutterites, and Mennonites are strongly committed to the Free Church principle of nonviolent resistance and conscientious objection to war. The Mennonites, Amish, Hutterites, and Moravian Brethren sing, read the Bible, pray, and preach in simple quiet worship and live in close communities separated from mainstream society. Brethren are known for their humble foot-washing ceremony. In 1995, the Amish and Amish Mennonite population was more than 250,000. In the same year, various types of Brethren churches in the United States combined to total about 284,000 members.[30] Since the 1960s, Mennonite worship is either more liturgical or more charismatic, each seeking in different ways to give more participation to ordinary members. The liturgical form offered responsive readings to the congregation, and the charismatic form encouraged raising hands during prayer and more ecstatic experiences. The faithful express their joys and concerns, gather children for a lesson, and pray silently, allowing anyone to pray aloud.

Amish   The Amish, close to the Mennonite Brethren, still wear simple clothes—often black, wide-brimmed hats for men and plain colors, ankle-length dresses, and head coverings for women. The Amish typically worship in district groups of about 30 neighboring families. Each family hosts a worship once a year in their home or barn. As many as 150 people may attend every other Sunday, starting at 8:30 AM and lasting more than three hours. Worship is a solemn service with Bible readings, prayers, and songs sung slowly in German, without musical instruments or harmony. Afterward, the host family serves a meal. Amish do not go to college or seminary to prepare for the ministry. A minister must sincerely feel a "call" to serve in this serious vocation. They serve for life with no salary. They are men (not women) chosen by lot from the district congregation. Each district usually has two or three ministers, a deacon, and a bishop.[31]

The Amish sing from a traditional Reformation hymnbook called the *Ausbund,* and the second hymn sung is always *"Loeblied"* (Hymn of Praise). Hymns have many verses and generally convey a feeling of deep sadness for the suffering of their ancestors in Europe. Songs are sung in unison, with no written notation, for they have been memorized. One of the "martyr" hymns, recalling early Anabaptists killed for their beliefs, goes:

> We alone, a little flock,
> The few who still remain,
> Are exiles wandering through the land
> In sorrow and in pain.

Quakers Traditional Quakers, or The Religious Society of Friends, have minimal institutional church structure, programmed formal worship, prayer books, priests, and visual art in worship. Friends may meet in a home, school, or "meeting house." For them direct communion with God makes the traditional sacraments unnecessary, because guidance from the Spirit did not stop in biblical times, as most conservative Christians believe. The Holy Spirit can come to anyone, anywhere, anytime. There is no time or place more sacred than another, for the entire world is sacred. They renamed Sunday "First Day" and they meet not in a church but a "meeting house" or even a home and sit in silence until the Holy Spirit moves someone to speak. Friends may read from books such as the Bible, or pray, or speak from personal experience, but what is said should come from the soul—the Inner Light. Spontaneous inspiration from God is still their guide, rather than planned worship. Some have said that they wait and listen inwardly until they feel a divine presence settle over the meeting. Characteristically Quaker songs include " 'Tis a gift to be simple, 'Tis a gift to be free." Leaderless meetings may be seen as a form of group mysticism. Quaker worship style has influenced other Free Churches.

Friends organize regionally under monthly meetings, quarterly meetings, and yearly meetings, where administrative business is conducted by consensus. Rather than voting, a consensus with good spirit is sought. Friends support private schools and colleges, retreat centers, and stress peace-making programs. Quakers have merged into the mainstream of society, no longer wearing special plain clothes, but still maintaining simple living, unstructured meeting for worship, and higher education through their secondary boarding schools and colleges. Some Friends maintain the original leaderless anticlerical tradition, while others appoint ministers to lead them. Today Friends tend to divide into the evangelical and liberal branches.

Some Friends have adopted a pastoral or "programmed" style of worship, with ministers, readings, prayers, hymns, a sermon, and perhaps baptisms and communion sacraments, with an additional time of un-programmed silence and spontaneous speaking. The form of worship does not matter as much as the spiritual reality.

Friends' Service Committees in several nations are strong international charities that support programs such as summer trips to aid in community building in impoverished areas. Friends maintain a long tradition of conscientious objection to war, as do other "Peace churches."[32]

Small in number but historically influential, Friends' worldwide membership numbers about 200,000, mostly in the 1,100 meetings in the United States.[33] The three major associations of Friends in the United States combine to total about 121,000 members.[34]

The conservative side of the Free Churches continuum emphasizes maintaining traditions, such as patriarchy, building strong, large families, and enforcing a conservative sexual ethic. Thus the Southern Baptists see women as subordinate to men, and the Amish reject most post–nineteenth-century technology and focus on family farms and businesses such as quilting, carpentry, and baking as nonindustrial, meaningful work.[35]

The radical side of Free Church continuum rejects strong regional organizations, a strong priesthood, and advocates separation from what they see as corrupting influences of mainstream commercial, industrial society.

Protestant Charities

Protestants support hundreds of charities. Major denominations have their own charitable organizations and also contribute to interdenominational charities, notably Church World Service (CWS). This is a major international charity for relief, development, and refugee ministry supported by 36 Protestant and Orthodox denominations. They work in more than 80 countries with indigenous organizations to foster self-reliance. In the United States, CWS responds to disasters, helps resettle refugees, provides educational resources, promotes fair national and international political policies, and sponsors programs to abolish hunger, and tools and blankets programs. Church World Service also works in partnership with other agencies in emergencies to distribute food, shelter, and medicine for disaster

Protestant staff organizing volunteers distributing food to rescue workers at collapsed World Trade Center, September, 2001, Ecumenical/Episcopal Seamen's Church Institute, New York City. © Susan Meiselas/Magnum Photos.

relief. For example, CWS regularly helps to provide shelter, food, blankets, and support for thousands of refugees. They supported the African singing tour of a choir from South Africa to raise awareness of the HIV epidemic. Some denominational charities have blossomed into interfaith programs, such as the Heifer Project, begun by a farmer member of the Church of the Brethren. The Heifer Project International raises funds for farm animals to be distributed to impoverished people worldwide, who are trained to raise and multiply their stock, then distribute the offspring animals to others, whom they also train. This project has expanded greatly into an interfaith movement.[36] This reflects the new direction in charitable aid, which is to promote projects that become independent, long-term improvements.

Conservative and Liberal Practices

Christianity incorporates a wide spectrum of approaches to varying issues, from liturgy to politics. Today we speak of conservative and liberal extremes of the spectrum, with a large middle ground, called the mainstream, or mainline churches. Many churches have both conservative and liberal elements and some may find more affinity with members of other denominations than with their own, as old historical debates, such as Calvinist predestination, lose importance.

Eastern Orthodox Church

Generally, today the Orthodox Church may be seen as conservative by holding to ancient, formal, prescribed liturgy in its retention of male priesthood, supporting monks on Mt. Athos who still refuse to admit any females, and identifying with various nationalities, such as the Russian and Greek. Conservatives, or traditionalists, seek to retain European customs even in American churches, such as having women cover their heads and all worshipers standing throughout the worship service. They also oppose abortion and reject ecumenical relations with other Christian churches. They typically retain the ancient Orthodox tradition of supporting their government. Traditionalists also want to retain the ancient Roman Julian calendar, which has a unique date for Easter *(Pascha)*. More modernist Orthodox Churches have shifted to the Christian Gregorian calendar that puts their Easter at the same time as Catholics and Protestants.

Orthodoxy may be seen as liberal or modernist organizationally for its fairly autonomous church structure with authority vested in more democratic councils (not a single highest leader), for encouraging its priests to marry, and for beginning to strengthen the roles of deaconesses. Armenian Orthodox churches have always had deaconesses, and the pre–eighth-century practice of allowing unmarried deaconesses in some Greek monasteries has been revived. The Russian Orthodox have monasteries for men and convents for women. Orthodoxy is also liberal in its participation in the World Council of Churches and for its Patriarch Bartholomew I of Istanbul's call for more attention to ecology.[37]

Roman Catholic Church

The Roman Catholic Church may be seen as conservative for its retention of a formal hierarchy with the Pope leading cardinals, archbishops, bishops, and priests and for retaining a formal prescribed liturgy. It may also be seen as conservative for holding to a male priesthood, for the requirement of celibacy for priests and monastics, for opposing politicians who favor women's right to choose abortion, and, in some countries, for supporting wealthy landowners. Some insist on holding Mass in Latin. Catholics hold to this conservatism not just to preserve tradition, but (like the Orthodox and evangelicals) to halt what they see as the moral and spiritual decay of secular society.

Staff serving soup at Loaves and Fishes ecumenical hospitality program at St. John's Episcopal Church, Ithaca, New York. Courtesy of the author.

Catholics may be seen as liberal notably in the changes made at the 1962–1965 Vatican II Council, which allowed for more lay and women's leadership, in opening to biblical historical-critical scholarship, in more informal worship, and in support for the poor in the Liberation Theology movement. This movement emerged when Latin American theologians began criticizing systematic injustices, poverty, and oppression not opposed by the church. Some priests in Latin America organized base communities to support the empowerment of peasants, and some were attacked, even killed. Archbishop Oscar Romero in El Salvador spoke out against the mistreatment of the poor, and he was assassinated while saying Mass in 1980. Other Catholics, including nuns, have also been assassinated. Criticized by Rome as too Marxist, Liberation Theology divided the Catholic Church in Latin America between those who did not question the social structure and those who challenged the institutional concentration of wealth in a few hands and the resulting poverty of the masses. Liberation Theology has expanded to South Africa and to North America to include racial and gender issues.

In countries where women are educated, there is a strong tendency to ignore the Church's ban on artificial contraception. Liberal Catholic theologians have called on the Church to liberalize its positions on sexual issues, mysticism, women, papal infallibility, ecology, human rights, and war.

Liberal Catholics also write about the urgency of restoring a sense of the divine presence in nature to repair the ecology crisis.[38]

Protestant Church

Protestant conservative and liberal variations have taken more diverse forms, because they lack a central hierarchy. Mainstream denominations have conservative and liberal branches within, but conservative Protestant church membership now outnumbers the mainstream Protestant churches, largely in the fundamentalist and evangelical movements. The U.S. Alliance of Evangelicals reports 23 million members. The more liberal mainstream Presbyterian Church USA reports about 3 million members and the United Methodists 8 million. Liberal debates came to a head in the 1960s "Death of God" controversy, followed by post-modernist movements that challenge the certainty of many cultural beliefs and press forward social justice and feminist, ecological, and gay rights issues. This has caused divisive conflicts among conservative, mainstream, and liberal Protestants.

Churches started by missionaries have grown worldwide, tend to be more conservative, and now outnumber European and North American churches. Measured in numbers, Christendom is becoming more conservative.[39]

Fundamentalists The fundamentalist movement is in large part a modern reactionary movement against industrial secular society's denial of God. The Civil War in the United States provoked conflicts between mostly southern fundamentalist and mostly northern liberal Christians over slavery, which led to some institutional divisions, such as the Baptists' and Presbyterians' split into southern and northern branches. Some have since reunited.

Fundamentalism is one of the largest interdenominational categories in Christianity. Many evangelicals, pentecostals, Mennonites, and the "confessing" movement in mainstream denominations believe in fundamentalist basics. Strict and puritanical in their moral codes and intolerant of others, they tend to demonize their enemies and see secular humanism as the work of Satan. Largely led by men, they criticize other denominations that ordain women to the ministry. Fundamentalists usually believe that they must separate themselves from nonbelievers in society. So some fundamentalists take their children out of public schools and home-school them or send them to Christian schools. Their apocalyptic end-of-of-the-world movements tend to lead them away from reform of the world.[40]

Evangelicals   From its early days, Christianity used the term "evangelical" broadly to mean following the teachings of Jesus. The German Lutheran Church is called the "Evangelical" Church. The Wesleyan Methodist movement was part of an eighteenth-century English "evangelical" stress on sincerity and enthusiasm in religion. Similarly the nineteenth-century U.S. revivalist "Great Awakening" movements were called "evangelical." It is now used in a narrower sense also, to mean a conservative, but not strongly fundamentalist, interdenominational Christian movement. Most evangelicals are not as extreme as fundamentalists and not as emotional in worship as pentecostals. They hold to many fundamentalist views but are more open to new thought. Evangelicalism crosses denominational boundaries, so they can be found in any church, such as the Southern Baptists, Lutheran Church-Missouri Synod, or "Bible" churches. Evangelicals are more actively involved in public moral issues than the more withdrawn fundamentalists. They have historically been involved in antislavery, prison reform, and anti-abortion movements. Broadly defined, evangelicalism and pentecostalism together make up a very large and rapidly growing percentage of Christianity. Evangelicals blend largely conservative Lutheran, Calvinist, and Free Church beliefs and practices.

The issue of the role of women in the traditionally patriarchal church is a controversial issue in Protestantism. Like Catholics and Orthodox, evangelicals also limit the role of women in leadership positions. The role of women leaders in Protestantism began to enlarge as the 1865–1914 Women's Boards of Foreign Missions multiplied across the Protestant spectrum. Beginning with the Methodists in 1910, women have been eligible for election to their representative conventions. Ordination into the ministry for women developed in this period in the Baptist, Congregationalist, and the new Holiness and pentecostal movements and expanded in most denominations, except fundamentalists and evangelicals.

The right-wing evangelicals argue the equal-but-separate position that men and women are created equal, but men are the head of the family and the church. Evangelical theologian Carl Henry argues that men and women have complementary roles, and men are granted a biblically based divine "headship" at home and in church. Men are subordinate to God, and women subordinate to men. But this gives no justification for male chauvinism or the lesser dignity and right of women. Ultimately, God has no sexual qualities, because "He" is pure spirit, Henry says. But God is not to be referred to in a feminine pronoun or image, because in the Bible God reveals himself as personal and overwhelmingly Fatherly. Henry argues that women are welcome to serve the church as Christian education directors in music, counseling, or chaplaincy, but they should not be pastors.[41] Many evangelicals agree with this, but some on the left wing are beginning to see the need to expand and explore this issue, and a few feminist left-wing evangelicals argue that gender is irrelevant to spiritual authority, and qualified women should be pastors.

The evangelical "Campus Crusade for Christ" and "Navigators" organize in many colleges and towns. Most evangelicals traditionally avoid overt political action, but some developed an aggressive political offshoot called the "Religious Right" and the "Christian Coalition," in the 1980s that lobbied strongly in Washington for conservative issues. Pat Robertson, host of the popular television show "700 Club," ran for U.S. president in 1988. By 2000 the Religious Right was less centrally organized but still had an influence in politics. The U.S. National Alliance of Evangelicals mobilized its 23 million members to support the failed Federal Marriage Amendment to the Constitution in opposition to homosexual marriages. In the 2004 presidential election, the Republican party actively sought to mobilize evangelical votes.

Liberal evangelicalism is represented by the magazine *Sojourners*, edited by Jim Wallis, which has expanded to embrace Christian liberals and progressives who seek to join personal biblical faith and social justice struggles. *Sojourners* focuses on social ethics such as abuses of global business practices, questions of just war, racism, and poverty. A popular left-wing evangelical social activist and educator is Tony Campolo, who has organized several educational and literacy programs in poverty-ridden communities worldwide. Feminist evangelical theologian Jann Aldredge-Clanton co-authored "Imagine God!," a musical for children that uses a variety of masculine, feminine, and nongender images of God. She is a Baptist minister, a chaplain at a hospital, and a teacher at Perkins/Southern Methodist University. She has really broken out of the evangelical framework by writing about reclaiming the divine feminine aspect of Christ-Sophia.[42]

The old rural style of early evangelicalism has now shifted to suburban churches. Half of all U.S. evangelicals live in the south, 29 percent have a college degree, 68 percent are married, 29 percent have been divorced at least once, 50 percent have children at home, 81 percent are white, and 62 percent are affiliated with the Republican political party, making them

14 percent of all registered Republicans. While Protestant mainstream churches experienced a decline in membership after the 1960s, conservative evangelical churches have grown. The wide spectrum of evangelicals makes their numbers difficult to ascertain but estimates range from around 11 percent to 15 percent (40,640,000) of Christians in the United States and around 210,603,000, or 11 percent of Christians worldwide by some to much more by others, depending upon which groups are included.[43]

Televangelism Fundamentalists in the United States have always promoted large revival meetings, often in large tents, to get people more enthusiastic about their faith, and they often included pentecostal-type faith healings. The radio was used by Roman Catholic Father Charles Coughlin, whose anticommunist message reached millions during the 1930s Depression. When television enlarged their audiences, "televangelism" reached millions more viewers. The most successful evangelical preacher has been Billy Graham, a Southern Baptist revival preacher who has attracted millions since the 1950s in his huge revival rallies broadcasted worldwide. He was a frequent visitor to the White House and co-founder of the leading evangelical magazine *Christianity Today.* As Graham approached retirement, his son Franklin Graham and daughter Anne Graham Lotz continued his work. Like some women evangelicals, Lotz does preach, but she is not in a leadership position.[44]

After some initial hesitation about preaching on television, more evangelical ministers soon brought in the cameras and gained huge followings. By the 1970s televangelists were broadcasting old-time fundamentalism mixed with modern media savvy. Televangelists typically preach in modern auditoriums with professional musicians, testimonials from well-known media stars, and frequent requests for donations.

But televangelism suffered from a few dishonest preachers repeating an old problem, portrayed in Sinclair Lewis's 1927 novel *Elmer Gantry.* With a highly visible $2.5 billion-a-year U.S. television ministry, well-publicized preachers who used deceptive methods and misused their trust to conceal sexual adventures and financial abuses were exposed in the 1980s. Jim Bakker and his wife, Tammy Faye, built a multimillion dollar "Praise the Lord" television ministry in South Carolina. But Jim was accused of having a sexual affair with a church secretary and paying her blackmail money. He was jailed for cheating his followers out of $158 million in misused donations. He was sentenced to 45 years in jail in 1989 but released after four and a half years to a Salvation Army halfway house.[45]

Mega-ChurchesA theology opposed to the Calvinist view of human depravity, but in fervent support of the rise of the middle class, is popular in the large U.S. evangelical "mega-churches." In contrast to John Calvin's dire pessimism about human nature as depraved, a completely opposite, optimistic view of human nature was preached in the 1950s by Norman Vincent Peale at Marble Collegiate Reformed Church in New York City. Stressing the Protestant support for the rise of the middle class after the discouraging 1930s Depression and World War II, Peale preached a half-Calvinist "Prosperity and Power Evangelism," beginning with his popular book "The Power of Positive Thinking," and helped initiate the pastoral counseling movement with a clinic at his Reformed Marble Collegiate Church in New York City.[46]

Robert Schuller followed in Peale's footsteps in his large "Crystal Cathedral" which he sees as the first mega-church, in Orange County, Southern California, with about 10,000 members, where he preaches only positive messages to more than 2,000 people in a service. He has written many books and broadcasts services on television worldwide on the "Hour of Power." Schuller's theology is not limited to denominational guidelines. He rejects original sin, promotes "self-esteem" and "be-happy" attitudes to solving life's spiritual and psychological problems, and welcomes interfaith dialogue. He criticizes the Calvinist emphasis on human sinfulness as crude and unchristian, wrongly turning away people who already feel shame, and need self-respect, not condemnation. Schuller is a universalist, seeing all people, not just Christians, as children of God.[47]

In the 1990s, a new generation of mega-churches grew in the suburbs of large cities. Yoido Full Gospel Church in Seoul, Korea, seats 12,500 people, making it one of the largest in the world. Conservative in theology, about half of the mega-churches are evangelical and a fourth of them are charismatic-pentecostal churches. In one survey, 604 of these churches averaged about 3,850 worshipers weekly. In 1999 a survey showed an average annual mega-church income of $4.8 million. Most U.S. mega-churches are in California, Texas, Florida, and Georgia. More than half are not affiliated with any denomination, but 20 percent are Southern Baptist. Nearly all mega-churches are conservative but use contemporary music, drama, and language. The Church of Joy in Phoenix has thematic services, such as a country/western music service for some and a more traditional musical service for others. Like other mega-churches, the Willow Creek Community Church in suburban Chicago set its goal to minister to the "unchurched," people who are "seekers" for a spiritual path.

Mega-churches typically have a more theatre-like building with theatre seats, a stage with polished theatrical performances, contemporary Christian music, skits, jokes, and professional music, video, and multimedia presentations with expensive overhead projectors, lights, sound equipment, web pages, and staff. The Lakeview Church in Houston, led by the charismatic preacher Joel Osteen, moved into a stadium in 2005 to accommodate 16,000 worshippers. Like other mega-churches, it preaches a gospel of personal "Victory," and reads the Bible literally. The pastors are usually men and a third have no seminary education. They see themselves as making a difference for those who feel battered by traditional religious guilt, have given up on church, and feel a need for spiritual healing.[48]

Protestant Liberals   One survey concluded that 18 percent of American adults are religious conservatives, 47 percent moderates, and 19 percent liberals. One group of experts called the following U.S. denominations liberal: Presbyterian Church USA, American Baptist Churches in the USA, Evangelical Lutheran Church in America, Christian Church (Disciples of Christ), United Methodist Church, Episcopal Church USA, and the United

Protestant minister baptizing a baby at St. Paul's United Methodist Church, Ithaca, New York. Courtesy of the author.

Church of Christ.[49] Support for the poor, ecology, gays, and feminism are leading liberal concerns. "Post-modernism" is a liberal intellectual movement that questions the certainty of any claim to absolute truth, whether religious or scientific.

Christianity and Ecology   Ecology is an issue gaining attention in North American churches. Some Christians reject industrial society's destruction of earth's biosphere and call for a renewed sense of the presence of the sacred in nature, even proclaiming that "Christ is Mother Earth." An Orthodox leader has called ecological damage a "sin."[50] The dualism of heaven and earth built into Christian theology has elevated God to a remote transcendent realm and left the earth a barren, spiritless world that was transformed into a set of "objects" by scientific philosophy. Now religious leaders are questioning such theologies and are arguing that the biblical injunction to have "dominion" over the earth is now invalid. They are also asking how religion can restore a heightened sense of human stewardship to care for the earth's ecosystems in books such as Mary Evelyn Tucker's *Worldly Wonder: Religions Enter Their Ecological Phase* (2003). The Vatican is increasingly supporting the environmental "sustainability" movement. The U.S. National Council of Churches joined with the Sierra Club to protest drilling for oil in Alaska's Arctic Wildlife Preserve. In response to the ecological problems of gas-guzzling and polluting vehicles, some evangelical church leaders asked: "What would Jesus drive?"

Christian Feminists   Liberal, progressive, radical, and post-modern Protestant women speak up against patriarchal control and oppression of women in the name of God, as in Elizabeth Cady Stanton's *Women's Bible* (1895). In 1848 the Women's Rights Convention in Seneca Falls, New York, called for sweeping reforms liberating women. The first mainstream woman minister was Antoinette Brown Blackwell, ordained in New York State in 1853. In the twentieth century, some European countries finally gave women the right to vote, then the United States did so in 1920. In the 1960s the feminist movement exploded and has continued to change religions and society.

Liberal Christian women argue that it is idolatrous to think of males more "like God" than women and blasphemous to attempt to justify patriarchal domination of women in the name of God. Theologian Sallie McFague emphasizes the metaphorical nature of religious language as opposed to literalism and argues that religions naturally need models of God that have human referents, so the "father" God, now an outdated model, should be replaced by imaging God as mother, friend, and lover. Women such as Barbara Harris (in 1989 the first woman to become a bishop in the Episcopal Church) are increasingly being ordained as ministers in Protestant churches.

In 1993 a Conference in Minneapolis-St. Paul, Minnesota, brought together about 2,000 women, including national leaders from mainline denominations, who felt marginalized. What they called the patriarchal environment of Christianity was condemned as "toxic." Some portrayed the divine as a pantheistic all-encompassing energy uniting, permeating, and healing all that exists. Many argued for the need to reinvent the family and sexual ethics. The ancient goddess Sophia was celebrated as the female side of God. In reaction, church officials condemned the conference as idolatrous. Mary Ann Lundy, who lost her job at Presbyterian Church USA headquarters after her leadership in the 1993 Re-Imagining God conference, was named Deputy Director of the World Council of Churches. A 5-year reunion brought together 900 women, and a 10-year reunion was also organized.[51] Since 2002, Catholic radicals have been ordaining a few women as priests.

Post-Modernist Christians

The Death of God movement in the 1960s was a culmination of nineteenth-century criticisms of conventional Christianity, notably by the German philosopher Friedrich Nietzsche (1844–1900) who proclaimed that "God is Dead," and we have killed him with scientific/industrial society. Some theologians argue that outdated views of God should be abandoned in order to clear the way for a new understanding of the God of the Bible. This view has had a strong impact in Europe, where excessive violence in the name of religion has jaded many, leaving scores of church pews empty.[52]

Yet, despite this strong critique, U.S. religiosity did not fade away, but increased. But it also became polarized between right-wing evangelicals and left-wing "New Age" spiritual seekers, while the large mainstream and liberal churches experienced declines in membership and leadership. And the critique of traditional religion has continued. Some theologians argue that religion is deeply influenced by human imaginative constructs in images such as God as warrior, judge, or king, as well as by violence in the Bible and abstractions such as absolute truth. Feminists, with a longer history, but also post-modernists, have been quick to apply this critique to the role of women in religion. If the biblical "father" is an imaginative construct, they argue, it is not the only valid one. So is "mother." Both are useful metaphors, not absolute truth.

Post-modernism is a wide-ranging category of thought open to new literary, scientific, technological, social, psychological, and theological thought that goes beyond liberalism. It expresses skepticism about the validity of all absolute truths, as expressed in religions, sciences, and philosophies, and thus the validity of major worldviews such as Christianity, Marxism, capitalism, liberalism, or fundamentalism. Post-modernists also charge that modernism's promise of the triumph of reason over superstition and technology over suffering has failed to fulfill its promises since, along with many valuable accomplishments, it has failed to prevent fascist holocausts and has created weapons of mass destruction that could destroy the human race. Nor is the gold standard of modernity's "objectivity" as neutral and detached from political agendas as it claims to be, as we see with massive financing of scientific research from military sources. This weakens the scientific claim to have absolute truth, but that applies to religions also. Postmodernists think that Christians must face the fact that exceedingly edited biblical texts most likely do not record what actually happened historically and that metaphysical claims may have limited truth value. [53]

While most Christians would reject post-modernism's denial of all religious absolutes, others accept some of their critiques, such as the patriarchal bias of Christianity, and seek to rethink the faith from the ground up. Christians would typically reject the radical relativism ("anything goes") of truth and ethics that some post-modernists have been accused of promoting. Building on the ground-breaking German philosopher Martin Heidegger (1889–1976), some Christian theologians, such as Paul Tillich (1886–1965) and Episcopal Bishop John Spong (1931–), have rejected fundamentalism and theism (a personal God) and rethought God as Being, or ultimate reality shorn of rigid human mythical accretions, notably the male image. Process philosophers such as David Griffin see all reality as constantly in flux and change, not as a static, fixed reality underlying the changing world. Thus, they see God as involved in changing, sensitive, caring relationships with the world, because God is personal and affected by these relationships and changes and develops. Other important process theologians, such as John Cobb, incorporated this idea into an ecological theology (see chapter 6, Major Figures).

Depth psychology uncovers another postmodern theme: the influence of the unconscious psyche in all thinking, which deepens the analysis of religion. Archetypal psychology perceived the divine psychologically in the soul's unconscious, its dreams and mythologies, symbolized in endless ways, not just as a father in heaven. Thus, religion cannot avoid mythical, metaphoric images expressing belief in ultimate reality, but these are flexible and not unchangeable. This approach has supported explorations of the Goddess in religion and the feminine psyche, as well as in healing.[54]

Post-modernists are influenced by European philosophers such as the deconstructionists, who challenge the certainty of "meta-narratives" or major cultural stories that religions provide, such as Jesus as cosmic savior overcoming suffering and assuring eternal life. The strong role of imagination and desire in thought is shown to have a powerful shaping force on both religion and science. Post-modernists criticize capitalist consumerism, social oppression, technological excess, ecological crises, and gender role rigidity, and some seek to harmonize religion with the best of scientific thought in order to work toward a new cosmology and ecology. Open to other world religions, some also welcome interfaith explorations that may some day change basic elements of traditional Christianity, such as theism, patriarchy, and separation from nature.

The Emerging Church

Numerous exploratory Christian groups have always sought new ways of adapting their faith to a new era, and a creative group of ministers in the early twenty-first century began what they call the "emerging church," which offers "vintage" Christianity but in a totally new context shorn of most traditional Christian liturgical arts. No church, no organ, no choir, no prayer book, but café-like settings with candles, popular music groups, and videos are their contexts for prayer. Some young people distrustful of the traditional church and the authoritarian, judgmental side of Christianity are drawn to the "emerging churches." They are hungry for spirituality, seeking some solace from commercialism and materialism, but need to find it in their familiar settings, the leaders say. They stress the pluralism of exploring various elements of other faiths, such as Buddhist meditation, focusing on experience rather than dogma, and cultivating mystical consciousness. For them, in an age of contraceptives and mass education, an open view of sexuality is necessary, not the repressive asceticism of the pre-contraceptive eras. Similarly, they need to feel that a variety of sexual orientations are acceptable, gay, lesbian, or straight. They use the increasingly familiar phrase "I am spiritual but not religious." They stress the need for an organic, free-flowing sense of deeply involving mystery, presented in a multisensory way, rather than professionals presenting a boring, linear, verbally oriented traditional performance to those who sit and watch.[55]

Global Growth

As the Protestant church historically spread worldwide with missionaries, a number of independent churches developed in various countries, such as the widespread African Independent Churches, especially in Nigeria and Asia, and notably in Korea and the Philippines. Protestants worldwide number about 647 million members, which are 29 percent of affiliated Christians and 13 percent of the world's population. The Christian Church is growing fastest in Latin America, Africa, and Asia (now about 60 percent of Christianity). Around 2000, the number of Christians there outnumbered those in Europe and North America (about 40 percent), where the religion began. This shift will have an impact on the church, likely pulling it in a more conservative direction.[56]

CHRISTIANITY WORLDWIDE

The Middle East

Today in Israel and Palestine, many branches of Christianity have churches. Most Christians are Palestinian Arabs, and others are married to Jews. Sites sacred to Christians, such as the Church of the Sepulchre, where Jesus was believed to be buried and resurrected, are owned and maintained by various Christian groups. There are about 294,000 affiliated Christians in Israel and Palestine (5.7 percent of the total population), mostly Catholic and pentecostal/charismatic.[57]

Eastern Europe

Today, Yugoslavia, combining Serbia and Montenegro, has 7,500,000 Christians (72 percent of the population), mostly Serbian Orthodox.[58] Poland is 96 percent Roman Catholic. Since being Catholic is part of the Polish personal identity for so many, the communist occupation had little effect on the popularity of the church.

In 1986, just before the collapse of the Iron Curtain, according to Western estimates about 68 percent of Hungarians were Roman Catholic, 20 percent Reformed (Calvinist), 5 percent Lutheran, 5 percent unaffiliated, and a number of smaller churches were affiliated with the national Council of Free Churches—Baptists and Methodists, for example. In the 1980s thousands of intensely active prayer and meditation groups, both Catholic and Protestant, emerged.

In Romania, the Romanian Orthodox Church is by far the largest church, claiming in 2004 about 20 million members, or about 89 percent of the total population of 22.4 million. The Church had about 12,000 buildings and 9,000 priests. The Catholic Church has two branches in Romania, the Eastern Rite (Uniates) and the Latin Rite (Roman Catholics). The Uniate Church is an Orthodox Church that accepts papal authority, while retaining its Orthodox rituals, laws, and calendar. Among Protestants were the Reformed, Lutheran, Baptists, and pentecostal.

In Bulgaria, the Bulgarian Orthodox Church helped retain the sense of Bulgarian nationhood during the communist occupation. After the fall of the communists, the Orthodox Church enjoyed a renewal. Bibles were sold at high prices, and Christmas in 1990 was widely celebrated. Seminaries reopened and attracted students, and the Synod published 300,000 Orthodox Bibles in 1992. By 1991, the pentecostals were the largest Protestant church, brought by Russian émigrés. They had 36 clergy in 46 parishes and 5,000 to 6,000 members. [59]

Latin America

Latin America is overwhelmingly Roman Catholic, in its own way. Perhaps 80 million Catholic and Protestant Christians in Brazil practice pentecostal or charismatic worship services. Indigenous Mayans and others quietly keep some old traditions, such as shamanic healing, and blend others with Christianity, such as the Black Madonna. Caribbean and Brazilian workers brought their indigenous religions from Africa and blended them in several varieties of new religions, generally known as "Spiritism," such as "Santeria" in the Caribbean, "Voodoo" in Haiti, and "Macumba" in Brazil. On their altars Christian saints stand next to African divinities, and African gods are often renamed as Christian saints. Their ceremonies include drumming, healing, and trance-induced "possession" by divinities.[60]

Latin American Christianity centers around town Catholic churches on a village plaza. Sunday masses often fill the churches with devoted believers. Colorful native cotton dress and busy markets fill the square. Mayday poles rooted in indigenous traditions provide a center for a spring dance in many towns when colorfully dressed dancers circle the pole to the rhythms

Roman Catholic congregation celebrating Mexican Independence Day, San Antonio, Texas. © Hiroji Dubota/Magnum Photos.

of drums and cheerful encouragement of the crowd. They intertwine bright ribbons tied to the top of the pole.

In Mexico 96 percent of the people are Catholics (95,169,000 in 2000). Christianity is commonly blended with indigenous Aztec traditions. An Aztec earth goddess was absorbed into Christianity as the Virgin of Guadalupe, who, according to tradition, appeared to the Indian Juan Diego in 1531. Guadalupe is the most important place of worship in Mexico, attracting 2 million pilgrims a year.

Liberation Theology and Evangelical Missionaries

The Roman Catholic Vatican II council (1962–1965) urged more identification with the poor. After this some Latin American priests began criticizing the oppression, injustice, and poverty of the aristocratic social structure that had long been approved by the Roman church. Religion is not just about personal salvation, they stressed, but about the liberating transformation of oppressive social institutions. Some priests used a Marxist economic and class analysis and spoke of the judgment of God on the rich. They helped found "base" Christian communities in support of the poor in the name of the "Liberating Christ." This provoked a critical response from conservative Catholics and the Vatican, for being too close to communist thought. This movement, called "Liberation Theology," spread across the globe, where in South Africa it attacked apartheid.

By 1990 a strong new movement of evangelicals into Latin America grew. Due to an influx of Protestant missionaries, by 1990 Brazil was about 18 percent Protestant and Chile, 25 percent. On the Caribbean Islands, Haiti became 15 percent to 20 percent Protestant and Puerto Rico up to 30 percent. Evangelicals in Latin America emphasize their themes of the total reliability and authority of the Bible, the need to be saved by a personal conversion to a relationship with Jesus, or to be "born again," and the duty to spread this message to others. The appeal partly seems to have to do with the lack of a strong clerical hierarchy, because lay members are allowed to become leaders and preachers. This was forbidden in Catholic parishes, where the priests retained leadership roles. The emotional worship style and healing practices of pentecostal and charismatic evangelicals has also been welcomed and, in some cases, blended with indigenous Latin American beliefs in spirits.[61]

Politically, the evangelicals usually adopt the view that, in view of Fidel Castro's communist conquest of Cuba, insurgent rebels fighting against the status quo are communists, and that any anticommunist government is divinely ordained. Conservative evangelicals generally support the elite regimes, even dictators, along with conservative Catholics, while Liberation priests press for human rights. Evangelicals teach a form of the conservative Calvinist "prosperity gospel." Belief will bring you material rewards in this life and the next, they preach. They seek to raise the poor into the middle class with their "redemption and lift" preaching. In 2002 Latin American Christians numbered about 471 million Catholics, 500,000 Orthodox, and 50 million Protestants.[62]

Africa

Sub-Saharan Africa

Christian Churches in Africa range from independent versions of traditional European churches to Christian blends with old African religions, even at times neglecting Jesus. They generally emphasize biblical authority and greatly revere charismatic preachers and prophetic revelations. Water is a common sacred medium of divine action, and sacred places are important. Beliefs in duties to ancestors and their presence in the landscape lingers. Thousands of new denominations range from hierarchical structure to local congregational control and spontaneous expressions of faith, including traditional drumming and dance.

The Anglican Communion developed strong local African leadership, and spread their message abroad. Nigeria's population is about 46 percent Christian (50,965,000). Many of these are in about 1,000 independent denominations (14,050,000) and Anglicans (20,070,000). Roman Catholics number 13,400,000. Among Indigenous churches, the Cherubim and Seraphim Church of the Lord was formed, which has spawned about 200 new churches. The U.S. African Methodist Episcopal and African Methodist Episcopal Zion Churches have also grown in Africa.[63]

South Africa

South Africa has the largest number of separatist Indigenous churches in the world. In 1995, there were 4,000 denominations with 13 million adherents, with names such as the Zionist Christians (5 million), and the Nazarite Baptist Church (700,000). They are fervently pentecostal, encouraging healing and spiritual experiences. In 2000 there were 313,800,000 affiliated Christians in South Africa (79 percent of the population), mostly Independent and Protestant.[64] Worldwide, Christianity has gained an increasingly large African component. In 2002, there were more active Christians in Africa than on any other continent. In 2002, Africa altogether had about 225 million Protestants, 127 million Catholics, and 37 million Orthodox.

Asia

Asia's and Oceania's affiliated Christians total about 366 million, with 34.4 percent Catholics, 3.6 percent Orthodox, and 61.9 percent Protestants. This is a growing portion of world Christianity.[65]

China

In 1926, the peak of Christian missionary work in China, there were about 8,000 Christian missionaries in China, and 70 percent of all hospitals were Christian. Mao Tse-Tung defeated the Nationalists in 1949 and founded the Communist People's Republic of China, which officially became an atheist state. Nationalists fled to the island of Formosa, now Taiwan, where Christianity continues. But Christianity has survived in mainland China as an underground movement. On the mainland, in 1995 the Han Charismatic House Churches reported 29,740,000 members, and the Han Chinese True-Self Churches had 10,500,000 members. In 1997, there were about 40 million house churches. Nationally, Christianity expanded to about 88,708,000 believers by 2000 (7.1 percent of China's population). More than 80 million belong to independent denominations, such as the True Jesus Church, with more than 1 million members, and about 12 million belong to the Catholic Church of China.[66]

Japan

After World War II, more than 2,500 missionaries poured into Japan. But as Japan became a more secular technological state, interest in Christianity faded. Yet freedom of religion is guaranteed in Japan today. Buddhism and Shinto remain the dominant religions (84 percent). In 2000, there were about 3,473,000 affiliated Christians (2.7 percent of Japan), including more than 100 indigenous denominations. The largest is the Spirit of Jesus Church, with 420,000 members.[67]

South Korea

In 2000, about 40 percent of South Korea's people were Christian. This is a remarkably high percentage for Asia, which is overall about two percent Christian. South Korea has the world's largest pentecostal, Presbyterian, and Methodist congregations, as well as the largest Christian theological seminaries. The Yoido Full Gospel Church, reputed to be the world's largest, has a congregation of 700,000 members. Some Christian converts see Christianity as a more democratic alternative that gives women more liberty than traditional patriarchal Confucianism.[68] In 2000, Korea's affiliated Christians numbered 18,681,000 (40 percent of the country). Most of those were Protestants and Independents, such as the Olive Tree Church. Since the 1960s, South Korea's churches have shown the most dynamic modern growth in the world. Amidst massive misery and despair, poverty and social oppression, postwar church relief efforts were appreciated. As discontent with rigid ancient Asian culture grew, Koreans seeking a modernized, democratic, less patriarchal culture and religion were attracted to Christianity.[69] Many blend mysticism, reverence for nature's forces, messianic claims, charms, exorcisms, healing, and stern moral codes.

The Philippines

The Philippine Islands are about 87 percent Christian (66,600,000) and of these 94 percent are Roman Catholic, due to its long colonization by

Spain (1542–1898). It is the only predominately Christian Asian country. During the U.S. Colonial period, 1898–1946, Protestant fundamentalists were active, and now a fundamentalist movement called "El Shaddai" has attracted a large number of Filipinos with its mass services and healing rituals. The pentecostal Assemblies of God Church is the largest Protestant church, with about 300,000 members. Christian radio and television broadcasting helps churches reach the dispersed islands.[70]

India

By 1995, there were 35 million Christians in India (3.7 percent of India), many attending prayer in Christian *ashrams* (communities). Several Protestant denominations merged to form two large churches: the Church of North India and the Church of South India. Pentecostal churches remained outside these organizations. Mother Teresa's Catholic Sisters of Charity Home for Destitutes in Calcutta is one of many mission services.[71] As in many mission countries, a radio ministry reaches about 9 million dispersed believers. Native missionaries increasingly lead contemporary Indian missions. For example, an evangelical organization in India called "Gospel for Asia" supports the training of thousands of native missionaries and reaches out to the downtrodden outcasts in slums with Bible schools, radio programs, and booklets. The Low-Caste Hindu Believers in Christ Church reports 7,500,000 members.

NOTES

1. United Nations, "Worldwide Adherents of All Religions by Six Continental Areas, Mid-2002," *World Population Prospects: The 1998 Revision* (New York: United Nations, 1999).

2. "Top 10 Largest Christian Populations," http://www.adherents.com; Russell Ash, *The Top 10 of Everything* (New York: DK Publishing, 2003), pp. 160–61. There are also many small countries with a very high percentage of Christians. Barrett, *World Christian Encyclopedia*.

3. Eileen Lindner, ed., *Yearbook of American & Canadian Churches* (Nashville: Abington Press, 2003), p. 11.

4. Lindner, *Yearbook*, Ch. 2; Neela Banerjee, "U.S. Catholic Bishops Agree to Join New Ecumenical Group," *New York Times*, 18 Nov. 2004, http://www.nytimes.com/2004/11/18/national/18bishops.html.

5. Council on Parliament of World Religions, http://www.cpwr.org.

6. United Nations, "Worldwide Adherents;" "Catholic Missions," in *Catholic Encyclopedia*, http://www.Newadvent.org.cathen/10375a.

7. Rev. Thomas Fitzgerald, "The Holy Eucharist," http://www.forministry.com/USNYGOARCSCGOC/vsItem.

8. Orthodox Christian Information Center, http://www.orthodoxinfo.com.

9. "Catholic Missions," in *Catholic Encyclopedia,* http://www.Newadvent.org/cathen/10375a.

10. "Mission Statistics," United States Catholic Mission Association, 2003, http://www.uscatholicmission.org/misstats.

11. Cathy Lynn Grossman, "Catholic Abuse Reports Paint Disturbing Picture," *USAToday,* February 29, 2004, Nation, http://www.usatoday.com/news/nation/2004-02-29-abuse-reports; Bishopaccountability.org Archives, http://www.bishop-accountability.org; "Fact Sheet about the Priest Shortage and Optional Celibacy," *Future Church,* June 9, 2004, http://www.futurechurch.org; Amy Welborn, "Bankrupt in Canada," March 19, 2005, http://amywelborn.typepad.com/openbook/2005/03/bankrupt.

12. " 'Recognitio' of the Holy see for the 'Essential Norms' Approved by the United States Conference of Catholic Bishops," 26 Oct. 2004, http://www.vatican.va.

13. Andrew Greeley, "For Priests, Celibacy Is Not the Problem," *New York Times,* Op-Ed, 3 March 2004.

14. Eugene Kennedy, *The Unhealed Wound: The Church, the Priesthood, and the Question of Sexuality* (New York: St. Martin's Griffin, 2001); Justin Pope, "Catholic Newspaper Questions Priest Celibacy," Associated Press, 16 March 2002; Andrew Greeley, "For Priests, Celibacy Is Not the Problem," *New York Times,* Op-Ed, 3 March 2004, http://www.newyorktimes.com; BBC NEWS, "Pope Condemns US Church Sex Abuse," 22 May 2002, http://www.newsbbc.co.uk; Anonymous, "Portrait of the Accused," *New York Times,* 12 Jan 2003, http://www.nytimes.com/imagepages/2003/01/12/national; Jonathan Finer, "Boston Torn by Parish Closings," *Washington Post,* 17 Nov. 2004, A03, http://wwwwashingtonpost.com/ac2/wp-dyn/a55-2004Nov16; and Al Baker, "Cardinal Law Given Post at Vatican," *New York Times,* National, 28 May 2004, http://www.nytimes.com/2004/05/28/national/28card.html.

15. Lee W. Bailey and Jenny Yates, *The Near-Death Experience* (New York: Routledge, 1996).

16. Evelyn Underhill, *Mysticism* (New York: E. P. Dutton, 1911). For classic concepts and Christian mystics see http://www.digiserve.com/mystic/Christian. See also Anne Fremantle, *The Protestant Mystics* (Boston: Little, Brown, 1964). For recent thought on mysticism see http://www.well.com/user/elliotts/smse_index.html.

17. Keith Sugden, *Pilgrims* (Andover, Hampshire, UK: Pitkin, 2001).

18. "The Lutheran Liturgy: Its Biblical Roots," http://www.goodshepherd.nb.ca/liturgy.

19. Lutheran World, http://www.lutheranworld.org; and David Barrett, et al., eds., *World Christian Encyclopedia*, 2nd ed. (New York: Oxford University Press, 2001), "Global Survey," II:10, and "Germany," I:298–308.

20. "Chart No. 63. Religious Bodies—Selected Data," *Statistical Abstracts of the United States* (Washington, D.C.: U.S. Department of Commerce, Census Bureau, 2002), p. 15; and "World Relief, Human Care," *The Lutheran Witness* (Lutheran Church Missouri Synod: St. Louis, Missouri), p. 19.

21. Evangelical Lutheran Church in America, http://www/ecla/org; "Chart No. 63," Census Bureau, p. 15; United Nations, "Worldwide Adherents"; "The Largest Lutheran Communities," Adherents, http://www.adherents.com; and "Lutheranism," Nationmaster, http://www.nationmaster.com.

22. The Anglican Communion Homepage/Provinces, http://www.anglican communion.org/tour/index.cfm; "Chart No. 63," Census Bureau; and United Nations, "Worldwide Adherents."

23. Carter Heyward, *A Priest Forever: One Woman's Controversial Ordination in the Episcopal Church* (Cleveland: Pilgrim Press, 1976).

24. "Methodism" and "United Methodist Church," Nationmaster, http://www.nationmaster.com; and Methodist Church of Great Britain, http://www.methodist.org.uk.

25. "Reformed Churches," Nationmaster, http://www.nationmaster.com; and the World Alliance of Reformed Churches, http://www.warc.ch.

26. Presbyterian Church USA, http://www.pcusa.org; and the United Church of Canada, http://www.united-church.ca.

27. Reformed Church of America, http://www.rca.org; and the Protestant Reformed Church of America, http://www.prca.org/prc.html.

28. The United Church of Christ, http://www.ucc.org and http://www.congregational.org.uk.

29. "Pentecostal" at Nationmaster, http://www.nationmaster.com; "United Pentecostal Church International," http://religiousmovements.lib.virginia.edu; the Assemblies of God, http://www.ag.org; on the Pentecostal union, see Eileen Lindner, ed., *Yearbook of American and Canadian Churches 2003*, (Nashville: Abington Press, 2003) p. 45.

30. Harold Bender, et al., eds. *Mennonite Encyclopedia* (Hillsboro, KS: Mennonite Brethren Publishing House, 1959); and Mennonite Church USA, http://www.mennoniteusa.org.

31. Amish and Country, http://www.amishanccountry.com/amish-religion.htm.

32. The Religious Society of Friends, http://www.quaker.org.

33. Quakerinfo, http://www.quakerinfo.com/index.shtml.

34. Friends General Conference, http://www.fgcquaker.org; Britain Yearly Meeting, http://www.quaker.org.uk; Barrett, *World Christian Encyclopedia;* and "Anabaptist," Nationmaster, http://www.nationmaster.com.

35. Amishnet, http://amish.net; and Steven Nolt, *A History of the Amish* (Intercourse, PA: Good Books, 1992).

36. Church of the Brethren, http:// www.brethren.org; and the Heifer Project International, http://www.heifer.org.

37. Melba Newsome, "The Green Patriarch and Environmental Orthodoxy: An Interview with the Patriarch of Eastern Orthodoxy," in *The Amicus Journal* 20, no. 4 (1999, Winter): 15–17.

38. Andrew Greeley, *The Catholic Myth* (New York: Collier MacMillan, 1990); Charles Curran, *The Catholic Moral Tradition Today: A Synthesis* (Washington, D.C.: Georgetown University Press, 1999); Thomas Berry, *The Dream of the Earth* (San Francisco: Sierra Club, 1988); and Hans Küng, *A Global Ethic,* http://astro.ocis.temple.edu/~dialogue/Antho/kung.htm.

39. Barrett, *World Christian Encyclopedia,* II:10; and Philip Jenkins, *The New Christianity* (Oxford: Oxford University Press, 2002).

40. "Fundamentalism," http://religiousmovements.lib.virginia.edu/nrms/fund.html; "Fundamentalism," Nationmaster, http://www.nationmaster.com; Martin Marty and R. Scott Appleby, eds., *The Fundamentalism Project* (Chicago: University of Chicago Press, 1995); Karen Armstrong, *The Battle for God* (New York: Alfred A. Knopf, 2000); and Max L. Stackhouse, "Fundamentalism Around the World," Religion Online, http://www. religion-online.

41. Carl F. H. Henry, *God, Revelation and Authority,* 6 vols. (Waco, TX: Word Books, 1982), vol. 5, pp. 157–64.

42. *Sojourners,* http://www.sojo.net; Campolo, http://www.tonycampolo.org; Jann Aldredge-Clanton, http://www.jannaldredgeclanton.com/speaker.htm; and Alan Cooperman and Thomas Edsall, "Evangelicals Say They Led Charge for the GOP," *The Washington Post,* 8 Nov. 2004, A01, http://washingtonpost.com.

43. The Barna Group, http://www.barna.org; Barrett, *World Christian Encyclopedia,* I:772, II:10; "Evangelical Christianity," Nationmaster, http://www.nationmaster.com; and Robert Liebman and Robert Wuthnow, eds., *The New Christian Right* (New York: Aldine Publishing, 1983).

44. Charles Coughlin, Biography Resource Center, http://galegroup.com.servlet/BioRC; and Billy Graham Evangelistic Association, http://www.billygraham.org.

45. "Televangelist" and "Jim Bakker," Nationmaster, http://www.nationmaster.com; Jeffrey Hadden and Anson Shupe, *Elmer Gantry: Exemplar of American Televangelism* (Norwood, NJ: Ablex Publishing, 1990); Religious Movements, http://religiousmovements.lib.virginia.edu/pubs; and "Jim Bakker Show," http://www.jimbakkershow.com.

46. "Turning America On To Positive Thinking: Dr. Norman Vincent Peale," http://www.usdreams.com/Peale28.html.

47. Crystal Cathedral, http://www.crystalcathedral.org; and "Robert Schuller," http://www.rapidnet.com/~jbeard/bdm/exposes/schuller/general.htm.

48. On mega-churches, see Hartford Seminary for Religion Research, http://hirr.hartsem.edu/bookshelf/thumma_article2.html; and Eileen Lindner, "Megachurches: How Do They Count?" in Eileen Lindner, ed., *Yearbook of American & Canadian Churches 2003* (Nashville: Abington Press, 2003).

49. The Princeton Religion Research Center (PRRC), "Survey Trivia from the PRRC." The PRRC is a nondenominational, interfaith research institute, founded in 1977. Its successor is the Princeton Center for the Study of Religion, http://www.princeton.edu/~csrelig.

50. On "Mother Earth," Matthew Fox, *The Coming of the Cosmic Christ* (San Francisco: Harper & Row, 1988): pp. 144–149; On "sin," Melba Newsome, "The Green Patriarch and Environmental Orthodoxy: An Interview with the Patriarch of Eastern Orthodoxy," *Amicus Journal* 20, no. 4 (1999, Winter): pp. 15–17.

51. Doug King, "Re-Imagining Gathering Explores New Realities in Feminist Theology," Witherspoon Progressive Presbyterians, http://www.witherspoonsociety.org/re-imagining_2000.htm. A critical view is presented in Parker T. Williamson, "Sophia Upstages Jesus at Re-Imagining Revival," Presbyterian Layman, http://www.layman.org/layman/news/reimagining-revival.htm.

52. Thomas Ogletree, *The Death of God Controversy* (Nashville: Abington Press, 1966).

53. For an introduction, see Christopher Butler, *Postmodernism: A Very Short Introduction* (Oxford: Oxford University Press, 2002).

54. Polly Young-Eisendrath and Terence Dawson, eds., *The Cambridge Companion to Jung* (Cambridge: Cambridge University Press, 1997).

55. Dan Kimball, *The Emerging Church* (Grand Rapids, MI: Zondervan, 2003).

56. United Nations, "Worldwide Adherents;" Barrett, "Global Table 18," *World Christian Encyclopedia;* and Philip Jenkins, *The Next Christendom: The Coming of Global Christianity* (Oxford: Oxford University Press, 2002).

57. Barrett, *World Christian Encyclopedia*, I:391–96; and S.P. Colbi, *A History of the Christian Presence in the Holy Land* (Lanham, MD: University Press of America, 1988).

58. "Yugoslavia," in Barrett, *World Christian Encyclopedia*, I:812–16.

59. Eastern Europe countries in United States Federal Research Division, Library of Congress, Country Studies/Area Handbook Series 1986–1998, http://countrystudies.us.

60. "Brazil" in Barrett, *World Christian Encyclopedia*, II:130–48.

61. David Stoll, *Is Latin America Turning Protestant? The Politics of Evangelical Growth* (Berkeley: University of California Press, 1990).

62. United Nations, "Worldwide Adherents."

63. "Nigeria," in Barrett, *World Christian Encyclopedia*, I:549–54.

64. "South Africa," in Barrett, *World Christian Encyclopedia*, I:675–81.

65. "India," in Barrett, *World Christian Encyclopedia*, I:359–371; S.C. Neill, *A History of Christianity in India*, 2 vols. (Cambridge: Cambridge University Press, 1985); and Gospel for Asia, http://www.gfs.org.

66. "China," in Barrett, *World Christian Encyclopedia*, I:191–98; and Daniel H. Bays, ed., *Christianity in China from the 18th Century to the Present* (Stanford, CA: Stanford University Press, 1996).

67. "Japan," in Barrett, *World Christian Encyclopedia*, I:412–19; and J. Breen and M. Williams, eds., *Japan and Christianity: Impacts and Responses* (New York: St. Martin's, 1995).

68. Grace Ji-Sun Kim, *The Grace of Sophia: A Korean North American Women's Christology* (Cleveland: Pilgrim Press, 2002).

69. "Korea," in Barrett, *World Christian Encyclopedia*, I:682–86; and D.N. Clark, *Christianity in Modern Korea*, Asian Agenda Report 5 (Lanham, MD: University or America Press, 1986).

70. "Philippines" in Barrett, *World Christian Encyclopedia*, I: 594–600; and C. Sabado, *Philippine Church History* (Manila: Salesiana, 1990).

71. Lush Gjergji, *Mother Teresa: Her Life and Works* (New Rochelle, NY: New City Press, 1991).

5

RITUALS AND HOLIDAYS

Ritual, ceremony, and celebration in Christianity here mean the formal acts of religious observance, sometimes outside of weekly worship, including holidays such as Christmas and Easter and occasions such as marriages and funerals. Rituals such as kneeling, chanting, or immersion in water are symbolic events that convey guiding meanings and spiritual realities deeper than words. They mark stages of life transitions, such as marriage, initiations, and participation in divine power. They are intended to be transforming, as when asking forgiveness and being reconciled with God. Holidays are times for special celebrations of the most significant beliefs and past events of the faith, especially Christmas and Easter.

The Christmas and Easter seasons extend for several weeks. Advent is a period of about four weeks leading up to Christmas, involving preparations such as decorations with evergreens, lights, Christmas trees, poinsettia flowers, gift-wrapping, and preparation of special foods such as cookies. Most Christians celebrate Christmas on December 25. Some Orthodox instead celebrate "Nativity" on January 6. Christmas Eve is traditionally celebrated with an elaborate church service, often with a children's pageant acting out the Christmas story. Churches typically decorate with evergreens and many lights and may conclude with a ceremony of each believer holding a candle while singing a Christmas carol such as "Silent Night." Christmas morning is of course a time for gift-giving, in the spirit of Christian benevolence, followed by a family meal and perhaps visits with family and friends. After Christmas, Epiphany is the celebration of the "showing forth" of the newborn Jesus. Eastern churches commemorate this as the baptism of Jesus, and Western churches celebrate Epiphany as the time when the wise men visited the infant Jesus in Bethlehem.

The second major holiday season centers around Easter, or *Pascha* for the Orthodox. This is a "movable" holiday, calculated as the first Sunday after the first full moon after the Spring Equinox. Lent is the 40-day season leading up to Easter, beginning with Ash Wednesday. On this day the faithful may receive on their foreheads a cross of ashes, symbolizing death. An optional period of self-restraint traditionally follows until Easter, usually in the form of fasting. Holy Week begins with Palm Sunday, the Sunday before Easter, celebrated with palm fronds to recall the tradition of Jesus's entry into Jerusalem marked by believers throwing palm fronds and robes on the ground in front of him. Next, Maundy Thursday is a sad day, for it recalls Jesus praying in the Garden of Gethsemane, the betrayal of Jesus by Judas, and his arrest for crucifixion. Good Friday, also a sad day, recalls Jesus's crucifixion.

Easter Sunday is a grand, joyous celebration in church services and expresses one of the most important Christian beliefs: that Jesus overcame death with resurrection, returning to life in his body for a short time before ascending to heaven. On this Sunday churches usually decorate with white lilies and have an elaborate celebratory service with special music such as the "Hallelujah" chorus from Handel's *Messiah*. In most Christian countries there is also a joy shared at the onset of the spring season, a time of renewal of life parallel to Christ's resurrection. Children happily hunt for "Easter eggs," and bunny or chick images, which are ancient symbols of the renewal of earth's fertility in spring. Eastern European decorated eggs may be very elaborate and jeweled. On the seventh Sunday after Easter, Christians celebrate Pentecost to remember the descent of the Holy Spirit onto Christ's apostles after the resurrection, as is described in the second chapter of the New Testament book of Acts.

Different churches have variations on these themes. Some denominations add many holidays, such as saints' days, and some have fewer and more restrained celebrations with less ritual.

THREE BRANCHES

The three branches of Christianity—Eastern Orthodox, Catholic, and Protestant—each have many colorful variations on Christian themes in liturgies. For the Orthodox, every day is a holy day. For Catholics, Most days

Greek Orthodox priest serving Communion bread at St. Catherine Greek Orthodox Church, Ithaca, New York. Courtesy of
the author.

are holy, but some are called "ordinary time." Protestants in general have
fewer holy days.

Eastern Orthodox

Sacraments

Orthodox sacraments are special mysteries believed to disclose the presence of God through the prayers and actions of priests and congregations.
The Orthodox retain seven medieval sacraments:

1. Baptism is the ritual of water washing away original sin for new initiates;
   infants are partially immersed in water in a special tub in the sanctuary, and
   adults are fully immersed in a larger tank.
2. Chrismation, or anointment, is marking a cross on the forehead right after
   Baptism with perfumed oil (myrrh). This is similar to confirmation for Catholics, when church membership is affirmed.
3. Holy Eucharist, or Communion, celebrates the death and resurrection of
   Christ, believed to bring salvation from suffering and eternal life.
4. Confession, Penance, or Reconciliation—its frequency is left to the discretion of the believer, but in case of serious sin, is required before Communion.
   The priest sits face-to-face with the parishioner.

5. Holy Unction is anointment of the sick with oil during times of physical or spiritual pain.

6. Ordination is being initiated into holy orders such as the priesthood; a deacon aids the priest; a priest serves a parish as pastor and teacher. Priests may marry before ordination, but bishops must be celibate or widowed. Ordination is limited to men. Orthodox priests outside of the liturgy wear a simple robe.

7. Matrimony is seen not as a social or legal institution, but as a sacred bond requiring mutual consent. In the service, after the couple has exchanged rings, they are crowned. In the case of a mixed marriage with someone of another faith, the Orthodox partner must promise to baptize and raise the children in the Orthodox Church. Divorce with the right to remarry in the church is discouraged, but granted in cases of adultery, desertion, incurable diseases, life imprisonment, or attempted murder of one spouse by the other.

Orthodox believers often repeat the "Jesus" prayer: "Lord Jesus Christ, Son of God, have mercy on me, a sinner." Saints are venerated and Mary is especially honored as the "Theotokos" (God-bearer). The Orthodox set aside fast days for abstinence from certain foods. Ethnic churches in the United States have festivals with their native foods, music, and dance.[1]

Roman Catholic

Sacraments

The sacraments are empowerments for the faithful to carry out the mission of the church in the world. There are seven major Catholic sacraments, divided into three kinds: initiation, healing, and service of communion.

The Sacraments of Initiation: Baptism, Confirmation, and Eucharist

1. Baptism is the first ritual of becoming a Christian, and it is a gateway to the other sacraments. Through it sins are forgiven so one can become a new creation, filled with the Holy Spirit. It is celebrated with water, by triple immersion, or by a triple pouring of water on the head. It symbolizes the washing away of the old personality and the rebirth of the new renewed by participation in the divine Father, Son, and Holy Spirit. The commitment of the parents, godparents, and the congregation to raise the child in the faith is also affirmed. It is performed on infant children of Catholics or adult converts.

2. Confirmation is a further initiation, binding believers to the church. It is administered when the age of reason has been reached by children,

Roman Catholic priest elevating the cup of Eucharist wine at Immaculate Conception Church, Ithaca, New York. Courtesy of the author.

after catechism has been learned, at various ages in various cultures, and is ordinarily performed by the bishop. The rite involves renewal of baptismal promises, confession of faith, and anointing the forehead of the baptized with sacred chrism (oil). The minister lays on hands and says: "Be sealed with the Gift of the Holy Spirit."

3. Eucharist is in tradition the pre-eminent sacrament, based on Jesus's Last Supper, the Thursday night before his crucifixion. In the Gospel accounts, sensing his impending death to be a sacrifice, Jesus took bread and said: "This is my body, which is given for you. Do this in remembrance of me." He gave new meaning to ordinary breaking of bread as a sign that his body will be broken in the next day's crucifixion, and that as the wine is poured out, so will his blood be shed, as a suffering servant. His death was believed to establish a new relationship with God (atonement, or reuniting), a new Covenant (promise), and the ritual communicates his saving power. Today the Catholic Church serves Eucharist in the form of the "host," a wafer of compressed wheat bread and wine diluted with a bit of water.

The Sacraments of Healing: Penance and Reconciliation, and Anointing the Sick

4. Penance and Reconciliation is the sacramental request for God's merciful pardon for an offense. It involves a confession of sins to a bishop or priest. Today this may be done anonymously in a booth with the priest separated from the confessor by a wall with a screen for communicating. Confession may also be done face-to-face, if the confessor chooses. Grave sins (formerly "mortal") such as idolatry, murder, or adultery, are distinguished from venial (everyday faults). Confession consecrates the confessor's contrite (sorrowful) penance. The priest is then authorized to absolve the sins, granting pardon from eternal and temporal punishment and peace. Interior, sincere conversion in the heart, as well as turning away from the wrong acts committed, are required for true penance and reconciliation. Since Vatican II, the minister is seen more as a healer than a judge. Many acts can express repentance: fasting, prayer, charity to the poor, efforts at reconciliation with those wronged, admission of faults, or sincere worship. The confessor bishop or priest is strictly bound under severe penalties to the confidentiality of the confession. The faithful, after attaining the age of discretion, are to confess serious sins at least once a year. They normally are not to take communion before confession of serious sins.

5. Anointing the Sick is the sacrament of commending the ill to the Lord by priestly laying on of hands, silent prayer, and anointment. Jesus's numerous healings of body and soul are the model for this sacrament. Illness is a trial that can lead to despair or be a time for self-examination that can increase faith. Before Vatican II this was called "Extreme Unction" and reserved for those close to death. It can be celebrated at home, church, or hospital, for one person or many. Anointing the sick is a preparation for return to the heavenly home.

The Sacraments of Vocation and Commitment: Holy Orders and Matrimony

6. The Sacrament of Holy Orders or Vocation is commitment to ministry in the tradition of Jesus's apostles for those committing themselves to service in the Church, serving as mediators between God and humans. Priests can exercise a sacred power coming only from Christ through his Church. This does not guarantee the perfection of the person of the priest, who may not be free from error. These flaws are to be overcome, but do not impede the effectiveness of the sacraments. Outside the Mass, priests usually wear black with a white clerical collar.

7. Matrimony for Roman Catholics is seen not as a human civil institution, but coming from God. A bride and groom prepare themselves by undergoing the sacrament of penance and receiving suitable instructions. The couple should express their consent before the Church, represented by a priest or deacon, being under no constraint, fear, or impeded by any law.

In some countries a mixed marriage between a Catholic and a non-Catholic, either baptized or not, requires special attention. Both parties should be clear that the Catholic member should preserve their Catholic faith and educate their children in the Catholic Church. With permission of the bishop, Catholics may be married in a Protestant church before a Protestant minister. It is hoped that non-Christian spouses will freely convert to the Church.

In some countries Catholics have access to civil divorce, but the Church deems these invalid and prevents them from receiving communion. Reconciliation of a divorced Catholic with the Church requires repentance and living in continence. The Pope can dissolve a marriage between a Christian and a non-Christian, and the Christian may remarry in the Church. A Church tribunal may examine a marriage later and declare the marriage null, having never existed. Such annulments may be granted in cases where the couple lack discretion, not understanding marriage, lack conjugal partnership or love, if one is a psychopathic, schizophrenic, sociopathic, emotionally immature, psychologically incompetent, morally impotent, or the marriage lacks interpersonal communication.[2]

Protestant

Protestant worship services are much more varied than Orthodox or Catholic, because Protestant churches have many more autonomous branches. The four major branches of the Protestant church—Lutheran, Anglican, Calvinist, and Free Churches—have varying liturgical traditions. Some Protestant services are formal, structured by liturgical books, and most are reverent and emotionally restrained. Others are reverent in a different way—spontaneous, excited and passionate, notably pentecostal services, which include baptism by the Holy Spirit, raising the hands, and healing. Protestants emphasize the "Word," or interpretations of the faith in longer sermons, rather than frequent Eucharist, and have the most congregational singing of all Christians. Communion is typically celebrated on varying schedules that local ministers may change, such as the weekly Anglican communion (plus more for special services such as funerals), bi-weekly for Lutherans, monthly for Methodists, quarterly for others (such as Presbyterians), perhaps yearly for Amish, or not at all for Quakers. Protestants generally welcome any Christian to Communion.

Lutheran Churches

Martin Luther reduced the two sacraments to those in the Bible: Baptism and Communion, and other Protestants followed this practice. Lutheran Baptism is for infants or adults, by sprinkling water on the head. Lutherans celebrate Communion frequently, perhaps twice a month. In a special way, traditional Lutheran "consubstantiation" means that the wine and bread exist alongside Christ's blood and body. But Luther denied the Catholic doctrine that sacraments have any supernatural effect in bringing God's grace from heaven. He also rejected the older idea of the power of a priest to transform the Communion. Rather, a Lutheran minister is seen as revealing the presence of God in the bread and wine.

Anglican Churches

In the Anglican communion, Church of England, Episcopal Church USA, and other branches of the Anglican Church, Communion is open to all Christians.

Each candidate for baptism is sponsored by a baptized person who intends to be an example of the Christian life. Sponsors of infants are commonly called godparents. The meaning of Baptism is explained, the candidates receive water on their heads, and perhaps chrism (perfumed oil), then prayers.

An Anglican marriage, performed by a bishop, or priest, or deacon, requires that the couple enter into marriage publicly by their free consent. A Eucharist may be included. *The Book of Common Prayer* has the groom say "In the Name of God, I (name), take you (name), to be my wife." and the bride says "In the Name of God, I (name), take you (name), to be my husband." If not married in the church, a couple may have a liturgy of the Blessing of a Civil Marriage.

Ministration to the Sick includes the laying on of hands, anointing, and communion by a priest, or if necessary, a deacon or layperson may do this, with oil blessed by a bishop or priest. Ministration at the Time of Death is a service of comfort in a time of grief, and pardoning of sins.

The Burial of the Dead liturgy begins with a funeral that may include

Psalms, Gospel readings, communion, then at the graveside, committal of the body, with the celebrant affirming eternal life, comforting the bereaved, and saying passages such as: "Earth to earth, ashes to ashes, dust to dust. The Lord bless him/her and keep him/her." Anglicans honor many saints and use rosary beads for prayer.

Methodist Churches Methodist communion may be served as each church chooses and is typically celebrated monthly. Methodist Communion is open to anyone who seeks to respond to Christ's love and to lead a new life of peace and love. Methodists believe that the bread and cup signify the body and blood of Christ and pray that the bread and cup may make them one with Christ, one with each other, and one in service to all the world. Like many Calvinist and Free Churches, Methodists serve grape juice in communion rather than wine to express their opposition to alcoholism. Methodist children may take Communion when their parents consider them to be ready. Methodist churches may pass plates of bread and trays of grape juice in small cups throughout the congregation, or serve up front from a common plate and cup, often by "intinction," or dipping the piece of bread into the wine before putting it in one's mouth. Members of the church may help serve Communion, along with the minister.

Baptism of children or adults is by sprinkling or pouring water on the head, or by immersion, as the parents or the baptized child chooses. Baptism of children is preferred, as part of the parents' responsibility to commit to raising their children in the church.

The local church may design its own confirmation program, which means receiving a person into church membership after a period of education in Christianity and Methodist beliefs. Children who have been educated in the faith may be confirmed at any age, usually around sixth grade up to twelfth grade, depending on the local church.

The minister may perform special services, such as weddings and funerals, with considerable flexibility.

Calvinist Churches

For Calvinists generally, Baptism is seen as the washing away of sins shortly after birth by dipping in or sprinkling water, for infants or adults. It is also a time of commitment of the family and church to raising the child in the faith. The Lord's Supper is a mysterious sign, not the physical presence of Christ, in the bread and wine, received in faith by believers. It is not meant for believers considering themselves to be perfect, but for those who sincerely seek to live by the faith with the aid of God's grace and Christ's spirit. Services are held for the ordination of deacons, elders, and ministers and for marriages and funerals. Christmas and Easter are special services, and other church holidays such as Lent and Pentecost may be celebrated moderately.

Free Churches

In their independence from hierarchy, Free Churches have a great deal of latitude in performing rituals and celebrating holidays. Baptism is not performed on infants however, but only on those of an age of understanding what they are doing. It may be by a simple sprinkling of water on the head, or by full immersion under water. The Lord's Supper may range from a communal "agape" feast, or dish-to-pass supper with prayers and songs to a traditional passing of plates with bread and wine on them, or coming forward to drink from a common cup or dip the bread in the cup ("intinction"). Free Churches do not celebrate the Lord's Supper weekly, because they focus more on the Word in the Bible and sermons. The emphasis should be on sincere participation, rather than routine repetition.

Baptists   Baptists combine Free Church and Calvinist traditions. For Baptists, the Lord's Supper is a symbolic act, partaking of bread and fruit of the vine, to memorialize Christ. It may be offered as each congregation chooses, but is not frequent. Baptism is always by total immersion under water of one old enough to understand the faith.

Mennonites   A version of the earlier Anabaptists today is the Mennonite Church, that stresses the importance of Baptism by immersion for those who understand its meaning. They will accept new members baptized upon confession of faith, but if a new member was baptized as an infant, he or she must be re-baptized. Communion may be celebrated quarterly, monthly, or otherwise, at the discretion of the congregation. Footwashing was practiced in early times, but is less so now.

Brethren   The Brethren baptize only believers who seek to follow Jesus and are old enough to understand the faith. In front of the congregation, a newly committed person kneels in the water of the baptistry, announces his or her decision, and is immersed underwater by the minister's hand three times to signify the Father, and of the Son, and of the Holy Spirit. Brethren also anoint those in physical or emotional difficulty with oil, and the minister and others may lay on hands for healing. For Communion they celebrate a "love feast" following the pattern of the Last Supper, when Jesus washed his disciples' feet and offered the bread and cup.

Quakers   Friends do not practice Baptism or Communion. Quaker weddings involve prior private preparatory discussions between the engaged couple with some elders, to seek approval for the match. The wedding vows are followed by a time when anyone in attendance may speak, sharing their memories and best wishes for the new couple. All who attend the wedding are welcomed to sign a paper testifying to the wedding. Funerals are also meetings for worship where anyone may speak.

Amish   Many Amish practice footwashing and the holy kiss (among close church members during worship). Communion is semi-annual, Christian holidays are traditional ones.

Black Protestants   Black Protestants in Africa are divided between the mission churches affiliated with European mission denominations, such as the Anglicans, and the African Independent Churches. The Independent churches incorporate more indigenous rituals.

In North America, the Black Protestants often join the Baptist church, which allows them a good measure of local autonomy, or other Free Churches, such as the pentecostals. Pentecostal baptism by the Holy Spirit may occur and is fully supported. Music is important, and sincere expression is highly valued. African American churches have contributed a major type of church music called gospel ("O, Happy Day," or "My Sweet Lord"), powerful in its lyrical sincerity, joy, and faith. Gospel music has influenced other Protestants, black and white, worldwide. One outstanding black gospel music group is "Sweet Honey in the Rock."

HOLIDAYS

The Christian calendar year has major holidays in common for all branches of the church and special additional days for each branch. Christmas, for all except some Orthodox, is December 25. Easter is a moving holiday, generally calculated as the first Sunday after the first full moon after the Spring Equinox. This usually falls in April but may come as early as March, and, for Julian calendar Orthodox, as late as five weeks following the Gregorian calendar Easter/*Pascha*.

The shared holidays for most all Christian churches are:

January 6: Epiphany celebrates the "manifestation" of Jesus to the wise men in Bethlehem, but for Gregorian calendar Orthodox, the baptism of Jesus; for Julian Calendar Orthodox, Christmas.

February: Lent is the 40 days before Easter, beginning with Ash Wednesday, when many churches have a service marking believers' foreheads with ashes in the shape of a cross.

April: Holy Week begins with Palm Sunday, through Maundy Thursday, Good Friday, and Easter Sunday (or *Pascha* Sunday for Orthodox), recollecting Christ's crucifixion and resurrection.

May: The Ascension of Christ to heaven in a cloud of light the fortieth day following Easter.

May: Pentecost is the gathering of apostles who felt the presence of the Holy Spirit as a rushing wind and flames above their heads; 50 days after Easter.

August 6: Transfiguration is when Jesus took Peter, James, and John to a hilltop and was transfigured into a bright light, speaking with Elijah and Moses, which showed them his divinity.

November 1: All Saints' Day commemorates martyrs and all the departed.

November: Advent is the season of four Sundays before Christmas.

December 25: Christmas celebrates the birth of Jesus in Bethlehem.

Orthodox Calendar

The Orthodox Church for many centuries followed the old Byzantine Julian calendar, attributed to the Roman Emperor Julius Caesar. But because it was not very accurate, the Catholic Church adopted a more accurate new Gregorian calendar in 1582, which is still used. In 1923, several Orthodox churches shifted to the Gregorian calendar, including Constantinople and Greece. But others did not change, including Russia and Serbia. So the dates for Christmas and Easter/*Pascha* will vary in different Orthodox churches. Christmas, or Nativity, in the Julian calendar is January 6.

The Orthodox Calendar contains two or three celebrations every day of the year, for saints, martyrs, church fathers, and others. Fast days are marked on the calendar. The major holidays are:

January 6: Epiphany (Gregorian calendar), the Baptism of Jesus; Christmas (Julian Calendar).

February 2: Presentation of Christ in the Temple (40 days after his birth).

March 25: The Annunciation, or announcement to Mary of her being pregnant with Jesus.

April (usually): Palm Sunday, Holy Week, and Easter, or *Pascha.*

May: Ascension of Christ to heaven, 40 days after *Pascha.*

May: Pentecost, when the apostles felt the presence of the Holy Spirit 50 days after *Pascha.* All Saints' Day, commemorating martyrs and those who have died.

July: Sunday of the Holy Fathers, the early church theologians.

August 6: Transfiguration, when Jesus was transfigured into a bright light.

August 15: The Dormition or Repose (death) of the Virgin Mary.

September 8: Nativity (birth) of the Virgin Mary.

September 14: Exaltation or Elevation of the Holy Cross.

November 21: Presentation of the Virgin Mary in the Temple.

December 25: Holy Nativity, or Christmas (Gregorian calendar).

The colors of Orthodox liturgical vestments are symbolic of various holidays. White is common, red is used for *Pascha* and Nativity, green for Pentecost, blue for holidays celebrating the Mother of God, and purple for Lent.[3]

Roman Catholic Calendar

The Catholic calendar has memorials for saints, apostles, theologians, kings, queens, and others, every day of the year. "Solemnity" means the highest or most important Holy Days. Certain ones are "Holy Days of Obligation" (to avoid needless work and attend Mass). The time between Holy Days is called "Ordinary Time."

January 6: Epiphany, the visit of wise men to newborn Jesus at Bethlehem.

February 2: Presentation of Jesus at the temple 40 days after his birth.

March 19: Solemnity of Joseph, husband of Mary

March 25: Annunciation, or announcement to Mary of her being pregnant with Jesus.

April (usually): Palm Sunday, Holy Week, Easter.

May: Pentecost, when the apostles felt the presence of the Holy Spirit, 50 days after Easter.

May, first Sunday after Pentecost: Solemnity of the Holy Trinity.

May, Sunday after Holy Trinity: Solemnity of *Corpus Christi* (body of Christ).

May, Friday following the second Sunday after Pentecost: Solemnity of the Sacred Heart.

June 24: Memorial of birth of John the Baptist.

June 24: Solemnity of Peter and Paul, Apostles.

August 6: Transfiguration, when Jesus was transfigured into a bright light.

August 15: The Assumption of Mary into heaven.

November 1: All Saints' Day.

November 2: All Souls' Day (in memory of the deceased).

November (usually), Last Sunday in Ordinary Time: Solemnity of Christ the King.

December 8: Solemnity of the Immaculate Conception, or Mary's freedom from original sin.

December 25: Christmas, Solemnity of Jesus's birth.

The Roman Catholic liturgical vestment colors—the color of the altar cloth and the celebrant's sash—are violet for Lent and Advent; white or gold for Easter, Christmas, Holy Days, and Feast Days; red for Feast Days and Holy Days; and green for ordinary time.[4]

Protestant Calendars

Protestant calendars vary, as there are so many independent branches. Individual ministers have more discretion in the less structured churches.

Lutheran Calendar

Lutherans follow a liturgical calendar year, with three major cycles and many festivals, each assigned liturgical colors for the minister's vestments and church art. The Christmas cycle includes Advent (blue, rose, purple), Christmas (white), Epiphany (white, green), and Transfiguration (white). The Easter season colors are white and gold and Pentecost is red.[5]

Anglican Calendar

The Anglican Church year typically observes major feasts such as Easter, Ascension, Pentecost (Whitsunday in England), All Saints' Day, Christmas, and Epiphany. Several other Anglican feast days include The Holy Name, the Annunciation, and St. Mary Magdalene. Fasting days are Ash Wednesday and Good Friday. Uniquely Anglican days of commemoration include those for English church leaders such as Dunstan, Archbishop of Canterbury. Holy Days include commemorations of St. Stephen (Dec. 26), and St. Paul (Jan. 25).[6]

Methodist Calendar

The Methodist liturgical year has two cycles: Christmas and Easter. The Christmas Cycle (Advent-Christmas-Epiphany), like most churches, culminates on Christmas Eve with a service dramatizing of Jesus's birth, accompanied by biblical readings, special music, and Christmas carols, surrounded by evergreens and candlelight. The Methodist Easter Cycle (Lent-Easter-Pentecost) culminates with the Easter Sunday service, with white lilies (as at many churches) and special music. Between cycles is ordinary time symbolized by green, indicating growth. Traditionally purple is used during Advent and Lent, symbolizing royalty and penitence. Blue may also be used during Advent to symbolize hope. During Christmas and Easter white and gold express joy. Red indicates the work of the Holy Spirit, like fire on the Day of Pentecost. During Holy Week, red symbolizes the blood of Christ. Red is also used for ordinations and church anniversaries.

Calvinist Calendars

Calvinist churches have more variation in calendars and liturgical colors. The Presbyterian Church USA, for example, changes colors annually.

Free Church Calendars

The Free churches may loosely follow the more structured church calendars and liturgical colors, but this is generally at the discretion of the local minister and church. For example, holidays observed by the Amish are Christmas, Good Friday, Easter, Ascension Day, Pentecost, and Whit Monday (the day after Pentecost). On these holy days they fast and meditate on related scriptures.

The Advent, Christmas, and Epiphany Season

The most popular of Christian holidays is Christmas, also known as Yule, Noël, or the Nativity, celebrating the birth of Jesus. It is observed in the West on December 25. The name comes from "Christ-mass." Christians worldwide celebrate the entry of the divine child into the world, thus bringing peace and good will to humanity. This spiritual meaning is the most important significance of Christmas, for the exact date of Jesus's birth is unknown and was celebrated on various dates for some time. In 354 Bishop Liberius of Rome set December 25 as the official date.

Christians place Christmas symbolically near the winter solstice, at the height of the earth's darkness (symbolizing suffering, depression, and evil), making the entry of God's divine son a mark of bringing new light, compassion, and healing to the world. The Christmas season begins with Advent, four Sundays before Christmas, or 40 days before for Orthodox, and continues afterward with Epiphany, the celebration of the showing of the newborn Jesus to the shepherds and wise men.

In early Christianity, Christmas was at first celebrated only by religious services. As Christianity spread, Christmas also became a time of merrymaking, singing, and dancing. The custom of gift-giving at Christmas goes back to the gifts brought to the infant Jesus by the Wise Men and kings from the East. Now some Christians strive to keep the meaning of Christmas's divine love from being overwhelmed by the potential commercialism of gift buying. The Christmas tree custom comes from a Germanic tradition of a sacred tree. Christmas in warm parts of the world in December celebrate more with flowers, feasts, or processions, as in Bethlehem. Contemporary Christmas Eve services include enactments of the Christmas story by youths, singing of popular Christmas carols, and candles held by each person.

Many Christians flock to celebrate Christmas in Bethlehem, five miles south of Jerusalem, where by tradition Jesus was born. The Church of the Nativity there is filled with crowds of travelers to see the Grotto of the Nativity, the traditional place of Jesus's birth.

In Europe there are many varieties of traditional Christmas rituals. English children hang up stockings, decorate a Christmas tree, and open gifts Christmas afternoon. The next day is traditionally Boxing Day, when money is placed in individual boxes for service workers. In Eastern Europe people in colorful clothes go to houses singing Christmas carols, where they are given sweets and good wishes. A traditional feast dish is a raisin, rice, and honey pudding called *kutya*. In France the legendary *Petit Noel* (Little Christmas) comes down the chimney with gifts to put in the children's shoes. People decorate their homes with mistletoe, an ancient, seemingly magical plant, for good luck. Christmas day is a religious holiday only; gifts are exchanged on New Years' Day.

In Italy, homes traditionally have a miniature Nativity scene of the birth of Jesus. The day before Christmas is a day of fasting that ends with the family gathering around the Nativity scene, praying and placing the *bam-*

bino (baby) Jesus in the manger. Then gifts are exchanged. In Rome on Christmas Day St. Peter's Church is traditionally filled with travelers from around the world. The Mass begins with a grand procession concluding with the Pope carried on a throne, blessing the people as he passes them. On the day of Epiphany, January 6, Italian tradition tells of *La Befans,* a female version of Santa Claus, who comes down the chimney. She rings a bell in one hand to announce herself and carries a cane in the other hand to warn unruly children.

In Spain, Christians traditionally try to do a good deed before midnight on Christmas Eve. Midnight Christmas mass fills the churches, and afterward people dance the *jota,* a special Christmas dance. Homes have a little nativity scene, the *nacimiento.* In Belgium, Christmas is a religious day when some towns traditionally have a long procession of hundreds of children parading through the streets carrying crucifixes or streamers. In Germany the Christmas tree is decorated with lights, tinsel, and sweets, and St. Nicholas comes on Christmas Eve. In Switzerland, *Christkindli* (Santa Claus) traditionally arrives in a sleigh pulled by reindeer. He wears wings, white robes, and a crown and distributes gifts.

Christmas is traditionally a more religious holiday in French Quebec and a blend of English and other immigrant traditions in the rest of Canada and in the United States. As Dutch, German, and other immigrants arrived, Christmas in the United States was revitalized after the limited Puritan traditions and is now celebrated with a family-centered ceremony of gift-giving around a decorated evergreen tree. Children hang up stockings for gifts and are showered with gifts Christmas morning, said to be brought by Santa Claus, who flies a reindeer-pulled sleigh through the night sky and slips magically down the chimney with his bag of gifts on Christmas Eve.

On Christmas Eve many churches have Christmas services, often re-enacting the birth of Jesus in a pageant with children playing roles as sheep, angels, and adults reading birth passages from the Gospels. Often the services end with a darkening of the sanctuary and a lighting of a candle held by each person while singing a hymn or Christmas carol, such as "Silent Night." Models of Jesus's birth in a stable are set up in church or outside, called a *crèche.*

Christmas is celebrated in Latin America with many Spanish-based customs blended with pre-Columbian Aztec traditions. During the weeks before Christmas, neighbors exchange tamales and drinks at parties *(posadas).* Midnight Christmas Eve, church bells toll and traditionally people fall to their knees and wish the nearest person *"Nochebuena"* (good Christmas

Eve). In Mexico large markets are filled with baskets, leatherwork, and pottery made by families for the season. Mexican Christmas is celebrated from December 16 to January 6 with much dancing and singing, flowers, and hanging *piñatas* filled with gifts for the children who break them open. Processionals go from house to house, led by a boy and girl carrying figures of Joseph and Mary, then place the baby Jesus figure in a manger, while they all sing thanks. In Brazil, Santa Claus, known as Papa Noel, is believed to come through the windows with gifts to put in the children's shoes for January 6.

The Lent, Holy Week, Easter, and Pentecost Season

Easter, the celebration of Jesus's resurrection, is a spring festival, echoing the pre-Christian rites of spring's renewal of nature after winter. It was named after the Anglo-Saxon spring goddess Estre. Lent is the period of 40 days before Easter, beginning with Ash Wednesday, when the faithful may receive a mark of ashes on their forehead, symbolic of Jesus's suffering, with the words: "Remember, O man, that dust thou art and unto dust shall thou return." Lent continues with recommended fasting for Orthodox and Catholics, and spiritual preparation until Easter, based upon Jesus's 40-day retreat into the wilderness in preparation for his ministry.

For the Easter season Jerusalem is filled with Christians of all branches who watch the processions during the Holy Week before Easter. They visit the traditional sites of Jesus's last week: the Last Supper; the Garden of Gethsemane, where Jesus is said to have prayed; the *Ecce Homo* ("Behold the Man") Arch, where Jesus was supposedly judged by Pontius Pilate; and the Via Dolorosa ("Way of Sadness"), the path on which Jesus is said to have carried his cross. Pilgrims carry crosses and stop at the 14 "Stations of the Cross" on the way to the place of crucifixion (Golgatha) and then to the traditional place of the tomb at the Church of the Holy Sepulchre. There Orthodox and other priests pass fire from their candles to the crowds outside, symbolizing the resurrection of Jesus.

The date of Easter is calculated as the first Sunday after the first full moon after the Spring Equinox, thus between March 21 and April 25. The week before Easter in the spring is called Holy Week, beginning with Palm Sunday, the Sunday before. On this Sunday church services typically use palm leaves that worshippers then carry home to celebrate Jesus's entry into Jerusalem on a donkey, when crowds spread palm branches and robes before him. For all Christians, Maundy Thursday grieves Jesus's betrayal, and Good Friday is the day of the Crucifixion. On Good Friday, parades in Mexico are filled with people wearing black, and statues are draped in black cloth. Good Friday is devoted to the Virgin of Sorrows *(Virgin de Delores)* with altars. Participants emanate deep feelings of sorrow and hope. Easter Sunday throughout Christendom is the culmination, with a joyous celebration of Jesus's resurrection, affirming belief in eternal life. Churches are decorated with white, symbolizing purity and joy.

Easter in North America is celebrated with special church services, such as outdoor sunrise services to greet the sun, symbolic of Jesus's resurrection and the power of the divine light to overcome darkness. The indoor services are graced with many Easter lilies and grand music. Easter also welcomes warm weather, celebrated with flowers, colored eggs, and bunnies, all ancient symbols of the rebirth of nature in spring.

For the Orthodox each day of Holy Week has a specific meaning, and the culminating day is called *Pascha,* or Easter. The *Pascha* egg decorations of the Orthodox tradition are elaborate and elegant, picturing crosses, flowers, and abstract designs of multicolored detail. *Pascha* is the most important Orthodox holiday. The Orthodox practice a 40-day Lenten fast before *Pascha.* Easter or *Pascha* is the celebration of Jesus's resurrection, which for believers overcomes death, suffering, and evil, and promises eternal life. It is tied in with the renewal of nature in springtime, long celebrated in archaic religions because of the sprouting of plants and the birth of baby animals.

Some cultures, especially in Spain and Latin America, celebrate Holy Week with elaborate rituals, such as the *Semana Santa* (Holy Week) in Seville, Spain, that involves a week of processions with elaborate floats. They are carried by men and portray Mary, Jesus crucified, and other scenes with statues, candles, and ornate decorations. Observing believers often react with great emotion. Robed and masked penitents process with musical bands and church organizations.

For Catholics and Protestants, Easter, with joyous music and lilies, is celebrated as much as Christmas. The popular use of Easter eggs and rabbits are remnants of pre-Christian fertility symbols.

Easter in Latin America is a major holiday. In Mexico, for example, it ends the prior weeks of Lent fasting with two weeks of Holy Week *(Semana Santa)* with Resurrection Sunday *(Pascua)* and the following week. On Palm Sunday, the week before Easter day, children sell palms in front of churches. In many towns the full Passion Play of Jesus's trial and crucifixion is enacted, often with deep emotion by actors in elaborate costumes, sometimes a man on a cross, and Resurrection. These two weeks are a constant flow of fireworks, parades with bands and costumed dancers, all-night parties, prayers, and pageantry. As in Spain, sweating men carry heavy platforms with life-size statues, such as The Virgin Mary, Mary Magdalene, Judas, John the Baptist, or a bleeding Jesus tied to a whipping post.

Crowded masses are held in the squares in front of churches. Crepe paper flowers and banners decorate the streets. Dancing *concheros* parade around to the beat of drums and trill of flutes, wearing elaborate feathered pre-Columbian costumes. On Easter Sunday after Mass, some towns feature the "Firing of Judas," with papier-mâché replicas of Judas and other hated figures, exploded with firecrackers.

Pentecost is the fiftieth day after Easter, celebrating the coming of the Holy Spirit to the Apostles (Acts 2) who experienced a rush of wind and visions of fire upon their heads when they were filled with the Holy Spirit and spoke in foreign tongues. In Great Britain, Pentecost is called Whitsunday, referring to the white clothing worn by those baptized that day.

NOTES

1. *The Divine Liturgy of Saint John Chrysostom* (Brookline, MA: Holy Cross Orthodox Press, 1985); Orthodox Christian Links, www.orthodox.net/Links; and Greek Orthodox Archdiocese of America, http://www.goarch.org/en/ourfaith/articles/article7101.asp.

2. *Catechism of the Catholic Church* (New York: Doubleday, 1995); and Richard P. McBrien, *Catholicism,* 2nd Ed. (New York: Harper & Row, 1994).

3. Orthodox Calendar, http://www.goarch.org; and Phillip Blyth, "Orthodox America: The Symbolism of Vestments," http://www.roca.org/OA/32/32f.

4. Catholic Calendar Definition, http://www.easterbrooks.com/personal/calendar/rules.html; and General Roman Calendar of Solemnities, Feasts, Memorials, http://www.cwo.com/~pentrack/catholic/romcal.html.

5. The Lutheran Calendar, http:/www.elca.org.

6. Anglican holidays are listed in the *Book of Common Prayer* (New York: Seabury Press, 2004).

6

MAJOR FIGURES

Christian history is filled with major figures who were inspired with spiritual wisdom. This chapter covers the lives and accomplishments of some major figures who were not explained in the previous chapters. The chapter is organized by major eras—Middle Ages, Reformation, nineteenth century, and twentieth century, and by birth date sequence within each era.

THE MIDDLE AGES

Hildegard of Bingen (1098–1179)

Hildegard was a German Benedictine nun who experienced visions of God's light and angels. She perceived that the Word of God is present in every living thing, expressed in its beauty. She stood strongly for her conviction of the spiritual equality of women and men and established an independent women's convent in Rupersberg, near Bingen, Germany. She wrote numerous important books, such as *Scivias Domini* (Know the ways of the Lord), poetry, plays, hymns, gospel commentaries, biographies of saints, medical studies, and natural histories. She was a popular cathedral preacher in a day when women rarely preached.[1]

St. Francis of Assisi (c. 1181–1226)

Son of a textile merchant in Assisi, Italy, Francis became a mystical monk who cast away wealth to live in poverty and service to others, and attracted many followers who still bear his name in the Franciscan Order. His early life was full of revelry, and he spent a year seeking military glory but became very discouraged. To his father's dismay, he renounced his inheritance in 1206 and declared himself "wedded to Lady Poverty." Francis gradually developed a deep spiritual life and devoted himself to serving the poor, saying that the lepers who used to horrify him were "transformed into sweetness of body and soul." He worked as a day laborer, scrounged for food, and rebuilt a crumbling church. He founded the new monastic order of the Friars Minor (humbler brothers) in 1209, which became the Franciscans. He loved nature and wrote the *Canticle of the Sun,* which praised the presence of God in nature, and the popular prayer "Lord, make me an instrument of your peace." Statues of him show him with a bird on his shoulder or hand, for it was said he understood the language of animals. He was made a saint in 1228.[2]

Dante Alighieri (1265–1321)

The culminating literary expression of the medieval Christian world was *The Divine Comedy,* written by Dante Alighieri. He was the greatest Italian poet, called "the chief imagination of Christendom."[3] He envisioned what the invisible metaphysical worlds after death might be like. The *Divine Comedy* (1321) is divided into three sections: the *Inferno* (Hell), *Purgatorio* (Purgatory), and *Paradisio* (Heaven). Dante's hero undertakes a mythical journey into cosmic space.

In the *Inferno,* Dante expresses the medieval world-picture's Hell as a funnel-like underworld that becomes increasingly horrid as it descends. He is guided through this inferno by the esteemed Roman poet Virgil, author of the *Aeneid.* Dante and Virgil emerge from the bottom of the *Inferno* and enter *Purgatorio,* where the shades of the dead linger until they are purged of their lesser sins. Than Dante meets Beatrice, his beloved guide who takes him closer to God.

In the *Paradisio,* Dante and Beatrice fly toward the celestial spheres and rise to the heights of mystical experience, singing the glories of the dazzling divine light that created the world and penetrates the universe. As they approach absolute reality, beyond time and space, God appears as Light eternal and as Father, Son, and Holy Spirit, adored by the Virgin Mary, angels, and saints. He sees that God's love and justice move the universe.

St. Brighid of Ireland (d. 525)

In ancient Ireland, a principal mythic Celtic goddess Brighid ("exalted one," "bride"), was a popular patroness of poetry, learning, healing and craftsmanship. She and her nuns were said to guard a sacred, perpetual fire. Historically, a woman with the same name (d. c. 525), whose accounts are mixed with folklore, was by tradition baptized by St. Patrick and founded a monastery at Kildare, where she is patron saint.[4]

St. Bridget of Sweden (1303–1373)

St. Bridget is the patron saint of Sweden. Swedish tradition tells of a woman Brigitta, or Bridget (1303–1373), who was married at age 13 or 14 and bore eight children. She joined the court of King Magnus Eriksson and had visionary revelations. After her youngest son and husband died, she entered a Cistercian monastery, then founded her own double monastery, for men and women separately, the order of Brigittines at Vadstenda. It had so many books that it was known as a literary center. She undertook pilgrimages—to Santiago de Compostella, Spain, to Rome, and to Jerusalem—and served the poor and sick.[5]

St. Sergius of Radonezh (1314–1392)

Sergius was an influential Russian Orthodox mystic and monk. With his brother Stephen he founded the important Holy Trinity Monastery, around 1334 CE, where the great icon painter Andrei Rublev developed his remarkable talent. The brothers went on to found 40 more monasteries. Sergius is now seen as the greatest Russian saint and one of the architects of the Russian nation, for he negotiated between warring Russian princes and inspired Prince Dmitri to fight against the invading Mongol Tartars during the thirteenth century.[6]

St. Catherine of Siena (1347–1380)

Catherine was one of 25 children of an Italian family. At the age of six she had a transforming vision of Jesus, and she subsequently spent most of her time in prayer and meditation, against her parents' wishes. At the age of 16, she became a Dominican nun and a nurse. She experienced mystical raptures of the divine presence and served the poor, imprisoned, and ill. She healed family quarrels, fearlessly criticized clerical evils, and persuaded wealthy priests to give away their luxuries and live simply. She was criticized for being such a popular laywoman preacher. But Catherine was respected by Popes, for she recalled believers to the Church's highest principles of humility, healing, and service to others. She was canonized a saint in 1461.[7]

St. Joan of Arc (1412–1431)

Joan, the French "Maid of Orléans," was an unusual young woman who was called to step outside traditional women's roles. An illiterate peasant, Joan, combining spiritual sensitivity with military toughness, became a mystic, a visionary, and a courageous warrior. At the age of 13 she had a mystical vision of St. Michael, a mighty warrior: "I saw him before my eyes ... surrounded by the Angels of Heaven.... I saw them with my bodily eyes as well as I see you; and when they left me, I wept."[8] These visions and voices urged her to wear men's clothes, take up armor and lead an army to free France from English armies during the Hundred Years War (1337–1453). She led and won several battles, but in 1430 she was captured and tried in an Inquisition court for witchcraft and heresy. She offended many for wearing men's clothes and taking on a strong, often successful military role normally reserved for men. But most troubling was her refusal of Church authority, as her judges accused: "she does not submit herself to the judgment of the Church Militant, or to that of living men, but to God alone," claiming to know God through her voices, which they deemed diabolical. Joan was burned at the stake at the age of 19 in 1431. She was re-tried post-mortem in 1455–1456, and found innocent. Joan became a symbol of France, and in 1920, a saint.

St. Teresa of Avila (1515–1582)

Teresa is the patron saint of Spain. She was 1 of 10 Spanish children in an aristocratic family. Her mother died when she was 15. She became a Carmelite nun but suffered painful, paralyzing illnesses. She developed a deep prayer life, had visions, and a vivid sense of the presence of God. She founded 17 convents for her new order of Discalced (meaning "barefoot")

Carmelite order of nuns living in poverty. She wrote *The Way of Perfection*, a spiritual direction for her nuns, and *The Interior Castle*, describing her own mystical experiences and "spiritual marriage." She was a friend of John of the Cross (1500–1569). She said: "Christ has no body now but yours." She was canonized a saint in 1622.[9]

THE REFORMATION

John Knox (1513–1572)

John Knox was a Scottish Catholic priest who supported reform, but when Protestant rebels captured Bishop Bedton's castle in St. Andrews (c. 1546), he was captured and endured 19 months as a navy galley slave. He later fled to Geneva, Switzerland, where he became an ardent Calvinist. Knox returned in 1555 to a Scotland still under Catholic rule, when to many Scots national independence involved the Protestant church. By 1558 Protestant Elizabeth was Queen of England and soon Catholic Mary Queen of Scots, was denounced and fled. The Scots began to respond to Knox's preaching by destroying monasteries and churches. The Scottish Parliament adopted a Calvinist creed largely prepared by Knox, and Scotland officially became Presbyterian in 1661. Nobles took over most Catholic properties, leaving the new church in poverty, but organized for congregational control. All practices without biblical basis were swept away. [10]

John Milton (1608–1674)

John Milton was an English poet who, like Dante, wrote a grand metaphysical poem, *Paradise Lost* (1667). He lived during a time of intense conflict and violence between traditional royalists and the rising middle class, between devoted Anglicans and rebellious Protestant Puritans. Milton opposed church hierarchy and favored democratically ruled churches.

The theme of *Paradise Lost* is: from what does evil ultimately derive? Milton proposes a number of non-biblical notions, including the idea that the Devil and his minions were fallen angels, expelled from Heaven. Satan arrives in the infernal realm defiantly crying "Better to reign in Hell than serve in Heaven" (1, 255) and proceeds to plot with his crew of demons and ancient gods how to exact revenge. He decides to spoil God's new creation by introducing sin.

The fiend travels to Eden, "squat like a toad," and tempts sleeping Eve. The Son of God arouses the army of angels to chase the demons back into Hell. The angel Raphael is dispatched to Eden to advise Adam to control the passions that Eve arouses in him and to follow his higher instincts. Satan re-enters Eden as a serpent. Flattering Eve, he persuades her to eat the fatal fruit, and she persuades Adam to eat also. Jesus intercedes with God for them, but they cannot avoid expulsion from paradise. Milton's evil is not simply Augustine's lack of goodness, but is the demonic will of a supernatural fiend lurking in every shadow. [11]

THE NINETEENTH CENTURY

Margarita Tuchkova (1781–1852)

A Russian noblewoman, Margarita Tuchkova was the notable founder of a large spiritual community of women. She was widowed in 1825 when her husband was among 45,000 Russian soldiers killed fighting Napoleon's army near Moscow. She found the spot where his body was blown to bits and retrieved his wedding ring. She grieved in a delirium until she was comforted by the Orthodox priest Filaret. So she built an Orthodox Church in Borodino on the spot where her husband died, But then she suffered again when her 15-year old son, Nikolai, died of scarlet fever. She descended into a grave spiritual crisis of despair. Father Filaret helped her slowly emerge, and she built a community of women around the Borodino church. She welcomed women, noble and poverty-stricken, abused and seeking spiritual refuge. She inspired many and gained the support of the church, which made the community a monastery, and Czar Nicholas, who gave her 25,000 rubles for buildings. She freed the serfs on her estate and sold most of her property to support the Borodino community, which grew to include 200 women.[12]

Elizabeth Cady Stanton (1815–1902)

Elizabeth Cady Stanton was the major leader in the religious side of the early women's liberation movement in the nineteenth century. She wrote most of *The Woman's Bible* (1895), because she believed that religion was part of the basis of society's oppression of women. In *The Women's Bible*, Stanton rejected the story of the temptation and subordination of Eve as ancient priestly additions to divine revelation. She similarly analyzed other biblical passages as self-contradictory social corruptions of the true Word of God. *The Woman's Bible* was widely criticized, but she was well ahead of her time. After a conversion experience, she befriended the Quaker leader Lucretia Mott, who encouraged her religious search. Stanton was a leading founder of the 1848 Women's Rights Convention in Seneca Falls, New York and an author of its famous "Declaration of Sentiments," asserting women's equal rights with men. She was the first person to publicly demand the right to vote for women. Stanton was active in Presbyterian, Quaker, Unitarian, Universalist, and Spiritualist circles. [13]

Antoinette Brown Blackwell (1825–1921)

Antoinette Brown Blackwell was the first woman ordained as a minister in a Christian church, in 1853. She grew up Antoinette Brown in a Congregational family in Upstate New York, attended Oberlin College, and finished the course in theology in 1850. But she was refused a theology diploma because she was a woman. Yet in 1853 she was ordained a Congregational minister in South Butler, New York, then in 1854 a Unitarian minister. She preached for the abolition of slavery and worked in New York City's slums. She married Samuel Blackwell, raised 5 daughters, and wrote 8 books, including *The Sexes Throughout Nature* (1875), which argued that Charles Darwin's male perspective limited his view of the role of the sexes. She lectured nationally and showed patriarchal Christians that women can be educated, speak persuasively, publish, and lead churches. [14]

THE TWENTIETH CENTURY

Pope John XXIII (1881–1963)

The young Angelo G. Roncalli was born into a poor family in Italy and was ordained a priest in 1904. He became a bishop, then Cardinal of Venice. Elected Pope in 1958, at the age of 77, he took the name John XXIII. Surprising some with his liberal views, Pope John spoke against weapons of mass destruction, urged social reforms for workers, the poor, and outcast, and promoted cooperation with other religions. Most important, he called the Second Vatican Council (1962–1965), which brought sweeping changes to the church. The first session voted to allow the Mass to be said in a country's vernacular language.[15]

Karl Barth (1886–1968)

One of the twentieth century's most important Protestant theologians, the Swiss Reformed Karl Barth, rejected Nazi idolatry, humanism, and liberalism, and developed "Neo-Orthodoxy." Teaching at Germany's Bonn University, Barth joined the "Barmen Declaration" of Germans who claimed the priority of the Gospel over the state, so he refused allegiance to Adolf Hitler. His theology of God as "wholly other" emphasizes humanity's utter inability to bridge the vast gap to God. He taught that only through God's grace and biblical accounts of Jesus can humans have access to God. He returned to Switzerland and continued to significantly influence Protestant theology. [16]

Paul Tillich (1886–1965)

Perhaps the twentieth century's most creative Protestant theologian, Paul Tillich was a German who was dismissed from Frankfurt University in 1933 because of his opposition to Adolf Hitler's Nazi regime. Then he taught at Union Theological Seminary in New York. Tillich was greatly influenced by the important German philosopher Martin Heidegger (1889–1976), developed his philosophy of Being into Christian form, and added elements such as depth psychology. Tillich saw God not as an anthropomorphic personal god, but as Being, or the ground of all existence, and he saw Jesus as the New Being. Tillich showed that Christianity can incorporate many scientific concepts without endangering its faith. Religious nationalism, he argued, is an all too common effort to give something finite an infinite significance. He taught that humans do participate in the universal, from matter to compassion, in a finite way, and that the purpose of life is to participate in the spiritual, divine sphere as much as possible. [17]

Charles Hartshorne (1897–2000)

Building on Alfred North Whitehead's *Process and Reality* (1929), American theologian Charles Hartshorne developed Process theology. He taught that, in contrast to transcendental theism whose God is absolute, distinct, and unchanging, all reality is in process, constantly developing in response to the environment. Physical stuff is not inert, changeless matter, he taught, but energy events. Both God and humans are affected by other parts of existence. God is distinct from the world, yet also embraces all things and leads them to fulfillment. All creaturely feelings, including suffering, are part of the divine life, he argues. God suffers with earthly suffering. God is the body and soul of the natural world. He taught at the University of Chicago, Emory University, and the University of Texas at Austin. David Griffin, John Cobb, and others have developed this theology further in ethical and ecological directions. [18]

Dorothy Day (1897–1980)

Tirelessly devoted to social justice, Dorothy Day was an American journalist who wrote for *The Catholic Worker* magazine. She combined a fierce criticism of capitalism and imperialism with a devotion to the church. She admired Jesus's compassion for the poor outcasts. She revered the many priests she knew who were poor, chaste, and obedient, and devoted their lives to service to God and humanity. She rejected the theology that sexual love was incompatible with love for God and became a mother. Day helped provide food and shelter for the dispossessed during the 1930s Depression. She was a pacifist, protested for civil rights in the 1960s, and spoke against abortion and for the Equal Rights Amendment.[19]

Dietrich Bonhoeffer (1906–1945)

Born in Berlin, Dietrich Bonhoeffer was a martyr in Nazi Germany and his writings have inspired many since. He was a Lutheran pastor and lecturer in theology at the University of Berlin. When Adolf Hitler came to power in 1933, Bonhoeffer became a leader in the Protestant resistance to the Nazis, the "Confessing Church," and was forced to flee to New York City's Union Theological Seminary. But troubled by his conscience, he returned to the dangers of Germany. Nazi Military Intelligence accused him of being part of a group planning the overthrow of Hitler, and he was imprisoned in 1943. Just before he was hanged in 1945, he said: "This is the end—but for me, the beginning—of life." He died in Flossenburg prison less than a week before the Allied troops reached it. His books, such as *Letters and Papers from Prison* (1951), have inspired many. He urged Christians to not underestimate the power of evil.[20]

Mother Teresa (1910–1997)

Born in Albania, Agnes Bojaxhiu became world-known for her aid to dying destitutes in Calcutta, India. She joined the Roman Catholic Order of the Sisters of Our Lady of Loreto in Ireland at the age of 18. She studied in Dublin and India, taking her vows in 1937. She first worked as a Roman Catholic high school principal in Calcutta, but she was grieved by the suffering of the neglected ill and dying in the city's streets. In 1948 she began her ministry among them, and Mother Teresa formed the Order of the Missionaries of Charity. Women members take vows of poverty, chastity, obedience, and service to the poor, whom she saw as the embodiment of Jesus. In 1952 she opened her Home for Dying Destitutes in Calcutta, whose nuns pick dying people up off the street and take them to their center. She extended her work worldwide, and she was awarded the Nobel Peace Prize in 1978. After her death in 1997, the process of moving toward her being canonized as a saint was remarkably fast, too fast for some critics, notably Christopher Hitchens, who criticizes her for opposing birth control and abortion, mis-managing money, and supporting right-wing politicians.[21]

Thomas Berry (1914–)

Thomas Berry is a Roman Catholic Priest who taught Religion at Fordham University in New York City. In 1970 he founded the Center for Religious Research in Riverdale, New York. His thought emerges from the theology of Teilhard but adds an ecological dimension. In his *The Dream of the Earth* (1988), Berry argued that the "fundamentalism" of industrial "progress" has attacked earth's basic life systems in an unprecedented pathology that has destroyed our sense of divine presence in the world, so we need to recover a spiritual sense of sacred presence in the earth's community of beings.[22]

Pope John Paul II (1920–2005)

The first non-Italian Pope since 1523, John Paul II spread the influence of the papacy with his unprecedented world travel and firm theological conservatism. Born Karol Wojutyla in Poland, he earned his Ph.D. and became Bishop, Archbishop, then Cardinal in Poland. He was active in Vatican II and was elected the first Polish Pope in 1978. In 1981 he survived an assassination attempt. His conservative encyclicals have criticized Marxism, Liberation Theology, atheism, and materialism. He warned against the dangers of rival nationalism and advocated economic justice for the poor. He consistently opposed artificial birth control, abortion, genetic engineering, and euthanasia. He took a strong stand against church dissent, homosexuality, and ordination of women.[23]

Dan Berrigan (1921–) and Phil Berrigan (1923–2002)

Brothers and Roman Catholic priests, Dan and Phil Berrigan have been notable civil disobedience and peace activists in the United States. They were part of the Catholic counterculture that protested nonviolently against racism, nuclear weapons, and war in the 1960s and afterward. Dan is a Jesuit, and Phil left the Josephites order to marry a former nun, Elizabeth McAlister. After burning draft records in 1968, Dan spent his first 18 months in jail. Phil organized the "Plowshares," a group that broke into military installations and poured blood on records and hammered on nuclear warheads. As a result, they both have spent up to 10 years in jail. Dan has written more than 50 books, including *The Trial of the Catonsville 9* (1970).[24]

Pope Benedict XVI (1927–)

The first Pope from Germany in over 1,000 years, Joseph Ratzinger was ordained a priest in 1951, earned his doctorate in theology in 1953, and until 1977 taught theology at German schools and universities. He was active in Vatican II in 1962–1965, and was appointed Archbishop of Munich and Freising in 1977, when he was soon chosen to be a Cardinal. Soon after the death of Pope John Paul II in 2005, when he spoke a sensitive and eloquent farewell, he was voted Pope. He is known for emphasizing strict obedience to church teachings. Since 1981, he served at the Vatican as Prefect of the Congregation of the Doctrine of the Faith, where he was known as the iron hand of the Vatican. He opposed Latin American Liberation Theology and efforts to rewrite scriptures in gender-neutral language. He takes a firm stand for priestly celibacy, against contraception, and against ordaining women. He also opposes European multiculturalism, but he pleases Catholic conservatives.

Mary Daly (1928–)

A professor of theology at the Catholic Boston College for 33 years, Mary Daly is a radical feminist who challenges basic Christian concepts. She does not want to place more women in patriarchal male roles in business or religion. She wants to radically alter consciousness so that abstract, detached theologies of God the Father do not justify injustices such as a husband dominating his wife. Religious institutions that harshly suppress women by refusing them approval of birth control or abortion, that tell them to submit to their husbands, and that impose a false sense of guilt seriously damage women's self-respect and their bodies. This patriarchal distortion of divinity must be undone, she argues. Women should be free to spin new relationships with each other as friends, sisters, and lovers, swirling in a cosmic dance together to nurture their Centering Selves. Thus, courageous women, feeling they belong to the whole cosmos, can seek wisdom, transformation, and happiness. Beginning with *Beyond God the Father* in 1973, Daly became increasingly radical and was forced to retire from Boston College in 2001 for refusing to admit men into her classes.[25]

Hans Küng (1928–)

A Swiss Roman Catholic priest and professor of theology at Tübingen University, Germany, Hans Küng has written many highly influential Catholic studies. He rejects papal infallibility, and his criticisms of the Catholic Church hierarchy provoked Pope John Paul II to ban him from teaching as a Catholic theologian in 1979. Küng wrote *A Global Ethic* (1992), which was adopted by the Parliament of the World's Religions in 1993. It does not propose a single global religion, a global ideology, or a blend of several religions. It requires human rights and demands that every human being must be treated humanely. The world needs a nonviolent and just economic order, he argues, promoting tolerance of minorities and human rights for men and women. He expresses "disgust" with the misuse of religion for warlike, purely political-power goals, opposes ecological destruction, and criticizes insatiable greed for money and prestige.[26]

Andrew Greeley (1928–)

Andrew Greeley is an influential Catholic priest, sociologist, and researcher at the National Opinion Research Center in Chicago. He researches the behavior and beliefs of American Catholics showing, for example, that most American Catholics reject papal restrictions on birth control. But this has not led them to leave the Church. His popular religious novels blend potboiler sexual conflicts with sin, grace, and redemption and have sold perhaps 20 million copies. He argues that sex is not inherently sinful and advocates the ordination of women priests. He argues that God is active in human passions and in all of creation. He also criticizes the media for over-exaggerating the problem of sexual abuse by priests, pointing out that,

horrendous as the problem is, no more than 4 percent of all priests are pred-
ators, and the remaining 96 percent are typically mature, happy men.[27]

Martin Luther King, Jr. (1929–1968)

Baptist minister Martin Luther King, Jr., earned his Ph.D. and became
the leader of the 1960s Civil Rights Movement that nonviolently over-
threw massive legalized racial discrimination. He organized boycotts and
marches that led to the U.S. Supreme Court's declaring bus segregation
laws unconstitutional. King was arrested and jailed repeatedly, his home
was bombed, and his family was threatened. But he insisted on confronting
injustices nonviolently and thus gained a high moral ground. His famous
1963 "I Have a Dream" speech has become a major speech in U.S. history,
and he received the Nobel Peace Prize in 1964. In 1968 he was about to lead
a protest march in Memphis, Tennessee, but was assassinated.[28]

Harvey Cox (1929–)

An American Baptist minister and Professor of Divinity at Harvard Divinity School, Harvey Cox made a great impact in 1965 with his book *The
Secular City,* where he argued that Christianity's role is not to promote
belief in an archaic metaphysical or mythical God "out there" but to support liberating values. In a later shift of emphasis, Cox wrote *Religion in the
Secular City* in 1984, which described the dramatic reawakening of traditional religions around the world. Cox expanded into studies of Liberation
Theology in South America, Christianity's encounters with other world
faiths, and the global rise of emotionally charged pentecostal spirituality.
He has chronicled many of the important trends in contemporary Christian history.[29]

Barbara Harris (1930–)

Barbara Harris marked an important milestone as the first woman to
become a bishop in the Episcopal Church, in 1989. An African American,
Harris was active in the 1960s Civil Rights Movement. She supported the
women deacons who were ordained priests in 1978, two years before the
Episcopal Church USA allowed women to be ordained. She was ordained
an Episcopal priest in 1980 then consecrated suffragan (assistant) Bishop of

Massachusetts in 1989. She speaks on issues such as racism, sexism, class discrimination, and AIDS.[30]

Desmond Tutu (1931–)

A major leader in the South African anti-apartheid movement, Desmond Tutu was ordained an Anglican priest in 1960. He taught theology, was Dean of the Cathedral in Johannesburg, and was the first Black General Secretary of the South African Council of Churches. He criticizes racial injustice and argues for equal civil rights and education. Tutu was awarded the Nobel Peace Prize in 1984, when he condemned the injustice of Blacks living in poverty-stricken ghettoes. He has publicized worldwide the cruelty of police shootings of Black children, the violence of police guns, dogs, and tear gas, detention without trial, exile, and death for hundreds of protesters. He argues that apartheid has no Christian justification. He is perhaps the greatest African leader for reconciliation between the races.[31]

John S. Spong (1931–)

Episcopal Bishop of Newark, New Jersey for over twenty years beginning in 1976, John S. Spong has been a controversial theologian who wrote several challenging books, beginning with *Living in Sin?: A Bishop Rethinks Human Sexuality* (1988), where he explores the issue of couples living together outside marriage and gay and lesbian marriage. Spong's books include *Rescuing the Bible from Fundamentalism* (1991) and *Why Christianity Must Change or Die* (1998). The theistic God has been defined by masculinity, which feminists have rightly condemned, he says, and it has died. Also, the church has relied too much on guilt and holy wars that must be rejected. Theism must be replaced by what the major theologian Paul Tillich called the "Ground of Being," Spong argues, the mystical presence of love and participation with all existence.[32]

Sallie McFague (1933–)

Sallie McFague, Professor Emeritus at Vanderbilt University Divinity School, challenges fundamentalist literalism that she sees has dangerous implications. She argues that comprehending theology is strongly based in understanding language. In her book *Metaphorical Theology* (1982), she argues that God can never be grasped by language, because God is beyond this human cultural construct. The parables of Jesus are good examples, where Jesus uses metaphors of light, pearls, and treasures to convey the meaning of presence of the divine. In her *Models of God: Theology for an Ecological, Nuclear Age* (1988), she charges that the model of God as father has slid into being an irrelevant idol. Better models would be God as mother, lover, and friend. To overcome the West's ecology and nuclear crisis, she writes, Christians must overcome the Christian error of dominion over nature and see nature instead as the "body of God."[33]

Charles Curran (1934–)

A major Roman Catholic scholar of social ethics and moral theology, Charles Curran has been a professor at Southern Methodist University in Dallas since 1991. He wrote and edited more than 40 books on moral theology and was an early leading proponent for the Catholic Church to change its teaching on sexual issues, such as artificial contraception and abortion. He taught at the Catholic University of America from 1965 to 1986 but was dismissed for challenging the Church's positions on sexual issues. Although he considers himself a good Catholic, he is one of the noted Catholic scholars dissenting from official Church authority. A recent book is *The Historical Development of Fundamental Moral Theology in the United States* (1999).[34]

Richard McBrien (1936–)

Priest and Professor of Theology at Notre Dame University, Richard McBrien has written many influential and controversial books, from to *Do We Need the Church?* (1969) to *Catholicism* (1980, rev. 1994). He raises controversial issues such as the literal nature of biblical texts (such as creation and virgin birth), the source of the theology of original sin, the strength of papal authority, the importance of church involvement in debates about sexual ethics, reproductive ethics, abortion, women's ordination, priestly celibacy, and the potential for positive change in response to the child abuse crisis.[35]

Rosemary Ruether (1936–)

Rosemary Ruether is a leading Catholic feminist who condemns the oppression of women and earth in the name of God. A professor at Garrett-

Evangelical Theological Seminary, she argues that whatever diminishes the full humanity of women cannot come from the divine, because it is idolatry to make men more God-like than women and blasphemy to use God to justify patriarchal domination. Ruether uses the term "God/ess" to designate the monotheistic Divine in its fullness. In *Gaia and God: An Ecofeminist Theology of Earth Healing* (1992), Ruether proposes that the Greek name for Earth Mother, "Gaia" should replace God as the focus of Christian worship, to lead us out of our ecological destructiveness.[36]

R.C. Sproul (1939–)

A leading evangelical theologian, R.C. Sproul wrote numerous books such as *Not a Chance: The Myth of Chance in Modern Science and Cosmology* (1994), arguing that the principle of chance could not be a causative force in creation, thus the universe could not have evolved by chance. He summarized the main themes of evangelical thought in *Essential Truths of the Christian Faith* (1992). He is on the council of the Alliance of Confessing Evangelicals, founded the Ligonier Ministries in Orlando, Florida, and has a radio show "Renewing Your Mind." [37]

James Cone (1939–)

A minister in the African Methodist Episcopal Church, James Cone is an outstanding African-American theologian who published the pioneering *Black Theology and Black Power* in 1969. Black Power is a more aggressive, militant and separatist black philosophy than Martin Luther King, Jr.'s nonviolent resistance movement. Cone said that Black Power means "complete emancipation of Black people from white oppression by whatever means Black people deem necessary," and "Christ is Black."[38] By blackness, however, he does not just mean only skin color. He means that blackness is a sign of oppressed people of all races, and whiteness is a symbol of oppressors in general. He sought reconciliation with God for all. As his thought developed, he saw Black Theology as part of a more global Liberation Theology emerging in Africa, Asia, and Latin America. He also welcomed the role of Black women into leadership in the Liberation struggle.

Matthew Fox (1940–)

Matthew Fox is a creative theologian who was a Roman Catholic priest silenced by the Vatican for his radical theology. He is founder and president of the University of Creation Spirituality in Oakland, California, known for its dramatic "Techno Cosmic Mass." He is the author of 24 books, including *The Coming of the Cosmic Christ* (1988), where he sees Christ as Mother Earth. He is critical of the Catholic Church's rejection of women priests and the scandal of priestly child abuse.[39]

Patriarch Bartholomew I (1940–)

The Ecumenical Patriarch, Bartholemew I is leader of the world's Eastern Orthodox Christians. Speaking up for ecological stewardship toward nature by Christians, he has organized several environmental forums, where he says that human destruction of species is a sin. He was one of the first religious leaders to equate the ecological crisis with sinful behavior. Self-restraint, he says, is an essential religious practice and must now be applied to our view of nature. To him nature is an extension of our bodies, just as the church is an extension of Christ's physical body.[40]

NOTES

1. Robert Van de Weyer, ed., *Hildegard* (London: Hodder & Stoughton, 1997).

2. Richard P. McBrien, *Lives of the Saints* (San Francisco: HarperSanFrancisco, 2003), pp. 404–7.

3. Dante Alighieri, *The Divine Comedy,* 3 vols. (New York: Oxford University Press, 1961.

4. Proinsias MacCana, *Celtic Mythology* (London: Hamlyn Publishing, 1970), pp. 34–35.

5. McBrien, *Lives,* pp. 291–93.

6. Lavinia Cohn-Sherbok, *Who's Who in Christianity* (New York: Routledge, 1998), p. 271.

7. McBrien, *Lives,* pp. 180–83; and "Catherine of Siena," in James Kiefer, Biographical Sketches of Memorable Christians of the Past, http://justus.anglican.org/resources/bio.

8. Anne L. Barstow, *Joan of Arc: Heretic, Mystic, Shaman* (Lewiston, NY: Mellen Press, 1986).

9. McBrien, *Lives,* pp. 421–24.

10. Williston Walker, et al., *A History of the Christian Church,* 4th ed. (New York: Scribner's, 1985), pp. 497–99.

11. John Milton, *Paradise Lost* (New York: Holt, Rinehart and Winston, 1965).

12. Brenda Meehan, *Holy Women of Russia* (San Francisco: HarperSan Francisco, 1993), pp. 17–40.

13. "Elizabeth Cady Stanton," Women of Achievement and Herstory, http://www.undelete.org/library; and June Benowitz, ed., "Elizabeth Cady Stanton," *Encyclopedia of American Women and Religion* (Oxford: ABC-CLIO, 1998), pp. 331–33.

14. Benowitz, "Blackwell, Antoinette Brown," *Encyclopedia of American Women and Religion*, pp. 39–40.

15. Geoffrey Parrinder, ed., "John XXIII" *A Concise Encyclopedia of Christianity* (Oxford: Oneworld, 1998), pp. 138–39.

16. "Karl Barth," Biography Resource Center, http://galenet.galegroup.com/servlet/BioRC.

17. "Paul Tillich," Biography Resource Center, http://galenet.galegroup.com/servlet/BioRC.

18. "Charles Hartshorne," Center for Process Studies, http://www.ctr4process.org and *The Stanford Encyclopedia*, http://plato.stanford.edu/entries/hartshorne.

19. Benowitz, "Day, Dorothy," *Encyclopedia of American Women and Religion*, pp. 84–85.

20. "Dietrich Bonheoffer," in Kiefer, Biographical Sketches.

21. "Mother Teresa," Biography Resource Center, http://galenet.galegroup.com/servlet/BioRC, and Christopher Hitchens, *Mother Teresa in Theory and Practice* (New York: Verso, 1995).

22. "Thomas Berry," Biography Resource Center, http://galenet.galegroup.com/servlet/BioRC.

23. Cohn-Sherbok, "John Paul II," *Who's Who*, p. 157.

24. Crystal Reference, http://www.crystalreference.com; War Resisters, http://www.warresisters.org; and Catholic Worker, http://www.catholicworker.com.

25. "Mary Daly," Biography Resource Center, http://galenet.galegroup.com/servlet/BioRC; and "Mary Daly Ends Suit, Agrees to Retire," *Boston College Chronicle*, 15 Feb. 2001, 9:11, http://www.bc.edu/bc_org/rvp/pubaf/chronicle/v9/f15/daly.html.

26. "Hans Küng," Biography Resource Center, http://galenet.galegroup.com/servlet/BioRC, and Center for Global Ethics, http://astro.ocis.temple.edu/~dialogue/geth/htm.

27. "Andrew Greeley," Biography Resource Center, http://galenet.galegroup.com/servlet/BioRC; and Father Andrew Greeley, http://www.agreeley.com.

28. "Martin Luther King," Nobel e-Museum, Laureates 2003, http://www.nobel.se/peace/laureates.

29. "Harvey Cox," Biography Resource Center, http://galenet.galegroup.com/servlet/BioRC.

30. Benowitz, "Harris, Barbara," *Encyclopedia of American Women and Religion,* pp. 147–48.

31. "Desmond Tutu," Nobel e-Museum, http://www.nobel.se/peace/laureates.

32. "John Spong," Biography Resource Center, http://galenet.galegroup.com/servlet/BioRC, and http://www.dioceseofnewark.org/jsspong.

33. "Sallie McFague," Biography Resource Center, http://galenet.galegroup.com/servlet/BioRC.

34. "Charles Curran," Contemporary Authors Online 2001, http://infotrak.galegroup.com; and Biography Resource Center, http://galenet.galegroup.com/servlet/BioRC.

35. Richard McBrien, http://129.74.54.81/rm/essays; and "Richard McBrien," Contemporary Authors Online, http://infotrak.galegroup.com.

36. "Rosemary Ruether," Biography Resource Center, http://galenet.galegroup.com/servlet/BioRC.

37. Ligonier Ministries, http://www.Ligonier.org.

38. "James Cone," Biography Resource Center, http://galenet.galegroup.com/servlet/BioRC, James Cone, *Black Theology and Black Power* (New York: Seabury Press, 1969), 6, 68.

39. "Matthew Fox," Biography Resource Center, http://galenet.galegroup.com/servlet/BioRC.

40. Olivier Clément, *Conversations with Ecumenical Patriarch Bartholomew I* (Crestwood, NY: St. Vladimir's Seminary Press, 1997); and Melba Newsome, "The Green Patriarch and Environmental Orthodoxy: An Interview with the Patriarch of Eastern Orthodoxy," in *The Amicus Journal* 20, no. 4 (1999, Winter): 15–17.

GLOSSARY

Albigensians: Followers of a late medieval dualistic theology common in southern France; leaders ("pure") practiced severe ascetic fasting, celibacy; defeated by Rome. See Cathars.

Anabaptists: Reformation "rebaptizers" who reject infant baptism for believers' baptism; expanded into Free Churches of many varieties, such as Brethren, Mennonite, and others.

Anathema: "Suspended" or excommunicated. Exclusion of members from church for breaching beliefs or rules.

Anglican: The term used to describe one of the four major branches of Protestantism, beginning with the Church of England during the Reformation, and expanding worldwide.

Antinomianism: Rejection of religious rules, moral laws, social norms, or conventional standards.

Apocrypha: Religious books not included in the official canon (Bible) of the church, such as the "Gospel of Mary."

Apostasy: "Withdrawal," or abandonment of one's religious faith or denomination.

Arianism: Early church belief that interpreted Jesus as not eternal and divine, but as human.

Arminianism: Rejection of John Calvin's doctrine of predestination that stresses free will and God's love for all people.

Asceticism: Practice of self-restraint in bodily concerns for spiritual enlightenment; fasting, celibacy, poverty.

Baptism: "To dip in water," the ritual of admission into Christianity, by total immersion or sprinkling water on the head of infants or adults.

Calvinism: One of the four major branches of Protestantism, founded by John Calvin in Geneva, Switzerland during the Reformation; also known as Reformed churches, Presbyterians, and Congregational (United Church of Christ) and others.

Canticle: Short liturgical songs, often placed between words by the priest.

Cathars: "Pure;" medieval believers in the evil nature of matter. Their leaders rejected marriage, war, and eating meat. Also called Albigensians.

Cathedral: The large main church of a diocese with a "chair" or office of the bishop; often built by or affiliated with monasteries or cities.

Charismatic: "Gifts of grace;" an inspiring leader or a liturgy stressing emotion, healing, miracles, prophesy, and speaking in tongues.

Communion, Lord's Supper, or Eucharist: "Thanksgiving," the major Christian sacrament, instituted by Jesus in the Gospels, and repeated in worship services regularly; he broke bread and blessed wine and shared it with his disciples, saying, in various forms in each Gospel text: "Take, eat, this is my body," and "this is my blood of the Covenant, which is poured out for many for the forgiveness of sins;" the meaning of the ritual is interpreted in various ways by different branches of the church.

Deacon/Deaconess: Assistant to the priest, some in preparation for priesthood/ministry, some in lifelong roles in pastoral, educational, or charity work.

Deity: Divinity, god, or goddess.

Deuterocanonical: "Second canon" biblical books accepted by Catholic and Orthodox churches in addition to the basic canon accepted by Protestants.

Diaconate: Rank or office of deacons.

Docetism: "To seem." Early belief later rejected by the church that Jesus's life was merely an appearance, and his humanity and sufferings were not real.

Ebionites: Early Christians who followed the Jewish law and denied the virgin birth of Jesus.

Encyclical: Originally a letter sent around to churches by a bishop or leader, now a letter sent from the Pope.

Eucharist: See Communion.

Ex Cathedra: "From the chair (of a bishop)"; solemn infallible rulings by the Pope.

Filioque: "And the son." Phrase added to original Nicene Creed by western churches to affirm that the Holy Spirit proceeds from both Father and the Son; rejected by Eastern Orthodox.

Free Churches: One of the four major branches of Protestantism developed during the Reformation; churches not affiliated with government; originally Swiss, German, and other nations, including the English Dissenters, nonconformists, Quakers, Baptists, Congregationalists; now has numerous denominations.

Genuflect: "Knee-bending." Liturgical kneeling before the altar.

Heretic: One who chooses to exaggerate, distort, or deny basic principles of a faith; a believer in false doctrines; the opposite of orthodox.

Hermeneutics: "Interpretation" theory and practice of interpreting biblical and other texts, using linguistic, historical, and literary "higher" criticism.

Indulgence: Pardoning punishment for sins, completely (plenary) or partially; was offered by medieval Catholic church to Crusaders, and sold to some; rejected by Protestants.

Intinction: Liturgical practice of dipping one's Eucharist bread/host into cup of wine rather than drinking wine from the cup.

Lay Investiture: Appointment of clergy by laymen, opposed by medieval Popes.

Liturgy: Christian public worship including music, prayers, Bible readings, a sermon and other elements of communion with God.

Manichaeanism: Belief in dualism of God and devil, evil of matter, need for celibacy and asceticism; began in Babylon, spread to Rome, affected Augustine, Christianity in view of Heaven and Hell.

Martyr: "Witness," one who dies willingly for their faith, believing in a rewarding life after death.

Missionaries: Messengers sent into foreign lands to teach the Christian Gospel and make new converts; often includes education, health and social services.

Monasticism: "Alone," solitary religious seekers or a community of men or women celibates who pray, worship, study, work, and do social services for the needy.

Monotheism: Belief that only one God (not many, as in polytheism) is the ultimate reality of the universe.

Neo-Platonism: Late Greek modifications of Plato, as with Plotinus (204–270 CE); affected Augustine; belief in mystical divine emanating down to earth via cosmic Intelligences and Soul in meditative states.

Nepotism: "Favoring nephews," the practice of a person in power hiring and favoring relatives and friends rather than the most qualified candidates; an ancient political tactic problematic in Renaissance Rome.

Nicene Creed: An early formative statement of Christian faith, emphasizing the divinity of Jesus against those who saw him as simply human; organized by Emperor Constantine in Byzantium in 325.

Ontology: Branch of philosophy studying Being or ultimate reality, today emphasizing intuition and experience rather than logic alone.

Ordinance: Authoritative command, long-established custom, or religious liturgy.

Original Sin: Belief from Paul and Augustine that Adam's "guilt" was transmitted to all humans; rejected by Pelagius, Abelard, and many modern Christians.

Pagan: "Peasant," derogatory term used to denote a non-Christian.

Patriarchy: A social system favoring men and subordinating women to male authority.

Pelagianism: From medieval Pelagius who rejected predestination and original sin but affirmed human ethical responsibility and cooperation with God's grace.

Polyphony: Simultaneous musical blend of two or more independent parts.

Polytheism: Belief that many gods inhabit the universe as sources of power in nature and society.

Prevenient Grace: Grace "coming before"; belief that God actively seeks lost people and that humans are predisposed to seek God.

Privatio Boni: "Lack of goodness" doctrine of Augustine that evil originates not with a devil but with a lack of human goodness.

Prophesy: Divinely inspired speakers and writers; common in world religions as those who discern the will of the divine; major Jewish and Christian prophets Isaiah, Jeremiah, and Ezekiel criticized early Israelites for insincere faith and promised a saving messiah.

Purgatory: Intermediate state between heaven and hell for period of purging and purification before entering heaven; described by Italian poet Dante, rejected by most Protestants.

Reformation: The historical period when Protestantism developed; with some forerunners, the four major branches were led by (1) Martin Luther's critique of church corruption in Germany in 1517, (2) King Henry VIII's rejection of papal authority in England in 1532, (3) John Calvin's book, *Institutes of the Christian Religion*, in 1536, and (4) the baptism of adults by each other near Zürich in 1525 that began the "Anabaptist" or "Free Church" branch of Protestantism, with many subsequent denominations.

Sacraments: Important outward and visible signs of inward and spiritual graces; a sacred ritual bringing the presence and power of God to transform a human event; Orthodox and Catholics have 7: Baptism, Confirmation, Communion, Penance and Reconciliation, Anointing of the Sick, Holy Orders, and Matrimony; Protestants returned to the biblical 2: Baptism and Communion.

Simony: The unethical buying or selling of religious offices, pardons, or services.

Slavonic: Branch of Indo-European Slavic languages used in the Russian Orthodox liturgy.

Synoptic: "Seeing together." The Gospels of Matthew, Mark, and Luke that report Jesus's life from a similar point of view, slightly different from Gospel of John.

Theism: Belief in a God who is seen in human male form.

Theodicy, problem of: "God's Justice," the conflict between the belief that God is all-good and all-powerful, despite the reality of human suffering in the world.

Theology: "Study of God," the knowledge of God learned from the Bible, experience, conscience, reason, nature, and church tradition.

Theosis: "Deification." Eastern Orthodox belief that descent of God to humans through Jesus has made possible human ascent to God through Holy Spirit.

Torah: The Hebrew term for the first five books of the Bible: Genesis, Exodus, Leviticus, Numbers, and Deuteronomy.

Transubstantiation: Roman Catholic belief that the Eucharist bread and wine are substantially changed into the body and blood of Christ at the consecration during Mass.

Trinity: Christian belief in the paradoxical unity of God the Father, Jesus the Son, and the Holy Spirit as the transcendent, historical, and ever-present aspects of the monotheistic divine.

Uniate: Churches of Eastern Orthodox tradition, language and liturgy, but in communion with Rome; mostly in Eastern Europe, notably Ukraine; priests marry.

Waldensians: Late medieval protest movement that appointed ministers, allowed lay preachers, was persecuted, and now are united with Italian Methodists.

BIBLIOGRAPHY

Abbott, Walter M., ed. *The Documents of Vatican II*. New York: The American Press, 1966.

Achtemeier, Paul, ed. *The Harpercollins Bible Dictionary*. San Francisco: HarperSanFrancisco, 1996.

Adherents. http://www.adherents.com.

African American Publications. http://www.africanpubs.com/Apps/bios.

African Christianity. http://cas.behel.edu/%7ELetnie/AfricanChristianity/SSAAICs.htm.

Alighieri, Dante. *The Divine Comedy*. 3 vols. New York: Oxford University Press, 1961.

American Baptist Churches USA. http://www.abc-usa.org.

Amish and Country. http://www.amishanccountry.com/amish-religion.htm.

Amishnet. http://amish.net.

"Amish," http://religioustolerance.org/amish.

Anglican Timeline. http://Justus.Anglican.org/resources/timeline.

Armstong, Karen. *The Battle for God*. New York: Alfred A. Knopf, 2000.

Assemblies of God. http://www.ag.org.

Augustine, Saint. *Confessions*. Trans. R. S. Pine-Coffin. New York: Penguin, 1979.

Augustine, Saint. *The City of God*. Trans. Marcus Dods. New York: Modern Library, 1950.

Bailey, Lee W., and Jenny Yates. *The Near-Death Experience*. New York: Routledge, 1996.

Bainton, Roland. *The Reformation of the Sixteenth Century*. Boston: Beacon, 1952.

Bainton, Roland. *The Horizon History of Christianity.* New York: American Heritage/Harper & Row, 1964.

Bainton, Roland. *The Medieval Church.* Huntington, NY: Robert Krieger Publishing, 1979.

Balderston, Daniel, et al. *Encyclopedia of Contemporary Latin American and Caribbean Cultures.* New York: Routledge, 2000.

Banerjee, Neela. "U.S. Catholic Bishops Agree to Join New Ecumenical Group." *New York Times,* 18 Nov. 2004. http://www.nytimes.com/2004/11/18/national/18bishops.html.

The Barna Group. http://www.barna.org.

Barrett, David. *World Christian Encyclopedia.* 2 vols, 2nd ed. New York: Oxford University Press, 2001.

Barstow, Anne L. *Joan of Arc: Heretic, Mystic, Shaman.* Lewiston, NY: Mellen Press, 1986.

Bartlett, W. B. *God Wills It!* Gloucestershire: Sutton, 1999.

Bays, Daniel H., ed. *Christianity in China from the 18th Century to the Present.* Stanford, CA: Stanford University Press, 1996.

BBC NEWS. "Pope Condemns US Church Sex Abuse." 22 May 2002. http://www.newsbbc.co.uk.

Bender, Harold, et al., eds. *Mennonite Encyclopedia.* 4 vols. Hillsboro, KS: Mennonite Brethren Publishing House, 1959.

Benowitz, June. *Encyclopedia of American Women and Religion.* Oxford: ABC-CLIO, 1998.

Berry, Thomas. *The Dream of the Earth.* San Francisco: Sierra Club, 1988.

Bettenson, Henry, and Chris Maunder, eds. *Documents of the Christian Church.* 3rd ed. New York: Oxford University Press, 1999.

Benowitz, June. *Encyclopedia of American Women and Religion.* Santa Barbara, CA: ABC-CLIO, 1998.

Billy Graham Evangelistic Association. http://www.billygraham.org.

Biographical Sketches of Memorable Christians of the Past. http://justus.Anglican.org/resources.bio.

Biography Resource Center. http://galenet.galegroup.com/servlet/BioRC.

Blyth, Phillip. "Orthodox America: The Symbolism of Vestments." http://www.roca.org/OA/32/32f.

Book of Common Prayer. New York: Seabury Press, 2004.

Boyd, Gregory, and Paul Eddy. *Across the Spectrum: Understanding Issues in Evangelical Theology.* Grand Rapids, MI: Baker Academic, 2002.

Brasher, Brenda, ed. *Encyclopedia of Fundamentalism.* New York: Routledge, 2001.

Breen, J., and M. Williams, eds. *Japan and Christianity: Impacts and Responses.* New York: St. Martin's, 1995.

Britain Yearly Meeting. http://www.quaker.org.uk.

Brooke, James. "Indian Lawsuits on School Abuse May Bankrupt Canada Churches." *New York Times,* International, 2 Nov. 2000. http://www.newyorktimes.com/2000/11/02/world/o2CANA.html.

Burgess, Stanley, ed. *New International Dictionary of Pentecostal and Charismatic Movement.* Grand Rapids, MI: Zondervan Publishing, 2002.

Butler, Christopher. *Postmodernism: A Very Short Introduction.* Oxford: Oxford University Press, 2002.

Campolo. http://www.tonycampolo.org.

Catechism of the Catholic Church. New York: Doubleday, 1995.

Bobin, Jean-Paul, ed. "Cathares: Les Fortresses de l'Hérésie." *Pyrénées Magazine Special Edition.* Toulouse: Milan Presse, 2002.

Catholic Calendar Definition. http://www.easterbrooks.com/personal/calendar/rules.html.

Catholic Worker. http://www.catholicworker.com.

"Catholic Missions." In *Catholic Encyclopedia.* http://www.Newadvent.org. cathen/10375a.

Center for Process Studies. http://www.ctr4process.org.

"Chart No. 63. Religious Bodies—Selected Data." *Statistical Abstracts of the United States.* Washington, D.C.: U.S. Department of Commerce, Census Bureau, 2002.

Chicago Statement on Biblical Inerrancy. http://www.iclnet.org.

Christian Apologetics and Research Ministry 2003. http://www.carm.org.

Christian Videos and DVDs. 2004. Gateway Films. http://visionvideo.com.

Church of the Brethren. http:// www.brethren.org.

Church of Scotland. http://www.churchofscotland.org.uk.

Clark, D. N. *Christianity in Modern Korea,* Asian Agenda Report 5. Lanham, MD: University or America Press, 1986.

Clément, Olivier. *Conversations with Ecumenical Patriarch Bartholomew I.* Crestwood, NY: St. Vladimir's Seminary Press, 1997.

Clenendin, Daniel. *Eastern Orthodox Christianity: A Western Perspective.* Grand Rapids, MI: Baker Academic, 2003.

Cohn-Sherbok, Lavinia. *Who's Who in Christianity.* New York: Routledge, 1998.

Colbi, S. P. *A History of the Christian Presence in the Holy Land.* Lanham, MD: University Press of America, 1988.

Cone, James. *Black Theology and Black Power.* New York: Seabury Press, 1969.

Constantelos, Demetrios. "The Historical Development of Greek Orthodoxy." http://www.myriobiblos.gr/texts/english/constantelos.html.

Contemporary Authors Online 2001. http://infotrak.galegroup.com.

Cooperman, Alan, and Thomas Edsall. "Evangelicals Say They Led Charge for the GOP." *The Washington Post,* 8 Nov. 2004, A01. http://www.washingtonpost.com.

Council on Parliament of World Religions. http://www.cpwr.org.

Creeds of Christendom. http://www.creeds.net.

Cross, F. L., ed. *The Oxford Dictionary of the Christian Church.* New York: Oxford University Press, 1997.

Crystal Cathedral. http://www.crystalcathedral.org.

Crystal Reference. http://www.crystalreference.com.

Curran, Charles. *The Catholic Moral Tradition Today: A Synthesis.* Washington, D.C.: Georgetown University Press, 1999.

Defining Evangelicism. http://www.wheaton.edu/isae/definingevangelicalism.html.

Demetrakopoulos, George. *Dictionary of Orthodox Theology.* New York: Philosophical Library, 1964.

Dillenberger, John, ed. *Martin Luther: Selections from His Writings.* Garden City, NY: Doubleday Anchor, 1954.

Dillenberger, John, and Claude Welch. *Protestant Christianity.* New York: Scribner's, 1954.

The Divine Liturgy of Saint John Chrysostom. Brookline, MA: Holy Cross Orthodox Press, 1985.

"Eastern Greek Orthodox Church Organization, Creed, and Catechism." http://www.bible.ca.seekers.map?162,14.

Ecumenical Patriarch of Constantinople. http://www.patriarchate.org.

Eliade, Mircea, ed. *The Encyclopedia of Religion.* 16 vols. New York: Macmillan, 1986.

Evangelical Lutheran Church in America. http://www.ecla/org.

Evans, G. R., ed. *The First Christian Theologians.* Oxford: Blackwell, 2004.

Fairbairn, Donald. *Eastern Orthodoxy Through Western Eyes.* Louisville, KY: Westminster/John Knox Press, 2002.

Fides quaerens internetum (Christian Theology). http://people.bu.edu/bpstone/theology/theology.html.

Fitzgerald, Rev. Thomas. http://www.forministry.com.

Forest, Jim. *Religion in the New Russia.* New York: Crossroads, 1990.

Fox, Matthew. *The Coming of the Cosmic Christ.* San Francisco: Harper & Row, 1988.

Fremantle, Anne. *The Protestant Mystics.* Boston: Little, Brown, 1964.

Fremantle, Anne, ed. *The Social Teachings of the [Catholic] Church.* New York: New American Library, 1963.

Friends General Conference. http://www.fgcquaker.org.

"Fundamentalism." http://religiousmovements.lib.virginia.edu/nrms/fund.html.

Future Church. http://www.futurechurch.org.

Gardner, Joseph L., ed. *Atlas of the Bible.* Pleasantville, NY: Reader's Digest, 1983.

General Roman Calendar of Solemnities, Feasts, Memorials. http://www.cwo.com/~pentrack/catholic/romcal.html.

Gjergji, Lush. *Mother Teresa: Her Life and Works.* New Rochelle, NY: New City Press, 1991.

Glazier, Stephen, ed. *Encyclopedia of African and African-American Religions.* New York: Routledge, 2001.

Gospel for Asia. http://www.gfs.org.

Greek Orthodox Archdiocese of America. http://www.goarch.org/en/ourfaith/articles/article7101.asp.

Greek Orthodox Church. http://www.greekorthodoxchurch.org.

Greek Orthodox Church of America. http://www.goarch.org.

Greeley, Andrew. "For Priests, Celibacy is Not the Problem." *New York Times,* Op-Ed, 3 March 2004. http://www.NYtimes.com.

Greeley, Andrew. *The Catholic Myth.* New York: Collier/Macmillan, 1990.

Hadden, Jeffrey, and Anson Shupe. *Elmer Gantry: Exemplar of American Televangelism.* Norwood, NJ: Ablex Publishing, 1990.

Hartford Seminary for Religion Research. http://hirr.hartsem.edu/bookshelf/thumma_article2.html.

Heidel, Alex. Chapter IV, "The Story of the Flood." In *The Gilgamesh Epic and Old Testament Parallels.* Chicago: University of Chicago, 1971, pp. 224–69.

Heifer Project International. http://www.heifer.org.

Henry, Carl F. H. *God, Revelation and Authority.* 6 vols. Waco, TX: Word Books, 1982.

Heyward, Carter. *A Priest Forever: One Woman's Controversial Ordination in the Episcopal Church.* Cleveland: Pilgrim Press, 1976.

Hillerbrand, Hans, ed. *Encyclopedia of Protestantism.* 4 vols. New York: Routledge, 2004.

Hillerbrand, Hans, ed. *The Oxford Encyclopedia of the Reformation.* 4 vols. New York: Oxford University Press, 1996.

Holy Bible. New Revised Standard Version with Apocrypha. New York: Oxford University Press, 1989.

Jann Aldredge-Clanton. http://www.jannaldredgeclanton.com/speaker.htm.

Janz, Bruce. "Who's Who in the History of Western Mysticism." The Mysticism Resources. http://www.clas.ufl.edu/users/gthursby/mys/whoswho.htm.

Jenkins, Philip. *The Next Christianity.* Oxford: Oxford University Press, 2002.

"Jim Bakker Show." http://www.jimbakkershow.com.

Ji-Sun Kim, Grace. *The Grace of Sophia: A Korean North American Women's Christology.* Cleveland: Pilgrim Press, 2002.

Johnson, Lucas. "Black Baptists Hope to Tackle Social Issues with Unified Voice." *Ithaca Journal/Associated Press,* 28 August 2004, B4.

Kennedy, Eugene. *The Unhealed Wound: The Church, the Priesthood, and the Question of Sexuality.* New York: St. Martin's Griffin, 2001.

Kerr, Hugh T., ed., *Readings in Christian Thought.* Nashville, TN: Abingdon Press, 1966.

Kiefer, James. Biographical Sketches of Memorable Christians of the Past. http://justus.anglican.org/resources/bio.

Kimball, Dan. *The Emerging Church.* Grand Rapids, MI: Zondervan, 2003.

King, Doug. "Re-Imagining Gathering Explores New Realities in Feminist Theology." Witherspoon Progressive Presbyterians. http://www.wither spoonsocicty.org/re-imagining_2000.htm.

Küng, Hans. *Christianity: Essence, History, and Future.* New York: Continuum, 1995.

Liebman, Robert, and Robert Wuthnow, eds. *The New Christian Right.* New York: Aldine Publishing, 1983.

Lindner, Eileen, ed. *Yearbook of American & Canadian Churches.* Nashville: Abington Press, 2003.

Lossky, Vladimir. *Mystical Theology of the Eastern Church.* London: James Clarke, 1957.

The Lutheran Calendar. http://www.elca.org.

"The Lutheran Liturgy: Its Biblical Roots." http://www.goodshepherd.nb.ca/liturgy.

Lutheran World. http://www.lutheranworld.org.

MacCana, Proinsias. *Celtic Mythology.* London: Hamlyn Publishing, 1970.

McBrien, Richard P. *Catholicism.* 2nd ed. New York: Harper & Row, 1994.

McBrien, Richard P. *Lives of the Saints.* San Francisco: HarperSanFrancisco, 2003.

MacDonald, Margaret, ed., *The Folklore of World Holidays.* Detroit: Gale Research, 1992.

Manschreck, Clyde. *A History of Christianity: Readings in the History of the Church from the Reformation to the Present.* Upper Saddle River, NJ: Prentice-Hall, 1964.

Marthaler, Bernard, ed. *New Catholic Encyclopedia.* 15 vols. Detroit: Thompson-Gale, 2003.

Marty, Martin, and R. Scott Appleby, eds. *The Fundamentalism Project.* Chicago: University of Chicago Press, 1995.

"Mary Daly Ends Suit, Agrees to Retire." *Boston College Chronicle.* 15 Feb. 2001, 9:11. http://www.bc.edu/bc_org/rvp/pubaf/chronicle/v9/f15/daly.html.

McFague, Sally. *Models of God: Theology for an Ecological, Nuclear Age.* Philadelphia: Fortress Press, 1987.

McGrath, Alister, ed., *The Blackwell Encyclopedia of Modern Christian Thought.* Oxford: Blackwell, 1993.

Meehan, Brenda. *Holy Women of Russia.* San Francisco: HarperSanFrancisco, 1993.

Melton, Gordon, ed., *Encyclopedia of American Religions.* 7th ed. Detroit: Thompson-Gale, 2003.

Mennonite Church USA. http://www.mennoniteusa.org.

Mennonite Central Committee. http://www.mcc.org.

Methodist Church of Great Britain. http://www.methodist.org.uk.

Milton, John. *Paradise Lost.* New York: Holt, Rinehart and Winston, 1965.

Nationmaster. http://www.nationmaster.com.

Neill, S.C. *A History of Christianity in India.* 2 vols. Cambridge: Cambridge University Press, 1985.

Newsome, Melba. "The Green Patriarch and Environmental Orthodoxy: An Interview with the Patriarch of Eastern Orthodoxy." In *The Amicus Journal* 20, no. 4 (1999, Winter): 15–17.

Nobel e-Museum, Laureates 2003. http://www.nobel.se/peace/laureates.

Nolt, Steven. *A History of the Amish.* Intercourse, PA: Good Books, 1992.

Ogletree, Thomas. *The Death of God Controversy.* Nashville: Abington Press, 1966.

Orthodox Calendar. http://www.goarch.org.

Orthodox Christian Information Center. http://www.www.orthodoxinfo.com.

Parrinder, Geoffrey, ed. *A Concise Encyclopedia of Christianity.* Oxford: Oneworld, 1998.

Pictorial Guide to the Quaker Tapestry. Friends Meeting House, stramongate, Kendal, Cumbria LA94BN, England, 1998.

Pinn Anne, and Anthony Pinn. *Fortress Introduction to Black Church History.* Minneapolis: Fortress Press, 2002.

Plato. *The Collected Dialogues of Plato.* Edith Hamilton and Huntington Cairns, eds. Princeton: Princeton University Press, 1978.

Pope, Justin. "Catholic Newspaper Questions Priest Celibacy." Associated Press, 16 March 2002.

"Portrait of the Accused." *New York Times,* 12 Jan. 2003. http://www.nytimes. com/imagepages/2003/01/12/national.

The Presbyterian Church USA. http://www.pcusa.org.

Princeton Center for the Study of Religion. http://www.princeton.edu/ ~csrelig.

Protestant Reformed Church of America. http://www.prca.org/prc.html.

Quakerinfo. http://www.quakerinfo.com/index.shtml.

" 'Recognitio' of the Holy See for the 'Essential Norms' Approved by the United States Conference of Catholic Bishops." 26 Oct. 2004. http://www. vatican.va.

Reformed Church of America. http://www.rca.org.

Religion-Online: Religious Information Source. http://Religion-online.org.

The Religious Society of Friends. http://www.quaker.org.

Richard McBrien. Essays in Theology. http://129.74.54.81/rm/essays.html.

"Robert Schuller." http://www.rapidnet.com/~jbeard/bdm/exposes/schuller/ general.htm, and Crystal Cathedral. http://www.crystalcathedral.org/.

Robinson, James M., ed. *The Nag Hammadi Library.* San Francisco: Harper and Row, 1977.

Russia: Christian Persecution in Russia. http://www.persecution.org/Countries/ russia.html.

Russian Orthodox Church. http://www.russian-orthodox-church.org.ru/hist_ en.htm.

Russian Orthodox Church Outside Russia. http://www.russianorthodox- church.ws/English.

Sojourners. http://www.sojo.net.

Southern Baptist Convention. http://www.sbc.org.

Stackhouse, Max L. "Fundamentalism Around the World." Religion Online. http://www. religion-online.

Stanton, Elizabeth Cady. *Women's Bible.* 1895; repr. Boston: Northeastern University Press, 1993.

Statistical Abstract of the United States. Washington, D.C.: U.S. Department of Commerce, 2002.

Stoll, David. *Is Latin America Turning Protestant? The Politics of Evangelical Growth.* Berkeley: University of California Press, 1990.

Sugden, Keith. *Pilgrims.* Andover, Hampshire, UK: Pitkin, 2001.

Throckmorton, Burton, ed. *Gospel Parallels.* 4th ed. Nashville: Thomas Nelson, 1979.

Tillich, Paul. *A History of Christian Thought.* New York: Simon and Schuster, 1968.

Tucker, Mary Evelyn. *Worldly Wonder. Religions in their Ecological Phase*. Chicago: OpenCourt, 2003.

"Turning America On To Positive Thinking: Dr. Norman Vincent Peale." http://www.usdreams.com/Peale28.html.

United Church of Canada. http://www.united-church.ca.

United Church of Christ. http://www.ucc.org.

United Methodist Church. http://www.umc.org.

United Nations. "Worldwide Adherents of All Religions by Six Continental Areas, Mid-2002." *World Population Prospects: The 1998 Revision*. New York: United Nations, 1999.

"United Pentecostal Church International." http://religiousmovements.lib.virginia.edu.

United States Catholic Mission Association, 2003. http://www.uscatholicmission.org/misstats.

United States Federal Research Division. Library of Congress, Country Studies/Area Handbook Series 1986–1998. http:countrystudies.us.

Vatican. www.vatican.va.

Vermes, Geza, ed. *The Complete Dead Sea Scrolls in English*. New York: Allen Lane/Penguin, 1997.

Virtual Religion Index. http://www.rci.Rutgers.edu/~religion.

Walker, Williston, et al. *A History of the Christian Church*. 4th ed. New York: Scribner's, 1985.

Weber, Max. *The Protestant Ethic and the Spirit of Capitalism*. New York: Scribner's, 1958.

Weststar Institute. http://www.westarinstitute.org.

Williamson, Parker T. "Sophia Upstages Jesus at Re-Imagining Revival." Presbyterian Layman. http://www.layman.org/layman/news/reimagining-revival.htm.

Wilson, Ian. *Jesus: The Evidence*. San Francisco: HarperSanFrancisco, 1996.

World Alliance of Reformed Churches. http://www.warc.ch.

Zeffirelli, Franco. *Jesus of Nazareth*. DVD, Artisan Entertainment, 1977.

INDEX